Man of the People,
Revised and Updated

Man of the People,
Revised and Updated

The Maverick Life and Career of John McCain

Paul Alexander

WILEY

John Wiley & Sons, Inc.

Published by John Wiley & Sons, Inc., Hoboken, New Jersey. Published simultaneously in Canada.

For general information on our other products and services, or technical support, please contact our Customer Care Department within the United States at (800) 762-2974, outside the United States at (317) 572-3993 or fax (317) 572-4002.

Wiley also publishes its books in a variety of electronic formats. Some content that appears in print may not be available in electronic books.

For more information about Wiley products, visit our web site at www.wiley.com.

Library of Congress Cataloging-in-Publication Data:

Alexander, Paul, 1955-
    Man of the people : the maverick life and career of John McCain /
Paul Alexander. —Rev. and updated.
      p. cm.
    Includes index.
    ISBN 978-0-470-39070-2 (pbk.)
      1. McCain, John, 1936-   2. Legislators—United States—Biography.
3. United States. Congress. Senate—Biography.   4. Presidential candidates—
United States—Biography.   I. Title.
E840.8.M26A44   2008
328.73092—dc22

                                    2008014506

Printed in the United States of America
10 9 8 7 6 5 4 3 2 1

*Once again, for Lauren Elizabeth Alexander
and for my family*

Contents

Acknowledgments

I would like to thank Congressman Gary Ackerman, Everett Alvarez, Tom Arrasmith, Charlie Black, Mike Briggs, Brooke Buchanan, Joyce Campbell, Erika Fortgang Casriel, Senator Lincoln Chafee, Senator Thad Cochran, Craig Crawford, Monica Crowley, Will Dana, Rick Davis, Ben Davol, Beth Day, Colonel George ("Bud") Day, Patricia Duff, Senator John Edwards, Congressman Eliot Engel, Kevin Fogerty, Frank Gaffney, Paul Galanti, Marina Garnier, Robert Giuffra, Jordon Goldis, Betsy Gotbaum, Mike Guy, Rebecca Hanks, Senator Gary Hart, Ann Hassinger (of the United States Naval Institute), William Haynes, Charles Hooff, Arianna Huffington, Nancy Ives, Senator James Jeffords, Congressman Peter King, Senator Patrick Leahy, Katie Levinson, Carolyn Licht, Robert Love, Beverly Lyall (of the Department of the Navy), Malcolm Matheson, Linda Mellon, Maggie Melson (of the Episcopal High School), Gary Meltz, Tim Meyer, Georgette Mosbacher, Meredith Mosley, Captain Chuck Nash, James Ortenzio, Lyn Paulsen, Lawrence Pike, James Pinkerton, Stephen Perrine, Phil Pulizzi, Governor Bill Richardson, Peter and Cindy Rinfret, Ed Rollins, Ken Ringle, Susan Russ, Mark Salter, Congressman Christopher Shays, Richard Shepard, George Shipley, Senator Alan Simpson, Carl Smith, Greg Stevens, Erik

Smulson, Admiral James Stockdale, Roger Stone, Orson Swindle, Dick Thomsen, General Paul Vallely, Jack Van Loan, Nanette Varian, Michael Vlahos, Senator John Warner, John Weaver, Bill White, Daniel White, Robert Whittle, Angie Williams, Carl Wilson, Robert W. Wilson, David Winters, and Patrick Woodson.

At International Creative Management, I would like to thank Tina Wexler and Lisa Bankoff. At John Wiley & Sons, I would like to thank Kate Wood and Pamela van Giessen. For the interviews they have given me over the years, I would like to thank John and Cindy McCain.

Prologue

An American Centrist

"When I was five years old, a car pulled up in front of our house in New London, Connecticut, and a Navy officer rolled down the window, and shouted at my father that the Japanese had bombed Pearl Harbor." John McCain was speaking in late March 2008 at the Los Angeles World Affairs Council. The speech represented a major foreign policy address for McCain, but from his opening comments it was clear he often felt a very personal connection to world events. "My father immediately left for the submarine base where he was stationed. I rarely saw him again for four years. My grandfather, who commanded the fast carrier task force under Admiral Halsey [during World War II], came home from the war exhausted from the burdens he had borne and died the next day. In Vietnam, where I formed the closest friendships of my life, some of my friends never came home to the country they loved so well." Using the same personal language, McCain moved on to his general thoughts about war. "I detest war," he said. "It might not be the worst thing to befall human beings, but it is wretched beyond all description. When nations seek to resolve their differences by force of arms, a million tragedies ensue."

Naturally, anything McCain had to say about war in March 2008 was heard within the context of his support for the war in Iraq, for after being an outspoken critic of the Bush Administration's execution of the war (especially the decision to maintain a comparatively small fighting force from the invasion on), he would become a strong advocate of Bush's stay-the-course policy for Iraq. McCain's reason is simple: al Qaeda. "Whether they were [in Iraq] before is immaterial," McCain said. "Al Qaeda is in Iraq now.... Civil war in Iraq could easily descend into genocide and destabilize the entire region as neighboring powers come to the aid of their favored factions." This was not the only example McCain invoked in Los Angeles to speak to the larger issue of the community of nations. "The United States did not single-handedly win the Cold War," he said. "[T]he transatlantic alliance did, in concert with partners around the world." As for Russia, the product of the end of the Cold War and the collapse of the Soviet Union, McCain was guarded, arguing membership in the G-8, from which he believes Russia should be excluded, should be reserved for "democracies committed to the defense of freedom." At the same time, "China and the United States," he added, "are not destined to be adversaries."

In describing McCain's approach to foreign policy, David Brooks, writing in the *New York Times* in March 2008, observed that, in the past when faced with circumstances similar to those in Iraq, McCain made significantly different decisions. In the fall of 1983, Ronald Reagan sought to send U.S. Marines into Lebanon, and McCain, even though he was new to the Congress, broke ranks and opposed his president. "I do not foresee obtainable objectives in Lebanon," McCain said on September 28, 1983. "I believe the longer we stay, the more difficult it will be to leave, and I am prepared to accept the consequences of our withdrawal." He was right, too. A month later, in Beirut, a terrorist attack killed 241 Americans, mostly marines.

So what can be made of John McCain and his willingness to embrace the global community of nations even as, according to Brooks, "he signaled that the foreign policy [in the future] will be very different from the one of the past six years"? One could argue that on foreign policy McCain is a centrist. He is neither an isolationist nor one who endorses nation building. His acknowledgment of the importance of the global community of nations suggests he may not pursue a unilateralism that can spell disaster—the type of unilateralism that drove the Bush Administration to invade Iraq in the first place.

In his overall political agenda, McCain can be seen as progressive on some issues, conservative on others. Consider his stand on the environment, where he is progressive. A skeptic about global warming when he first arrived in Congress, he has evolved over time to become one of the most ardent proponents of initiatives to protect the environment. "We need to be good stewards of our planet," he said in Los Angeles, "and join with other nations to help preserve our common home. The risks of global warming have no borders. We and other nations of the world must get serious about substantially reducing greenhouse gas emissions. We need a successor to the Kyoto Treaty." Indeed, McCain argued against Bush's withdrawing from the Kyoto Treaty in 2001, and he has consistently voted against allowing drilling for oil in the Arctic National Wildlife Reserve in Alaska—positions that have put him at odds with those forces sympathetic to the establishment energy industry in the United States.

While a progressive on the environment, McCain can be considered a conservative on fiscal issues—at least to a point. During the Reagan Administration, he voted for tax cuts proposed by the president. Historically, McCain has supported a ban on taxing the Internet as well as the use of cell phones. But, during the Bush Administration, he opposed Bush's major tax cuts. In 2001, he voted against the tax cut, saying, "I cannot in good conscience support a tax cut in which so many of the benefits go to the most fortunate among us at the expense of the middle-class Americans who most need tax relief."

A social motivation may have led him to vote against Bush's first tax cut, but fiscal responsibility forced him to oppose the second one, in 2003. "The tax cut is not appropriate," he said, "until we find out the cost of the war [in Iraq] and the cost of the reconstruction." By 2008, once he had hit the presidential campaign trail, McCain had decided not to repeal the Bush tax cuts he had voted against as long as spending cuts are implemented to balance the cuts. Then again, McCain has based a good part of his political career opposing earmarks and pork-barrel spending of any type. In this way, McCain is old-fashioned: He believes tax cuts must be made in conjunction with budgets cuts, and of paramount concern is achieving a balanced budget. In short, he endorses the fundamental tenet of fiscal conservatism, which says spend only what you have.

On social issues, McCain is harder to define. In his career he has been a steadfast defender of the right to life, yet in interviews through the years he has used language that would suggest he is not in favor of overturning *Roe v. Wade,* and, implying that John Roberts has been much more to his liking than Samuel Alito, he has maintained he would nominate to the United States Supreme Court justices in the tradition of Sandra Day O'Connor. On the issue of gun control, while he has supported the Second Amendment to the Constitution, he has demanded qualifications to the right to bear arms, such as a ban on assault weapons and Saturday night specials and a mandate for safety locks on some guns.

On gay issues, he has shown some moderation. While he continues to support "don't ask, don't tell" and opposes gay marriage, he attacked the Federal Marriage Amendment, the cornerstone of Bush's reelection effort in 2004, by describing it as "un-Republican." Because he has embraced the Log Cabin Republicans as well as numerous friends and colleagues who are gay, James Kirchick, writing in *The Advocate* in March 2008, argued that McCain "isn't so bad" on gay issues. Kirchick concluded: "In a 1999 interview, McCain said he'd be 'comfortable' with a gay president. This gay writer would be more than comfortable with John McCain in the Oval Office."

In his congressional career, McCain has also become known for teaming up with Ted Kennedy, the very symbol of American liberalism. The two senators advanced a patient's bill of rights and comprehensive immigration reform—the latter of which was deemed by some conservative critics as being amnesty for the millions of immigrants who are currently residing in the United States illegally.

However, the one topic on which many conservatives most fervently disagree with McCain has been his signature issue of campaign finance reform. After years of struggle, McCain was finally able to pass McCain-Feingold, the name for campaign finance reform legislation in the Senate, in Bush's first term. Critics saw the bill's intention of limiting the way money can be contributed to a candidate as an infringement of individual freedom, even though McCain argued that regulating how and how much money can be given to a candidate prevents large single contributions from affecting a campaign. "The First

Amendment is an important safeguard of pro-growth policies," Pat Toomey of the Club for Growth wrote in the *Wall Street Journal* in early 2007. "When government strays from sound economic policies, citizens must be free to exercise their constitutional rights to petition and criticize those policies and the politicians responsible for them. The 2002 McCain-Feingold bill (or the Bipartisan Campaign Reform Act) . . . seeks to squash political dissent by imposing grossly unconstitutional restrictions on citizen participation in political debate."

Parts of the legislation—such as what became known as the Millionaire Amendment, which attempts to place restrictions on self-financed campaigns—eventually ended up the subject of protracted litigation. But, despite the legislation's flaws, McCain argues that campaign finance reform has served to make the process of financing elections more transparent to the public at large.

So, in the end, because of the varying positions he has taken on domestic issues—conservative on some, progressive on others—he can again be described as a centrist. What's more, there is no one group to which McCain aspires to have any unique appeal. Conservatives generally support some of his social and fiscal positions, though by no means all of them, and liberals applaud his efforts on such topics as the environment and immigration, but they have concerns about other parts of his political agenda. Ultimately, McCain is virtually impossible to pigeonhole as he, more often than not, strives for the middle ground, which is why he so often teams up with Democrats to produce meaningful legislation that can be passed by Congress and signed into law. His affinity for the common ground, his desire to govern from a consensus, is what makes him appealing to Independents. A centrist, not just on foreign policy but on domestic policy as well, he is running for president to return the country to the middle of the political spectrum.

"I run for president," McCain said that day in Los Angeles, "because I want to keep the country I love and have served all my life safe, and to rise to the challenges of our times, as generations before us rose to theirs. I run for president because I know it is incumbent on America, more than any other nation on earth, to lead in building the foundations for a stable and enduring peace. I run because I believe, as strongly as I ever have, that it is within our power to make in our time another, better world than we inherited."

Chapter 1

Admiral McCain

On September 5, 1945, during a peaceful and beautiful evening in the San Diego area, Vice Admiral John Sidney McCain settled into his home in Coronado, California. His wiry frame had become dangerously slim—he weighed just over 100 pounds—and his face was weather-beaten from his years at sea. Nicknamed "Slew" by his fellow officers and "Popeye" by the sailors he commanded, McCain was exhausted. Dragged down by a cold, he may have also suffered an undetected heart attack within the previous few months. The summer, which had finally brought an end to World War II, had been especially hard on him. He had commanded the Second Carrier Task Force, Pacific Fleet, since August 1944. In the final year of the war, operating in conjunction with the Third Fleet under the command of Admiral William F. Halsey, McCain's Task Force 38 "spearheaded the drive in the Philippines," to quote from his official naval biography, "supported the capture of Okinawa, and rode rampant through the Western Pacific from the Indo-China Coast to the Japanese home island. The force knew only one word—'Attack!' "

Task Force 38's motto fit its commander. Slew McCain was gruff, hard-edged, quick-tempered, frequently profane, sometimes suspicious, always hardworking, and prone to sullenness. He liked to slam down bourbon, play the horses, shoot craps, and roll his own Bull Durham cigarettes. He was unwaveringly patriotic, stubbornly ambitious, and brilliant. Most important, he was a leader. In the last six months of the war in the Pacific, McCain's Task Force 38 was cited for damaging or destroying 6,000 Japanese airplanes and either sinking or damaging an estimated 2,000,000 tons of Japanese warships. The task force's airplanes once sank 49 Japanese ships in a single day.

Indeed, Slew McCain, with his trademark ill-fitting sailor cap (hence the Popeye reference), had established a reputation that would become mythic in naval lore. Regarding the Japanese, he once proposed "killing them all—painfully." At the signing of the peace accords on the battleship *Missouri* in Tokyo Bay on September 2, 1945—a ceremony Halsey insisted McCain had to attend, even though he was sick and anxious to go home—McCain glared at the deck, unable to bring himself to look at his just-defeated enemy. "The Jap warlords are not half licked yet," he said after the ceremony, a comment that made headlines. That same day, he made his point with authentic "McCain" humor. "He went from group to group [on the *Missouri*]," one newspaper reported, "greeting old acquaintances, and announced he was at work on the concoction of three new drinks, the 'Judy,' the 'Grill,' and the 'Zeke,' each named after a Japanese plane. 'Each time you drink one you can say, "Splash one Judy" or "Splash one Zeke,"'" he explained."

The last year of the war had not been without tragedy for McCain. Besides fighting the Japanese, McCain and Halsey had to contend with the horrendous forces of nature. On December 17, 1944, Halsey and McCain's fleet of ships was hit by a typhoon. In the lead ship, Halsey—tired, and focused on fighting the Japanese, not the weather—had failed to anticipate the approaching storm. He was also given insufficient warning about meteorological conditions by the central command in Pearl Harbor. The result was catastrophic. The overwhelming waves capsized and sank three destroyers—the *Hull*, the *Spence*, and the *Monahan*—and damaged six other ships, killing 778 men in all. In addition, 146 airplanes were destroyed when they were swept overboard.

Later in December, at a board of inquiry held in Hawaii, Halsey defended his decisions. Admiral Chester Nimitz, one of the navy's power brokers, personally lobbied Secretary of the Navy James Forrestal to keep him from relieving Halsey of his command. It is believed that it took no less than Chief of Naval Operations Ernest King to prevent the board from making McCain the fall guy. With the war in the Pacific going so well, it made no sense, it was argued, to remove either Halsey or McCain.

Recommendations Halsey made were obvious enough. The navy, he said, should take steps to improve its weather-tracking methods; it should also beef up its communications links to Pearl Harbor. The navy failed to act on either recommendation. Six months later, on June 2, 1945, when Halsey and McCain again found themselves in severe weather conditions, they were unprepared for the second typhoon that hit their fleet. The storm damaged 33 ships, destroyed 76 airplanes, and killed six men. It was decided McCain should come in from the sea and take a job in Washington—he was to become an assistant to General Omar Bradley in the Bureau of Veterans' Affairs—but the war ended before his orders were activated. McCain witnessed the historic surrender ceremony on the *Missouri*. Then he began a leave at his home in California.

He was born on August 9, 1884—not quite two full decades after the end of the Civil War—in Teoc, Mississippi, a tiny town in rural Carroll County. The son of John Sidney and Elizabeth-Ann Young McCain, he grew up on a plantation. The McCains of this era even owned slaves, as reporters would later reveal. McCain attended high school in Carrollton, then matriculated at the University of Mississippi. After his freshman year, he entered the United States Naval Academy in Annapolis, Maryland, on September 25, 1902. When he graduated on February 12, 1906, *The Lucky Bag,* the academy's yearbook, described McCain this way: "The skeleton in the family closet of 1906. A living example of the beneficial course of physical training in the N.A. having gained 1⅜ ounces since he entered. A man of exemplary habits which make him very popular."

Social, fun-loving, and often mischievous, he was as big of spirit as he was slight of build. In 1909, Ensign McCain served on the battleship *Pennsylvania* and the cruiser *Washington*. On August 9 of that year, in Colorado Springs, Colorado, he married Katherine Daisy Vaulx, a beautiful and personable woman from Arkansas and a daughter of an Episcopalian minister. The couple had three children—Catherine Vaulx McCain, James Gordon McCain, and John Sidney McCain Jr., born on January 17, 1911, in Council Bluffs, Iowa. Slew McCain's son—nicknamed "Junior" and "Mac" but most often called "Jack"—was born in Council Bluffs because his father, during an extended tour of duty on the *San Diego,* was sailing around the southern tip of South America, and Katherine had traveled to Iowa to stay with a sister who had moved there.

In 1918, the year World War I ended, McCain was still stationed on the *San Diego,* which was performing escort duty in the Atlantic Ocean. Between 1918 and 1927, he served in various capacities on a number of ships—among them, the *Maryland* and the *New Mexico.* He traveled constantly, but when he was stateside, he usually worked in Washington at the Department of the Navy. His family, for the most part, was raised in Washington, not far from the Capitol. "My mother was the real parental control," Jack McCain would say later, "because my father was gone part of the time that I was growing up."

Describing his father, Jack was unequivocal. "My father," he would say, "was a great leader, first, and people loved him, and he knew how to lead. He also knew when the time came to be a strict disciplinarian, versus the time to be a more easy-going commanding officer. And he had an intense and keen sense of humor. My mother used to say about him that the blood of life flowed through his veins. . . . [H]e was also . . . extraordinarily well read. So this gave him an outstanding command of the English language. He was a man of great moral and physical courage. The fact that he had the first carrier task force under Halsey bears witness to that."

In September 1927, as his father had before him, Jack McCain entered the Naval Academy, which was his goal "from the time that I was old enough to begin to realize there was such [a place]." He had attended, first, Central High School in Washington and, finally, Columbia Preparatory School. When he got to his father's alma mater, Jack, having just turned sixteen, discovered he was among the youngest students in his class—and one of the few to enter with a presidential appointment. "I went in there at the age of sixteen, and I weighed one hundred and five pounds," he would say, referring to another trait he shared with his father—a decidedly puny build. "I could hardly carry a Springfield rifle. Getting out there and holding an oar was another unique experience in my life." Perhaps because he was so much smaller than his classmates, Jack seemed to go out of his way to break academy rules. He routinely got into scuffles and amassed a daunting number of demerits.

When he graduated on May 1, 1931, his yearbook citation avoided the behavior issue: "Mac was born with one weakness which he strives in vain to conquer: his liking for the fair sex. . . . 'An officer and a gentleman' is the title to which he pays absolute allegiance. Sooner could Gibraltar be loosed from its base than could Mac be loosed from the principles which he has adopted to govern his actions."

Upon graduation, Jack sought advice from his father, who told him simply, "The only thing I say to you is to make a good job of it"—whatever he chose to do. Jack decided to pursue a naval career that focused on submarines. Beginning in June 1931, as his first post-academy assignment, Jack served on the *Oklahoma*. At its home port—Long Beach, California—he met Roberta Wright, the daughter of Archibald Wright, a rich and strong-willed oil wildcatter. Originally from Mississippi, Wright had retired from his business in Oklahoma and Texas and moved his family to Los Angeles for a better life.

Roberta and her twin sister Rowena, born on February 7, 1912, in Muskogee, Oklahoma, were their father's darlings. Each summer, the family escaped the Oklahoma heat by traveling to the West Coast. Los Angeles became their permanent home in 1924, the year Archie had retired so he could spend all of his time with his daughters. Roberta's mother, Myrtle, was horrified that one of her daughters would take up with a sailor, so when Jack and Roberta decided to marry, over the objections of Roberta's parents, the couple eloped to Tijuana, Mexico, where they were married on January 21, 1933, at Caesar's Bar. "Not exactly in the bar," Roberta would later say. "It was really sort of upstairs." Naturally, her mother "had a cat fit," as Rowena would put it. But there was little she could do. Jack and Roberta went about their lives—they survived the Long Beach earthquake that occurred not long after their return from Mexico—and Jack tried to find humor in their lives whenever he could. "Asked once how he could tell his beautiful wife from her identical twin," the *Washington Post* would one day write, "[Jack McCain] replied . . . : 'That's their problem.' "

In July 1933, Jack reported to the Naval Submarine Base in Groton, Connecticut, to follow his interests and study submarines. At about the same time, Rowena married John Luther Maddox—who later founded an airline that eventually became part of TWA—and settled down in Los Angeles. In December, Jack graduated and took up his first of numerous submarine assignments.

In June 1935, Slew McCain, now age 51, decided to return to school and reported to the Naval Air Station in Pensacola, Florida, to study flight training and aviation. On August 19, 1936, having been designated a naval aviator, Slew was appointed Commander of Aircraft Squadrons and Attending Craft at the Coco Solo Air Base in the Panama Canal Zone. Jack happened to be stationed there; he and Roberta were awaiting their first child. Ten days into Slew's new command, Roberta entered a navy hospital. On August 29, she gave birth to a son. In keeping with the McCain family tradition, he was named John Sidney McCain III. Jack's son, too, would be given a nickname, just as Jack and Slew had been before him. This John Sidney McCain would be known as "Johnny."

Slew McCain remained at Coco Solo until May 1937. Next, he commanded the *Ranger*, before he was named commander of the Naval Air Station in San Diego, California, a post he held from July 1939 until January 1941. (In 1939, Rowena's husband, John Maddox, died; years later, she married an investment counselor.) When Slew assumed the command of Aircraft Scouting Training on January 23, 1941, he was promoted to rear admiral. During these years, Jack was advancing in his assignments as well. He taught in the Department of Electrical Engineering at the Naval Academy from June 1938 to May 1940. Then he served on the submarine *Shipjack* until, in April 1941, he was made commanding officer of the *USS O-8,* which was being recommissioned in the Philadelphia Navy Yard. While he held this post, Jack's family—which now included another son, Joseph, and a daughter, Jean—lived in New London, Connecticut. Johnny was five years old when the Japanese attacked Pearl Harbor. He rarely saw his father for the next four years.

During World War II, Jack McCain tried his best to live up to his father's reputation. He commanded the submarine *Gunnel,* which was part of the naval armada involved in D-Day, and the submarine *Dentuda,* which was on patrol in the Pacific when the cease fire was announced on August 14, 1945.

As a submarine commander during the war—McCain was in charge of three subs altogether—he sank, according to one published report, "twenty thousand tons of Japanese shipping" and "once spent 72 hours on the ocean bottom, riding out a depth charge attack. 'It gives you a new outlook on life,' [McCain] said of the experience." For his service during the war, Jack McCain received the Silver Star Medal (for "conspicuous gallantry and intrepidity," the citation said), the Bronze Star Medal with Combat "V" (for "sinking an enemy vessel of 4,000 tons and damaging two small crafts totaling 350 tons"), and two Letters of Commendation.

As for Slew, he served, at the beginning of World War II, as Commander of Air Forces for the Western Sea Frontier and the South Pacific Force. He was named Chief of the Bureau of Aeronautics in October 1942, and, in August 1943, became a vice admiral in his capacity of Deputy Chief of Naval Operations (Air). McCain much preferred sea duty to the Washington bureaucracy, so, in 1944, he returned to the Pacific Theater to command Task Force 38, which became infamous by the war's end. As Task Force 38's leader, he received the Navy Cross and Gold Stars in lieu of the Second and Third Distinguished Service Medals. The citation that accompanied the award reflected Slew McCain's lust for fighting: "[H]e devised techniques and procedures to locate and destroy grounded enemy planes, accounting for 3,000 planes smashed throughout his sustained attacks against Japan's home islands with only one of our destroyers damaged during the intensive operations between July 10 and August 15 [1945]."

The historic drama of the last months of the war in the Pacific—the relentless fighting, the around-the-clock anxiety, the never-ending presence of death—had taken a toll on Slew McCain. On September 5, 1945, his first day back home in California, he had greeted his wife

Katherine and then visited a navy doctor who had voiced concern about McCain's fragile health. But McCain didn't want to dwell on the negative. He wanted to look to the future, when he would report for duty in Washington and then submit to the Chief of Naval Operations, Admiral Ernest J. King, a white paper he and a friend, Admiral John Thach, had written. The landmark McCain-Thach report argued that navy air power should be used to support troop action in the coordinated air–ground effort that would become commonplace in the future. That first day, Slew spent much time with Katherine, whom he had badly missed during his long months at sea. He especially enjoyed telling her about a lunch he had with Jack on the submarine *Proteus* in Tokyo Bay just after the peace accords were signed. Admiral Charles Lockwood gave the luncheon on the *Proteus*. "During the process of the luncheon," Jack would recall, "I got my father off to one side, and I said to him that I would like to talk to him alone in that little stateroom they used to give commanding officers. And we went back there, and we talked for a little while. . . . And my father said to me at that time, he said, 'Son, there is no greater thing than to die for the principles— for the country and the principles that you believe in.' I considered myself very fortunate to have had a chance to see him at that particular moment."

On Slew's second day home, September 6, Katherine had arranged a welcome-home party for him. As he stood in a room packed with friends and naval personnel, Slew was the picture of the vaunted warrior having returned home from victory, but he appeared tired and subdued. Everyone there was thrilled the war was over, and most people who noticed Slew's lack of energy chalked it up to the stress he had experienced during the preceding months. Then, as the party roared noisily around him, Slew approached his wife to tell her he didn't feel well. He suddenly collapsed to the floor. A doctor attending the party rushed to his side but Slew was already dead. His heart had simply stopped beating.

McCain's body was flown to Washington, D.C., with full honor guard. On September 10, following a funeral service, McCain was buried in Arlington National Cemetery with military honors. His first namesake, Jack, was a navy commander; his second namesake, Johnny, was nine years old. They stood in the grey haze of the cemetery and watched the proceedings in silence—the 21-gun salute, the presentation of the folded flag to the widow, the last rites given by the navy chaplain. In the immediate wake of McCain's death, which was deemed significant enough that President Truman sent condolences to the family and the *New York Times* ran his obituary on the front page, the United States Congress moved to recognize McCain's considerable achievements in World War II by posthumously awarding him a fourth star, a reward the navy, no doubt, would have bestowed on him had he lived.

In the years after World War II, with the example of his father urging him on, Jack McCain continued to excel in the navy his father had loved so much. In November 1945, Jack assumed the position of Director of Records for the Bureau of Naval Personnel in the Department of the Navy in Washington. "They brought me back and put me in charge of the records activity," Jack McCain would recall. "And there was something like one million enlisted men records, and I forget how many officer records, see. But there was a backlog of filing of papers into these records in the neighborhood of several million sheets. And when you get into several million of anything, you're getting into real problems of management. . . . I had a team up there of five hundred sailors, three or four hundred Waves [women sailors]. . . . I must admit it's an interesting job because you read all sorts of strange things about people that you don't ordinarily get your hands on."

McCain held that post until January 1949. In those three years, he spent a good deal of time with his family in Washington. Then he was again ordered to sea, this time to command two different submarine divisions (Seventy-One for eleven months and Fifty-One for two months). In February 1950, he was made executive officer of the heavy cruiser *St. Paul* and held that post until November, when he was sent back to Washington to become the Director of the Undersea Warfare Research and Development Branch of the Office of the Deputy Chief of Naval Operations. In July 1951, he was named commander of the *Monrovia*.

By the 1950s, the McCain name had become famous in the navy, and revered in Mississippi. "We were all steeped in the tradition and history of the McCain legacy," Senator Thad Cochran of Mississippi recalls. "I trained as a naval reserve officer (NROTC) in McCain Hall at the University of Mississippi. That was where we would go to classes. I knew all about the family history. It was the first Admiral McCain who the building was named for at the University of Mississippi. We would also have a McCain Field, where the army national guard would train, not too far from the McCain homestead."

In the early 1950s, Jack's son Johnny was poised to enter the family "business" by first attending Slew's and Jack's alma mater—the Naval Academy. In four years, Jack McCain would earn the rank of admiral. Before his career ended, his promotion to four-star admiral made the McCains the only family in American history to have both a father and a son reach that rank. But that distinction came much later. In the summer of 1954, as he prepared to enter the Naval Academy, Johnny McCain already felt enormous pressure to live up to the remarkable accomplishments of his father and grandfather. Even so, throughout his early years, it never occurred to Johnny McCain that he could choose *not* to go into the navy. He was, simply, born to be a sailor.

Chapter 2

Anchors Away

If there was ever a military brat, it was Johnny McCain. He was born in a navy hospital in the Panama Canal Zone while his father was stationed there, but that was just the beginning of the long, odd childhood of a boy who grew up under the pressure of being the son and grandson of navy brass. From 1936 until 1946, Jack McCain held posts that took him from New London, Connecticut, to Pearl Harbor to the Pacific Ocean battle areas where he fought during World War II. He served on— or so it seemed—countless ships and submarines. With his father's active duty defined by such a rapid rate of reassignment, Johnny would barely get used to one home before his family would be uprooted and assigned to the next. His education was gained in whatever school happened to be on the base where his family was living at any given time. More than once he found himself in a "combined class" attended by students of varying ages. Routinely, naval-base schools did not have the facilities needed to achieve even the most basic education standards.

As a young boy, Johnny exhibited one behavior trait about which he would often comment as an adult—a hair-trigger temper that could be set off by even the slightest provocation. When he was a toddler and young child, it was not unusual for him to become so mad he would hold his breath until he passed out on the floor. As his body developed, another notable factor emerged. Although he was healthy, robust, and athletic even at an early age, he was still slight of build, as were his father and his grandfather.

In the early years of his life, Johnny's parents made one decision about which they would be unwavering: When Johnny grew up, he would follow the family model, attend the Naval Academy, and then enter the navy. Jack and Roberta used a subtle tactic to make Johnny's future life known to him. Neither parent ever told Johnny directly he had been born with a life plan over which he had little control. Instead, they simply talked about his future as though the plot for it were a *fait accompli*. "You know, Johnny is going to the Academy one day," Jack would say to a friend. Or Roberta would simply state at a family gathering, "Naturally, Johnny is going to be a midshipman."

The first demonstrative move Jack and Roberta made toward realizing their goal came in September 1946 when they enrolled Johnny, then 10 years old, in St. Stephen's School in Alexandria, Virginia. After Jack had returned to Washington following the war, the family had settled down in northern Virginia. To make Johnny ready academically for acceptance into the Naval Academy, Jack and Roberta had to remove him from the inferior educational system provided by the nation's naval bases. At the time, St. Stephen's was a relatively new, up-and-coming private day school, but it was an improvement over the schools Johnny had been attending.

At the end of the 1948–1949 academic year, McCain left St. Stephen's so he could spend the next two years traveling with his family as his father held positions of command on submarines. Then, for the fall of 1951, with acceptance into the Naval Academy looming only three years away, Jack and Roberta sent Johnny to boarding school. This time, taking into account both his emotional and intellectual developmental needs, Jack and Roberta chose for Johnny one of the most famous all-boys boarding schools in the South: the Episcopal High School in Alexandria, Virginia.

"Episcopal was one of the better prep schools in the South," says Dick Thomsen, Episcopal's principal from 1951 until 1967. "It was always ranked with the best schools in New England. The two Southern schools that stood out with Andover, Exeter, Groton, and so on, were Episcopal and Woodberry, the two rival schools in Virginia. Academically, Episcopal was good. Our students were very bright because the South was beginning to rise again . . . at least economically, and people there were looking for better schools. We were getting boys from major Southern centers like Charlotte, Charleston, and Atlanta, as well as leading cities in Virginia."

Jack and Roberta were enrolling Johnny in a school that emphasized his Southern heritage, which was traceable to his grandfather's early years on a plantation in Mississippi. Episcopal was so completely associated with the South that, from Virginia to Louisiana, it was often referred to simply as "The High School." Located just across the Potomac River from Washington, on a sprawling campus that featured rolling green lawns, Episcopal marked its beginning in 1839, the year when 35 boys attended school on an 80-acre piece of land under the directorship of the Reverend William Nelson Pendleton. Because it was the first high school in Virginia, Episcopal's student body expanded to 100 within a year. Only the Civil War could stop its growth. In 1861, after Union troops occupied Alexandria, the school shut down and served as an army hospital for Union soldiers during the next four years. When the school reopened in 1866, a memorial was constructed in Pendleton Hall to commemorate the 68 Episcopal alumni who had been killed fighting for the Confederate cause during the war.

When McCain arrived at Episcopal in the fall of 1951, he found a place steeped in heritage and traditions that demanded rigid adherence to social and cultural codes. By then, the 275 boys who comprised the student body lived on a campus that had grown to 130 acres to accommodate large athletic facilities, especially playing fields for football, baseball, and track. The boys spent a good deal of their time on sports. In fact, a student's day could be divided into two parts. The morning and early afternoon were taken up with rigorous academic pursuits; each boy was required to select a college-preparatory core curriculum plus electives. From mid-afternoon on, the students retired to the sports fields for mandatory athletics. The weekly schedule, which ran from

Tuesday to Saturday—Sunday and Monday were off days—was intense, by calculation.

"In a word, it was brutal," says Charles Hooff, who, like McCain, moved from St. Stephen's to Episcopal. "You were allowed off the campus only three weekends a year. You could leave the campus one Monday a month. We went to school on Saturday and were off on Monday because Sunday was a pious day and they didn't want you studying on Sunday. You had mandatory chapel every morning and mandatory church on Sunday. The school was built on the old tradition of hazing. There weren't a lot of masters—30 at the most. The school was really run by the monitors and the seniors. They handed out all of the discipline, and it was swift and severe. They wouldn't physically abuse you; they would mentally abuse you. Now, occasionally they might work you over, but the hazing and punishment were mostly verbal. I mean, you were 14, and they were 18. They intimidated you. It was the seniors going after the freshmen. Some kids absolutely collapsed under the pressure. There was a real requirement to conform. John McCain had a problem with this at first, but then he grew into being a leader in that area, when he was a senior."

In this constricting environment, each boy also dealt with living conditions that were less than luxurious. A contemporary of McCain, Ken Ringle, later wrote: "We lived in curtained alcoves like hyperglandular adolescent monks; slept in sagging pipeframe beds; drank milk drawn from some dairy where, it seemed, the cows grazed on nothing but onions; and amused ourselves at meals by covertly flipping butter pats with knives onto the ceiling, where they would later melt free to drop on other, unsuspecting skulls." Ringle and McCain lived in the same building. "It had been used by the Union during the war and hadn't been renovated since then," Ringle says. "There were cockroaches in there. One day, they swarmed in, and you couldn't see the floor. The curtained alcoves we slept in were like the pictures you see of hospitals in the Civil War."

Almost from the start of his first year there, McCain had trouble fitting into Episcopal's environment. More a navy brat than a "good old boy," he found it easier to embrace his family's military background than its Southern heritage. Indeed, in his first year at Episcopal, he did more than his share of rebelling against both the school's traditions and the practice of intimidation against the freshmen (and any sophomores experiencing their first year at Episcopal). Before long, the brash and in-your-face McCain had earned the nickname "Punk." He seemed to go out of his way to underscore that characterization by wearing a funky-looking overcoat and smoking cigarettes. Clad in blue jeans, motorcycle boots, and his overcoat, smoking a cigarette that dangled from his lips, McCain would sneak into Ninth Street in Washington, go to Waxy Maxy, and buy the latest record by Elvis Presley or Stick McGee. Or, if he was feeling lucky, he'd slip into a bar and try to buy a beer. "There was illegal smoking at Episcopal and the one way to do the illegal smoking was to sneak off to the woods," Ringle recalls. "His coat was a sign that he was always skipping off, because in the winter it was cold out there. McCain also skipped off into Washington."

"As headmaster, I actually saw very little of him," Dick Thomsen says, "because I mostly dealt with cases that needed special attention. While he was not what you'd call a happy camper, he was never so bad he came to me as a student to deal with. My impression of him was: I knew he walked around with his jacket and tie all messed up. The tie would be at half-mast and the jacket collar turned up. He'd have this sort of surly look on his face, that 'Don't tread on me' type of expression. He traveled with a gang that was, I guess you could say, dissidents. On the other hand, he wasn't a bad student. Not outstanding; a good student. He was small but a good athlete. He was an excellent wrestler—a tough competitor on the wrestling mat."

During his junior year, he was voted runner-up to "Sloppiest," and in his senior year, he got runner-up to "Thinks he's hardest." He certainly cut a "hard" image. One way he did this was to show off in his job as waiter. "That was another subculture, being a waiter," Ringle says. "We got paid a little something for it. It was kind of a macho thing. Every waiter waited on two tables. Each table had 14 people. You brought out platters and plates. At the end of the meal, the guys who sat in the middle of the table had to scrape the plates, and then the waiters took them off. They carried them out to the kitchen on this oval aluminum tray they balanced on their shoulder. If you were a waiter, one of the big deals was if you could balance the tray and go out kind of swinging it a little bit, with a swagger. If you were strong, you could lift this thing off your shoulder—28 of these plates and all of the silverware. On Sundays, we had salad too. So we had what you called 28 and 28. And if you were strong enough to lift—to press— 28 and 28, you were a heavy mother. McCain could get 28 and 28 up, even though he was a fairly small guy."

By his senior year, McCain had gotten in line enough to collect his share of achievements. He lettered in wrestling, starred on the junior varsity football team, played on the tennis team, and participated in the Dramatic Club and the E-Club. He served on the staffs of the school newspaper, *The Chronicle,* and the yearbook, *Whispers.* He spent time on athletic and extracurricular activities, but McCain was able to maintain an academic performance good enough to position himself for acceptance into the Naval Academy.

Years later, McCain would single out one master who played a meaningful part in shaping his character: William B. Ravenel, who devoted his life and career to teaching young men. The effort Ravenel expended on McCain was profound: He tried to make McCain become a better person. "William Ravenel was a leader of men," says Robert Whittle, a student at Episcopal whose uncle also taught there. "Mostly, he used a sense of humor instead of force. He was a guy you knew was smarter than you and funnier than you. He used both traits to move you along. He coached football and taught English. Specifically, he had a wry sense of humor. He understood what you were going through as a 16- or 17-year-old, and he turned it around and used it on you. You were very cynical, if you were at a boarding school. And he let you know he was more cynical than you were. He used that positively. He was, simply, a wonderful English teacher."

In the end, Ravenel was one of the main reasons why McCain matured as much as he did at Episcopal. Ultimately, McCain left the school more seasoned than the 15-year-old who had arrived there, but he was still full of fire and contentiousness. McCain's citation in his school yearbook would attest to that fact. Underneath his senior portrait, McCain, whose home address was listed as 540 New Hampshire Avenue in Norfolk, Virginia, was described as follows: "It was three fateful years ago that 'Punk' first crossed the threshold of the High School. In this time he has become infamous as one of our top-flight wrestlers, lettering for two seasons. His magnetic personality has won for him many lifelong friends. But, as magnets must also repel, some have found him hard to get along with. John is remarkable for the amount of grey hair he has; this may come from his cramming for Annapolis or from his nocturnal perambulations on Ninth Street. The Naval Academy is his future abode—we hope he will prosper there."

McCain *did* prosper there, almost from the start—or so it appeared. "Following his first summer at the Naval Academy," Dick Thomsen remembers, "John came back to the Episcopal campus during the opening days of school. He was dressed in his midshipman uniform and looking absolutely spit-and-polished. Everything was in order—necktie up, the very model of the modern midshipman." That day, McCain sought out Thomsen with a purpose. "Sir," McCain said to his former principal, "I know I gave you a lot of trouble while I was here at the school, and I'm sorry for that. But some of my buddies from last year are still here and I wonder if you'd like me to talk to them and try to get them to have a little bit better senior year than they might have otherwise."

Thomsen was thrilled. "John," he said, "I'd be delighted for all the help I can get. So be sure to talk to them and see if you can give them a straight year ahead."

McCain sought out his old classmates and talked to them. Impressed, Thomsen thought to himself, "Boy, can the Naval Academy really straighten a young man out!"

Eventually, Thomsen got the real story. "About a year or so later," Thomsen recalls, "I learned McCain was one of the greatest hell raisers the Naval Academy ever had. He was always about one or two demerits removed from dismissal from the Academy."

McCain entered the Naval Academy when he was 17 years old. Right from the start, he displayed a bad attitude. "I was basically told when I was young," McCain says, "that I was going to the Naval Academy. And that caused resentment in me—and obviously affected some of my wild behavior. Or *caused* some of my wild behavior." He had been rambunctious at Episcopal. "I would fight at the drop of a hat" because "I was very defensive of my individuality—much too much so." That behavior didn't let up at the Academy. During his years there, his conduct earned him so many demerits that, as one newspaper later reported, "by the end of his sophomore year he had marched enough extra duty to go from Annapolis to Baltimore and back 17 times."

For McCain, all of the nervousness, tumult, and anger he felt did not necessarily come from an outside influence. "He had a little bit of internal conflict," Frank Gamboa, one of his roommates, would say later. "His legacy weighed heavy on him. I was there because I wanted to be there. He was there because it was the family business. He felt he didn't have a choice. He was very proud of his father and of the navy—and he felt comfortable—but at the same time his lack of freedom, of choosing his own way, bothered him." McCain dressed shoddily, left his room a wreck, and maintained a generally bad disposition a good part of the time.

In his first year—"Plebe Year"—McCain often engaged in insubordinate behavior, such as the time he and other plebes gathered in his room and, wearing only their underwear, had a water-balloon fight. He also found a way to keep a contraband television set hidden in his room. However, these were nothing compared to the traditional rituals of Plebe Year with which McCain had to deal. "The plebe will be barked at, shouted at, forced to memorize and recite at all times," John Karaagac, an authority on the military, later wrote. "He will be ordered to stand in that demeaning and exaggerated attention known as 'the brace.' His first year will comprise an extended test of memory and endurance, of conspicuous obedience to the thousands of wearisome chores and indignities that make up the hazing process. His superiors will judge who can take the abuse and who cannot, who reacts well under pressure and who breaks. . . . The plebe will grow accustomed to the timetable, punctuated by bells, that dominates his whole existence; he will grow accustomed to drill and marching and quickly eating in the cavernous mess hall; he will, by degrees, accommodate himself to the constant inspection of room and uniform—aggressive, probing, minute inspection. Above all, he will learn the reality of sleep deprivation and come to dread the shrieking alarm raising him from his sweet slumber at half past six on cold, cruel, and dark mornings."

McCain survived Plebe Year. He struggled academically during his sophomore and junior years, but somehow got by. He excelled in sports, becoming a standout in boxing. When he sailed off on his first class cruise in June 1957, he was looking forward to his senior year.

One highlight of the cruise was a nine-day stay in Rio de Janeiro, where he and friends rented an apartment. "The next four days," one journalist later wrote, "were a blur, involving liquor, women, and night-clubs, everything except sleep, as Rio embraced McCain and his pals in its many charms, X-rated and otherwise." Through an invitation from a fashion designer, McCain met a Brazilian model and spent five days escorting her to various Rio social events.

When he returned to Annapolis for his senior year, McCain knew he would do what his grandfather and father had both done—join the navy with the intention of being a "lifer." At Christmas break, he spent four days with the fashion model in Rio. Then he returned to the Academy for his final semester. When his graduation was imminent, McCain discovered that, of the 894 midshipmen graduating, he was fifth from the bottom. Nevertheless, he proudly attended his graduation exercises on June 4, 1958, and received his bachelor of science degree. The audience listened carefully as President Dwight D. Eisenhower delivered the commencement address.

"John, better known as Navy's John Wayne," read his yearbook citation, "was always reputed to be one of our most colorful characters. Following his family forbears to our sacred shores, he thought the Navy way was the only way. A sturdy conversationalist and party man, John's quick wit and clever sarcasm made him a welcome man at any gathering. His bouts with the Academic and Executive Departments contributed much to the stockpile of legends within the hall. His prowess as an athlete was almost above reproach. . . . John looks forward to a long and successful career in the Navy; he is a natural and will not need the luck we wish him."

Upon graduation, McCain was commissioned an ensign. He spent part of the summer in Europe, where he dated an heiress to a tobacco fortune. In August 1958, he reported to Pensacola, Florida, to start his training as a naval aviator. Pensacola was home to the Blue Angels, the navy's world-famous precision flying unit. While in Pensacola, McCain lived the life of a navy playboy, driving a Corvette, partying around the clock when he was not in training, and dating many women, including an exotic dancer headlined as "Marie, the Flame of Florida."

For the next two-and-a-half years, McCain attended flight school. Part of that time he spent at the Naval Air Station in Corpus Christi, Texas, where he continued to train as a pilot. One Saturday, as he was making a practice run, his engine died. Unable to reach the landing strip, he crashed into Corpus Christi Bay. The plane sank to the bottom of the bay, and McCain, knocked out temporarily when the plane slammed into the water, came to and somehow broke the canopy, wedged his way out of the cockpit, and swam up to the surface of the bay. He had escaped the crash, which could have killed him, with no major injuries, just some bumps and bruises.

Eventually, McCain graduated from flight school in Corpus Christi. During the Cuban Missile Crisis in October 1962, he was a navy flier stationed in the Caribbean. By 1964, he had returned to Pensacola and began a relationship that would change his life. While he was at Annapolis, he knew a young woman named Carol Shepp. Originally from Philadelphia, she had dated a midshipman whom she married. The couple had two sons, Douglas and Andrew, but, like many first marriages, it ended in divorce. Carol was tallish, rail-thin, dark-haired, and her air of sophistication and class appealed to McCain.

Soon after he and Carol rekindled their friendship, McCain was transferred to Meridian, Mississippi, where he served at McCain Field, named for his grandfather. McCain continued with his partying ways, but the longer he stayed in Mississippi the more he became serious about Carol, who still lived in Philadelphia. In time, McCain was flying up to Pennsylvania on weekends to see her. He was a pilot, so flying himself anywhere he wanted to go was not a problem. The couple married on July 3, 1965, in Philadelphia, at the home of Connie and Sam Bookbinder, close friends of Carol. A reception followed at the Bookbinders' restaurant. As soon as he could, McCain adopted Carol's two sons and the new family settled into their life in Mississippi.

McCain continued to fly himself to destinations around the country. A trip in the autumn of 1965 almost ended in disaster. He had flown to Philadelphia to see the Army-Navy football game. On his way back, as he was flying to Norfolk, Virginia, where he planned to stop before proceeding to Mississippi, he had just started his descent when his plane's engine failed. He tried to recrank the engine three times—with no luck. As the plane headed toward the ground, McCain ejected at

1,000 feet. The plane crashed in a wooded area as he floated peacefully to the earth. Because he had radioed ahead to the Norfolk tower, McCain was soon picked up by a helicopter. For the second time, he had survived a plane crash.

On September 2, 1966, Carol gave birth to the couple's first child, a daughter named Sidney Ann McCain. It *seemed* McCain had three children since he always treated Doug and Andy as if they were his own. Soon after Sidney's birth, McCain was transferred to Jacksonville, where he joined a squadron scheduled to go to Vietnam. In the spring of 1967, the squadron set out for Vietnam on the carrier *Forrestal.* Because McCain's parents were stationed in London, Carol decided to move to Europe and live there while McCain served his tour in Vietnam.

On November 9, 1958, McCain's father, Jack, had been made a rear admiral. On August 10, 1960, he was named Commander Amphibious Group Two. Less than a year later, on May 26, 1961, he became Commander Amphibious Training Command, Atlantic Fleet. By late 1963, he was promoted to vice admiral for his duties as Commander Amphibious Force, Atlantic Fleet.

"When Admiral McCain was commander of the amphibious forces, the symbol was an alligator," says Tom Arrasmith, McCain's aide. "An amphibian that's mean! One of the ships brought him back a real alligator from the Okefenokee Swamp once. I tried to talk him out of it, but he thought it was a great public relations thing. So we ended up traveling with an alligator. The sailors loved it. They thought it was the coolest thing in the world. It was about two and a half feet long. You bet your ass he bit. You would be surprised. I have a number of scars on me that would prove that. His name was Spike.

"Admiral McCain was in charge of an operation in the Dominican Republic. When it was wrapping up, the Organization of American States said it would take over. The general in charge of the Brazilians was not someone you would want to meet on a dark night. He came out to visit the admiral, and the admiral said, 'Tom, bring Spike out here.' So we brought Spike out and the general, being very macho, said, 'Oh, yes, we have lots of these.' The admiral said, 'You want to play with him?' I took the top off the box and the general said, 'I believe I will have a cup of coffee.'"

On May 1, 1967, Jack McCain was named Commander-in-Chief, United States Naval Forces, Europe, which was why he was living in London when Carol and the children moved to Europe. Jack McCain would hold that post until July 1968, when he became Commander-in-Chief, Pacific.

Chapter 3

Vietnam

For Lieutenant Commander John McCain, July 29, 1967—a Saturday—started out like any other day he had spent as a naval aviator assigned to fly missions against the North Vietnamese. Since Tuesday, the *Forrestal,* the carrier on which he had served for eight months, had been in Yankee Station in the Gulf of Tonkin, 175 miles north of the city of Da Nang. After tours in the Mediterranean and the Atlantic, the *Forrestal* had been assigned to join in the American bombing of North Vietnam. To sustain this ongoing bombing campaign, carrier-based airplanes had been flying between 30 and 40 missions a day. During the past several months, a sense of routine had come to identify the entire process for the American airmen.

Each day, like clockwork, American jets took off from the carriers in the Gulf: the *Oriskany,* the *Bon Homme Richard,* and now the *Forrestal.* On average, the North Vietnamese shot down 21 planes a month—a statistic that McCain tried to put out of his mind as he got ready for the day's bombing mission. The high number of losses was one reason pilots loved routines; reassurance came from the sameness of the days. Like many other pilots, McCain was superstitious. He always stuck to a certain sequence, no matter what. Before each flight, as one detail of his routine, McCain had his parachute rigger clean his helmet visor. A person prone to superstition might have been troubled on Thursday when, barely 48 hours into the *Forrestal's* new assignment in the Gulf, two small fires broke out on the ship—one below deck and one in an airplane. The fires had been put out quickly, but they were bad omens.

On the morning of July 29, between 10:15 and 10:30, McCain left a lower deck and proceeded upstairs to the flight deck. It was a beautiful, crystal-clear day on the Gulf. McCain walked over to his plane, an A-4 Skyhawk, parked near the carrier's island about halfway from either end of the ship's 1,000-feet-plus flight deck. Carefully, McCain climbed into his fighter jet. A dozen or so other pilots were boarding their planes to get ready for the day's bombing missions.

When he was strapped down and buckled into the cockpit, McCain pulled shut the plane's canopy and cranked the engine. With the deafening roar of the engine engulfing him, he went through the preflight procedure—a careful check of all gauges and instrument settings. It was not yet 10:55 and the first plane was scheduled to take off at 11:00. Then, as he sat quietly in the cockpit, suddenly all hell broke loose. Only later did he learn that, while the planes were idling on the flight deck, a plane parked several positions down from his experienced what naval aviators call "a wet start." A large burst of flame shot out of the plane and ignited a missile on a nearby aircraft. The missile zoomed across the deck and crashed into either McCain's plane or the one parked to his right. The resulting explosion shocked McCain. All around him, the deck was almost instantly consumed in flames.

His survival instincts taking over, McCain disengaged himself, climbed out of the cockpit, stepped onto his plane's refueling pipe, jumped onto the burning deck, rolled quickly through the flames, and came out on the other side of the inferno. Miraculously, he was relatively unscathed. As he ran away from his plane, he saw that another pilot, about 50 feet away, had jumped from a plane, but his clothes were on fire. As McCain ran to the pilot's aid, a bomb exploded with such force that McCain was thrown backward, and the pilot he had hoped to save was blown up.

While McCain watched helplessly, the fire rapidly consumed much of the four-acre flight deck, setting off bomb after bomb. In no time, half of the carrier's flight deck was overtaken by flames as airplanes caught fire and bombs exploded. Sailors ran from the fire with their clothes aflame; several jumped into the sea. Crewmen shoved planes and bombs overboard, hoping to prevent more deadly explosions. Before long, roughly two-thirds of the ship's 4,800 crew members were involved in the effort to contain the fire.

"I saw so many guys running from the planes, all on fire," Lieutenant James J. Campbell recalled. "Then there were yellow shirts, brown shirts, blue shirts—all jumping on them, trying to smother the flames. They were burning head to foot, screaming. A guy ran past me with no clothes left, burnt off, and not much skin left. I saw two guys with a fire hose. Then there wasn't any more water. A bomb went off. Then they weren't there any more, just the stump of the hose, flopping around."

The fire raged all day and into the night. The last of the fire was not put out until 12:20 A.M. on Sunday. Even then, as the carrier made its way to Subic Bay in the Philippines before proceeding to the United States for repairs, fires continued to break out. In all, four massive holes had resulted from the explosions on the deck of the ship, and four more holes had to be cut in the deck to fight the fires below. In total, 26 planes were lost—either blown up or shoved overboard—and 31 planes and three helicopters were damaged. But the most devastating statistic was the casualties: 135 men died, while countless others were injured. The *New York Times* would describe the fire as "the worst calamity to strike a United States navy ship since World War II and constituted one of the darkest hours in the history of carrier operations."

Press coverage of the fire was extensive. One of the front-page stories in the *Times* featured a striking photograph of McCain. His eyes, dark and foreboding, were looking away from the camera, and his face reflected shock and anguish. The article, "Start of Tragedy: Pilot Hears a Blast As He Checks Plane," described McCain as having "a disarming disregard for formal military speech or style," adding, "He is wiry, prematurely gray and does not take himself too seriously."

"We're professional military men and I suppose it's our war," McCain told the *Times* reporter, "and yet here were enlisted men who earn $150 a month and work 18 to 20 hours a day—and I mean manual labor—and certainly would have survived had they not stayed to help the pilots fight the fire. I've never seen such acts of heroism."

"The ship went back to the Philippines," John McCain would write. "Then [it] had to return to the United States, and I made one of the several tactical blunders I made in my life, when the recruiters came over from the *USS Oriskany* and said they were looking for volunteers because they'd lost a number of pilots. And for reasons I still can't explain, my arm shot up and I found myself on the *USS Oriskany* in a very famous squadron, VA-163. The air wing on the *Oriskany*, I'm told, had the highest losses of any air wing in the war. Part of that was because the *Oriskany* was in the middle of the escalation that took place in the summer and fall of 1967."

That escalation, of course, was not devoid of controversy. It had already become obvious to many of the military personnel involved in the Vietnam War that the United States did not have in place a tactical agenda directed toward winning the conflict. Perhaps the greatest source of their frustration was their belief that Washington was not allowing them to do what they needed to do to win. The most constant criticism centered on President Lyndon B. Johnson, who had become so concerned about provoking a nuclear conflict with either China or the Soviet Union that he, or rather a committee he controlled, had drawn up a list of approved bombing targets in North Vietnam. Some targets were bombed repeatedly since a certain number of missions had to be run every day.

"It was dumb the way we were doing it," says Roger W. Smith, who served in the air force in Vietnam at that time. "I wasn't sure there was any value to what we were doing. You had to be an idiot not to know that, because nothing changed. And we knew, better than the protesters back home, the fact of what was going down and how ineffectual it was. We had rules of engagement that put us at greater risk in order to not put the enemy at greater risk—like rolling in over Hanoi. We did not want to have collateral damage from a stray bomb. Here we were going to Hanoi, their capital, and we were told to keep the bomb and pull up on a run if a little cloud rolls over in front of you."

Many members of the military blamed the United States' unsuccessful approach to the war on Robert McNamara, who was secretary of defense under President Johnson. In later years, McCain insisted on calling him by his full name: Robert Strange McNamara. Their complaint about McNamara was simple. He made uninformed decisions that directly affected the war effort because he did not understand the military and he would not listen to those who did. It was not until 1968 that Johnson replaced McNamara with Clark Clifford.

During the summer and fall of 1967, McCain flew bombing missions over Vietnam with VA-163 off the *Oriskany*. He could have chosen to go to the *Intrepid,* the carrier that had replaced the *Forrestal* after the fire—he had been stationed on the *Intrepid* twice before and had enjoyed the tours—but McCain joined the *Oriskany* attack squadron because he had come to Vietnam to fly combat missions. It would be one of those missions that would prove to be disastrous for McCain.

On the morning of October 26, Lieutenant Commander John McCain climbed into his A-4 Skyhawk to fly his twenty-third bombing mission. McCain's plane was one of 24 aircraft that were catapulted off the *Oriskany* that morning. They headed away from the carrier and formed their flight pattern as they started toward Hanoi. None of his earlier missions had taken McCain over the center of Hanoi, so he was more than a little apprehensive as he flew above the blue waters of the Gulf.

McCain's mission required flying over downtown Hanoi, since his target was the Hanoi Thermal Power Plant. By now, the issue of targets had become sensitive to a number of pilots, McCain among them. Combat pilots like McCain believed it made no sense to have the bombing of North Vietnam masterminded, for all intents and purposes, by the White House. Because Washington wanted the bombing to continue, American pilots were often risking their lives to bomb installations they had bombed and destroyed the day before. But military personnel must follow orders; therefore, the pilots flew their missions, regardless of what they thought about some of them.

Knocking out a power plant at least made sense. So, as McCain flew the number-three aircraft in the first division of his strike group, he was anxious to conduct his mission. Before long, the American planes arrived over Hanoi, a city that had become one of the most guarded in recent history. American pilots who flew over Hanoi knew they would meet a more or less constant barrage of surface-to-air missiles (SAMs), which the North Vietnamese were buying from the Soviets. The pilots feared the huge SAMs—each missile was the height of a telephone pole—because any plane hit by a SAM was probably going to crash.

So far, McCain's twenty-third mission seemed like it was going to be successful, though the planes were encountering more than their share of surface-to-air missiles. As he flew over the city, McCain spotted his target. The power plant, 4,500 feet below, was just waiting to be hit, so McCain cut his steering wheel and rolled into a dive. The dive was quick and effective; he released his bombs. Then, just after the release—the unthinkable! BAM! A SAM smashed into his plane's right wing. The explosion blew the wing off completely. Immediately, the plane twisted into an inverted, straight-down spiral as it plunged toward the ground.

McCain had no choice but to eject, even though the plane was upside-down and hurtling downward. When he pulled the cord, the force of the ejection knocked him unconscious. He could not know it at the time, but the ejection had broken his right leg at the knee, his left arm, and his right arm in three different places. The knee break had occurred because his leg crashed into the control panel as his body shot out of the cockpit. The jerk of the parachute had probably broken his arms. While his limp body drifted down toward the ground, McCain regained consciousness only to discover himself hanging precariously in midair, underneath his parachute. With much noise, his airplane crashed before he was completely aware of what was happening. Then, glancing down, McCain could see he was approaching a body of water. As luck would have it, he had been shot down over the largest urban area in North Vietnam, yet he was going to land in water—apparently a lake. Later, he would learn it was Truc Bach Lake.

McCain glided through the air and plunged into the lake. His helmet and oxygen mask had been blown off during the ejection, but because he still had 50 pounds of equipment strapped to his body, he began to sink. Somehow he rose up to the surface, but no sooner had he taken a gulp of air than he descended again. He tried to swim—to no avail; his right arm and right leg could not function. Miraculously, he resurfaced again; when he sank the third time, he went to the bottom of the lake. In danger of drowning, he was able to bite the toggle of his life preserver with his teeth and pull it free. Quickly, the life vest inflated, and McCain floated to the surface. As he shot out of the water, he gasped for air. Then he began bobbing in the middle of the lake.

The spectacular sight of a plane being shot down and a pilot parachuting to earth drew the attention of North Vietnamese onlookers, who began to gather on the edge of the lake. One of the Hanoi locals was a young man who worked as a storeroom clerk at the Department of Industry. His name was Mai Van On.

Carrying a bamboo pole, On swam out to where McCain was floating in the water. With the weighty equipment pulling McCain under, more of his body was under the water than above it. McCain was also all tangled up in his parachute cords. The first thing On did was to pull the upper part of McCain's body out of the water. "His head was drooped and his eyes were closed," On later said. "They gradually opened, and I saw a look of relief that he was still alive." With the pole engaged among the parachute cords, On pulled McCain toward the shore. When they were drawing close to the lake's edge, a neighborhood teenager, Le Tran Lua, swam out to help On bring McCain the rest of the way. In the shallow water, On could see that, under his badly ripped flight suit, McCain was wearing a chain around his neck. It was McCain's good-luck charm.

Once On and Lua got McCain near the shore, a group of locals helped pull him the rest of the way. On could not stave off the crowd of 40 or more people who moved in to curse and spit at the downed pilot. So crippled he was unable to move, McCain could not defend himself. Soon after, members of the mob stripped McCain to his underwear. As others in the mob kicked him, McCain looked down at his leg. His right foot was resting at a 90-degree angle against his left knee. Horrified at how badly his leg was broken, McCain shouted, "My God, my leg! My leg!" And when he said this, the mob became infuriated.

A Vietnamese soldier slammed his rifle butt into McCain's shoulder, crushing it. Another soldier stuck a bayonet first into his left foot, then into his groin. In unimaginable pain, McCain lay on the ground unable to move. He was at the mercy of a mob that seemed intent on killing him. Then, out of nowhere, the Hanoi police arrived, forced the crowd to back off, and prepared to take McCain to the place where they took all American pilots who had been shot down over Hanoi. Positioning him on a stretcher, they put McCain's crumpled body in a car and drove him across town to Hoa Lo Street, a thoroughfare that had just one address on it. Hoa Lo Street was the address of Hoa Lo Prison, a place the Americans had nicknamed the Hanoi Hilton.

"I was taken into a cell and put on the floor," McCain later wrote. "I was still on the stretcher, dressed only in my skivvies, with a blanket over me." For the next four days, McCain remained in that spot. Periodically, one interrogator or another would come into the room and try to get information from him. McCain would give up only his name, rank, serial number, and date of birth—the procedure stipulated in the military Code of Conduct for prisoners of war. When McCain refused to provide information, the interrogator would slap him, but McCain was so injured that if he was hit too hard, he blacked out. The North Vietnamese made his status clear: He would get medical attention if—and only if—he gave them information. He was also given little food and water.

One day, two guards came in and pulled back the sheet to look at McCain's body. When they did, McCain saw his knee for the first time. He was shocked to see that it had swollen to the size of a football. Realizing how bad his knee was, McCain said to one of the guards, "Get the interrogator." Before long, a man arrived whom the prisoners would call The Bug. McCain later described him as "a psychotic torturer."

Calmly, McCain said to The Bug, "Look, take me to the hospital, give me some treatment, and then maybe we can talk about military information."

The Bug left, then returned with the camp doctor, whom the prisoners called Zorba. Zorba examined McCain, took his pulse, and spoke to The Bug in Vietnamese.

"Are you going to take me to the hospital?" McCain asked.

"It's too late," The Bug said.

"Take me to the hospital," McCain said, "and we'll talk about military information. If you take me to the hospital, I'll get well."

Ignoring McCain, The Bug repeated, "It's too late. It's too late." Then he and Zorba left. A few hours later, The Bug burst back into the room. "Your father is a big admiral," he said, almost shouting. "Now we're going to take you to the hospital." In his excited speech, more than once The Bug referred to McCain as the "Crown Prince." Men soon came and took McCain to the hospital where, for the next three or four days, he was given blood and plasma. This probably saved his life.

McCain's guard was a 16-year-old boy, who ate nearly all the food he was supposed to feed him. Eventually, the doctors tried to administer some medical treatment. McCain was taken to a room where a doctor attempted to put a cast on his right arm. The bone was broken in three places, and the doctor had a problem getting the bone pieces into proper alignment. For three excruciating hours, without the benefit of a sedative or novocaine, McCain endured the doctor's fumbling attempt to fit the bone pieces together. Repeatedly, McCain passed out from the indescribable pain. Finally, the doctor gave up and simply placed the arm in a cast.

McCain was rolled into a clean, white room where he was placed in a bed. Exhausted by the ordeal, he felt as if he had no energy left in his body. An hour or so later, a man the prisoners called The Cat came in, accompanied by a man known as Chihuahua. McCain later learned The Cat, a neatly dressed, lithe, well-mannered man, was the supervisor of all the POW camps in Hanoi. The Cat showed McCain the identification card of Colonel John Flynn of the air force, who had been shot down on the same day as McCain. The Cat, it seemed, wanted McCain to know that the Vietnamese had captured another senior officer. The Cat told McCain he had to speak to a journalist, but McCain refused.

"You need two operations and if you don't talk to him," The Cat said, "then we will take your cast off and you won't get any operations. You will say that you're grateful to the Vietnamese people, and that you're sorry for your crimes."

McCain was joined by a French journalist named Chalais and a two-man television crew. At one point as Chalais questioned McCain, he asked him to describe how he was being treated. McCain said it was satisfactory. Standing behind Chalais and alongside Chihuahua,

The Cat told McCain to say he was grateful for the lenient and humane treatment he was receiving from the North Vietnamese, but McCain refused. The Cat insisted he say it, but again McCain refused. Finally, Chalais turned to The Cat and said, "I have enough." Only then did The Cat back off. As soon as the filming was over, McCain was taken back to his filthy room, where his young guard continued to eat his food.

On Saturday, November 11, the *New York Times* ran an article entitled "Hanoi Says McCain's Son Terms U.S. 'Isolated.'" In the article, which repeated comments attributed to McCain in the Hanoi press, McCain, identified as "son of Admiral John S. McCain Jr., commander of United States naval forces in Europe," was said to have given an interview to North Vietnamese journalists in which he said: "The morale of the Vietnamese people is very high, the Vietnamese people are very strong, present events are moving to the advantage of North Vietnam, and the United States appears to be isolated." To make the comment sound plausible, the Hanoi press included remarks presumably made by another American serviceman, John Flynn. The Hanoi press reports said, according to the *Times,* that both McCain and Flynn had mentioned the effectiveness of the antiaircraft artillery being used by the North Vietnamese to guard Hanoi.

Two weeks after the surgery on his right arm, McCain was subjected to an operation on his leg. In the days following the operation, McCain's condition worsened. His spirits were not lifted when the doctors told him his leg needed two more operations but they were not going to perform them because he had a "bad attitude." Finally, one day, when it was obvious McCain was not improving, The Bug visited him and asked what could be done to make him feel better. "Well," McCain said, "I would get better if I was put with some Americans who would take care of me."

Six weeks had passed since the Vietnamese moved McCain from the Hanoi Hilton to the hospital. He now weighed 100 pounds; in those six weeks, he had lost 55 pounds. That night, McCain was taken by truck to a nearby prison the Americans had named The Plantation. He was placed in a cell with two other POWs—Major George ("Bud") Day and Major Norris Overly, both of the air force. At first, Day and Overly were not sure McCain was going to make it. But the two airman fed him, bathed him, and attended his wounds. Finally, after several days, McCain began to perk up and Day and Overly decided he might make it after all. Years later, McCain was clear about what he believed: Day and Overly saved his life.

"My first thought was that they had dumped John on us to die," Day says. "He was filthy. He hadn't been washed, since he had been shot down. He had a bunch of food in his hair, and a beard, and he just smelled like he was rotten. So Overly started cleaning him up and washing him up and taking care of him. John was determined to live. Overly also started getting some food in him. Soon John started gaining some weight and doing better. I sensed very quickly that I was dealing with a remarkably brilliant guy."

After Christmas, the three Americans were moved to another room in The Plantation. In early February, Overly was released, along with David Matheny and John Black. They were the first three POWs freed by the North Vietnamese. "When Overly left, John and I were alone," Day says. "By then, John was doing wonderfully. He'd probably gained about seven or eight pounds. We got really well acquainted. We talked about everything imaginable."

In March, the month in which President Johnson announced an end to bombing north of the twentieth parallel and W. Averell Harriman was dispatched to Paris to prepare for peace negotiations with the Vietnamese, the Vietnamese moved Day to another cell. McCain was then kept in solitary confinement. "I was not allowed to see or talk to or communicate with any of my fellow prisoners," McCain would write. "My room was fairly decent sized—I'd say it was about 10 by 10. The door was solid. There were no windows. The only ventilation came from two small holes at the top in the ceiling, about six inches by four inches. The roof was tin and it got hot as hell in there. The room was kind of dim—night and day—but they always kept on a small light bulb, so they could observe me. I was in that place for two years."

One day in mid-June, McCain was taken to an interrogation room much larger than the others he had seen. He was met there by The Cat and a guard the POWs nicknamed The Rabbit. For two hours, The Cat spoke randomly to McCain. Then he asked flatly, "So you want to go home? The doctor says your condition is still very poor. Would you like to go home?"

McCain knew exactly what The Cat was up to. If the North Vietnamese released him—the son of a famous American admiral—they could use the episode for propaganda purposes. McCain said, "Well, I'll have to think about it back in my room." That response allowed McCain to buy time. He was suffering from a case of dysentery that had terribly debilitated his system, so The Cat's offer was tempting, even though he knew he would not be able to go home. For he was familiar with the military Code of Conduct: Prisoners could be released only in the order in which they were taken prisoner. Many POWs—Everett Alvarez and James Stockdale, to name two—had been there much longer than McCain.

"I was in a cell that was catty-corner from the cell block that John, Norris Overly, and Bud Day were in," says Jack Van Loan, who was shot down on May 20, 1967. "The only way we could communicate with those guys was when they were in the shower. We'd get down on our hands and knees, and we'd whisper in the shower drain. That's how I first heard about John McCain. After they let Overly go, that left Bud in there. In time, they moved Bud too.

"Then one day I was peeking out through a little hole that I had in my door and I saw this group of high-rankers coming through the courtyard of The Plantation. They had with them one of the really good English speakers. He and one or two of the senior guys went into the cell block that John was in and they in essence told him that they had a plane out there waiting and all John had to do was say he had been treated well and he could go home.

"Immediately John started to yell, which you could hear all over the camp. Let me tell you, I picked up a couple of new words that day, because he called them everything in the book. Now this was really dangerous stuff. To start calling them what he was calling them was unacceptable by any standard. I was just standing in my cell cringing, thinking, 'For God's sake, what are you doing?' Of course, John was telling them: 'I'm not going home early.' They could have killed him right there. But they had been told these were valuable blue chips, so John got away with it."

Three days after the previous meeting, McCain was brought back to the interrogation room. The Cat and The Rabbit were waiting for him; they would try to achieve what the high-rankers had not been able to. The Cat got right to the point. "Did you think about our offer?" he said.

"Yes," McCain said. "I can't accept that offer."

"Why?" The Cat said.

"Our code of conduct says you go home by order of those who have been shot down first, then the sick and injured."

"But you're injured," The Cat said.

"Yeah, but I'm going to survive."

"President Johnson has ordered that you go home."

"Show me the orders."

"We don't have them."

"Show me the orders and I will believe it."

"The doctors say you cannot live if you do not go home."

McCain said calmly, "The prisoners must be sent home in the order in which they were captured, starting with Alvarez."

With this, the interrogation session ended abruptly. The Cat was clearly unhappy with McCain. A few days later, McCain was brought in for a third session with The Cat, but he was too weak to talk. Finally, on the morning of the Fourth of July, the day on which McCain's father was named the commander-in-chief of the United States forces in the Pacific, McCain was taken into another interrogation room to meet with The Cat and The Rabbit.

"Our senior officer wants to know your final answer," The Rabbit said.

McCain looked at The Cat, who sat there silently fiddling with an ink pen and a copy of the *New York Herald Tribune*.

"My final answer is the same," McCain said. "It's 'no.'"

"That is your final answer?" The Cat said.

"That is my final answer."

Standing up, The Cat kicked the chair over. "They taught you too well," he said. "They taught you too well." Turning, he stalked out of the room, slamming the door behind him.

There was a pause. Finally, The Rabbit said, "Well, you better go back to your cell. Things will be very bad for you now."

The Rabbit was right. For the next year and a half, McCain lived through nothing short of hell.

One night in August 1968, a guard the prisoners had named Slopehead took McCain into a room where 10 other guards had gathered. "You have violated all the camp regulations," Slopehead said. "You're a black criminal. You must confess your crimes." Specifically,

Slopehead wanted McCain to sign a statement saying he was sorry for the crimes he had committed against the Vietnamese people and thanking his captors for treating him well as a prisoner of war.

McCain refused. "Why are you so disrespectful of the guards?" Slopehead said.

"Because the guards treat me like an animal," McCain said.

At this response, the guards knocked him to the floor and beat him. "After a few hours of that," McCain later wrote, "ropes were put on me and I sat that night bound with ropes. Then I was taken to a small room. For the next four days, I was beaten every two to three hours by different guards. My left arm was broken again and my ribs were cracked."

The beatings continued. The Vietnamese wanted McCain to sign the statement, which of course they intended to use for propaganda purposes. "I held out for four days," McCain later wrote. "Finally I was at the point of suicide, because I saw that I was reaching the end of my rope. I said, 'Okay, I'll write for you.'"

McCain was taken to another room where, for 12 hours, he worked on a statement with an interrogator. The interrogator wrote the final statement, which McCain signed. "It was in their language," McCain would write, "and spoke about black crimes, and other generalities. It was unacceptable to them. But I felt just terrible about it. I kept saying to myself, 'Oh, God, I really didn't have any choice.' I had learned what we all learned over there: Every man has his breaking point. I had reached mine."

After he signed the statement, McCain was allowed to rest for two weeks. But because the Vietnamese decided they could not use the statement he had signed, they tried to break him again. This time, he was both physically and mentally strong enough to resist. He never signed the document they wanted. Because of this, the beatings continued, sometimes two or three a week. The severe treatment went on until October 1969. In August of that year, Navy Lieutenant Robert F. Frishman, along with Air Force Captain Wesley Ramble and Seaman D. B. Hegdahl, had been released. On September 2, in a press conference held at Bethesda Naval Medical Center, Frishman and Hegdahl detailed the abuse they had suffered as POWs in North Vietnam.

Frishman had been shot down on a bombing mission over Hanoi on October 24, 1967. In the crash, his elbow was crushed, but instead of treating his injury the Vietnamese doctors simply removed the elbow, leaving him disabled. Hegdahl, who had been captured when he fell overboard from his ship, had been kept in solitary confinement for a year.

The testimony of the former POWs so disturbed Secretary of Defense Melvin Laird—who had replaced Clark Clifford following Nixon's victory over Hubert Humphrey in November 1968—that he released a statement, that day, which included this sentence: "There is clear evidence that North Vietnam has violated even the most fundamental standards of human decency." In the *New York Times* article "Ex-POWs Charge Hanoi with Torture," Frishman mentioned McCain. "It's bad enough just being in solitary confinement," Frishman said of McCain, "but when you're wounded like John, it's harder." Starting in October, as a result of the news conference, the treatment of the POWs improved significantly.

One morning during Christmastime, the guards came for McCain. "We're going to take you to a Christmas service," one said. Enthusiastic at first, McCain became furious when his guards took him to a room equipped with five or six television cameras. Obviously, the Vietnamese were going to film the POWs holding a Christmas church service. The guards had barely gotten McCain inside the room before he started shouting. Soon, his yelling included foul language. When he was forced to sit in one of the pews, he said loudly to the man beside him, "Hi, my name's John McCain; what's yours?" Single-handedly, McCain had all but ruined the attempt made by the North Vietnamese to create a propaganda tool. "That was the fun part," McCain later wrote. "They let me enjoy the rest of Christmas day but the next few weeks were pretty rough."

McCain was removed from The Plantation and sent back to the Hanoi Hilton. Specifically, he was placed in an area called Las Vegas. Years would pass before he was allowed to leave the prison he later described as "the hotel where they didn't leave a mint on your pillow."

"He had landed in that Ho Chi Minh pond," says Admiral James Stockdale, a prisoner since September 1965, who knew both McCain and his father. "Without having the guts and kicking himself off the bottom, he would still be down there. After that, he probably got a bit mellower. But he was no mellow guy then. He wasn't going to give anybody anything. As a result, I don't think anybody got beaten up as much as John McCain. He was obstreperous, and he hated people that tried to work him over. He was contemptuous of those goddamned gooks and he let them know it. Being the son and grandson of navy admirals, he knew more than most that when you get into prison camp, the story changes. He knew the rules of the game, and he was not about to kiss ass to get out of there. In fact, the last thing you want to be is cooperative. He conducted himself as a belligerent, and that is the only way to go. They wanted to kiss him because he was the prince of an admiral. He wasn't there for that. He was there to keep his mouth shut and get out of prison when the war was over. What they had was really an extortion prison, where you were expected to make pacifistic comments or take a beating. And anybody who was anybody was taking beatings."

"**M**y first encounter with John McCain was through a wall between Rooms Six and Seven in the Hanoi Hilton," says Orson Swindle, who was taken prisoner on November 11, 1966. "I was put in Room Six adjacent to John. We started communicating through the wall. I was tapping, 'Who is this?' 'John McCain,' he replied. Then he told one of these really lousy jokes. 'How can you identify an Italian airline?' 'I have no idea,' I tapped back. 'It's the one with the hair in the wheel wells.' This guy has been shell-shocked or something, I thought."

At the time, the Hanoi Hilton held about 450 POWs. Many of them, like Swindle and McCain, had come to know the history of the facility well. The structure had been built in 1945 on a site once occupied by local families who made earthenware hibachis, known as "hoa lo." Throughout the prison, the cells had leg shackles so the prisoners could be chained to their beds. The steel doors had peepholes for spying on the prisoners. The first American POWs had landed in the Hanoi Hilton in August 1964. Over time, as more and more Americans arrived, the place developed a folklore that included labels provided by the POWs. The prison's sections had names like Camp One, Camp Unity, Heartbreak Hotel, New Guy Village, and Las Vegas. Some of the larger areas had subdivisions. Las Vegas was made up of the Thunderbird, the Stardust, the Riviera, the Desert Inn, and the Golden Nugget. When he arrived in late 1969, McCain was put in the Golden Nugget, a sub-area consisting of only three rooms.

McCain remained in solitary confinement in the Golden Nugget until March 1970, when John Finley, an air force colonel, moved in for two months. In May, the Vietnamese wanted McCain to meet with an antiwar group that was visiting the prison. McCain refused. In June, because of his unwillingness to meet with any of these groups, McCain was moved into a room called Calcutta, a six-foot-by-two-foot cell with no ventilation. The tiny space was incredibly hot, and McCain quickly came down with another case of dysentery. In September 1970, when he was moved to the Riviera, he was able to communicate with other prisoners by tapping on the wall in code. He remained in the Riviera until December, when he was moved to a huge space called the Thunderbird. On Christmas night, he was transferred to Camp Unity. For the first time since he was brought to the Hanoi Hilton a year ago, he was in a part of the prison outside Las Vegas.

"In late 1970," McCain later wrote, "there was a change in our treatment. Ho Chi Minh died. We were put into large cells of two or three together in each cell. I was put in a cell with Admiral Stockdale, Robinson Risner, the other famous ones. But it didn't last very long because [in March 1971] we had a riot over having church services. The Vietnamese wouldn't let us have a church service. The Vietnamese came and selected 36 of us, and we were taken out to a punishment camp called Skid Row."

"I called it Skid Row," Orson Swindle says, "because it was a single long building with about 36 cells and a long dark walkway in front of us. They told us we were the bad apples in the barrel and they were isolating us. The first thing we did was establish who was there, because we were taken out there in typical fashion: blindfolded and handcuffed. Instinctively, we knew that we were put in cells. We started peeking through doors and cracks, and soon we concluded that there were no guards in the area and the doors were closed. But we could whisper, talk, or bounce our voices across the wall in front of us. We learned all these ingenious ways of communicating.

"John is a compulsive communicator. As soon as we got there, he said, 'Hey, Orson, it's John McCain. I am down in Room Nine. Orson,' he continued, 'I wanted to tell you this when we started tapping through the wall the other day. Ever since I graduated from the Naval Academy in '58, I wanted to be a marine in the worst way.' 'That's interesting, John,' I said. 'Why weren't you?' 'I was going to apply,' John said, 'but they told me I wasn't qualified.' 'How can that be possible?' I said. 'You're a Naval Academy graduate. Why weren't you qualified?' 'Well,' John answered, 'my parents were married, so therefore I wasn't qualified.' Those were his first words to me in Skid Row."

McCain and the group remained in Skid Row from March until August. They returned to Camp Unity for one month because Skid Row flooded; then they were sent back to Skid Row until November. "Finally," Swindle says, "in November 1971 they moved us back to the Hilton. They moved about 25 of us into a room together. John and I ended up sleeping side by side on this stone pedestal." It was the first time McCain had been kept with a large group of Americans since he had arrived at the Hanoi Hilton four years earlier. "Believe it or not," McCain would write, "we had a wonderful time in that cell. We played cards. We had church services. I taught a history course. We had a choir. Our choir director was a guy named Quincy Collins who had been the choir director at the Air Force Academy Glee Club. We had guys with wonderful voices. When people say how terrible it was in prison, this was wonderful, especially after what we had just gone through."

"We had hours upon hours of time to talk and get to know each other in infinite detail," Swindle says. "We talked about everything we ever did in sports personally, and all of our heroes from the great sports events we had witnessed or listened to on the radio. We talked about books. John is one of the most well-read people I've ever met. He has an incredible memory. John and I tried to put together a history of the English and American novels. We tried to recollect the sequence of the novels as they were written, going back to *Robinson Crusoe* and *Moll Flanders*. We just made up what we didn't remember.

"John would also tell movies by narrating them from memory. We would have 'Monday Night at the Movies,' 'Tuesday Night at the Movies,' and so on. There was a Hemingway movie made in the early 1960s about the adventures of a young man, Nick Adams. A biography of Hemingway, really. We told it with all the sequences of the punch-drunk fighter. One of the best things John did was tell stories of Damon Runyon. He could imitate the dialect of the New York bookies. He told us all about the Harvards and the Yales playing football, and going up to Saratoga. John was a great entertainer."

In 1971, the POWs were finally able to have a proper church service on Christmas because, after numerous requests from prisoners, the Vietnamese belatedly found a copy of the Bible. Since he had gone to Episcopal High School, which required attendance at chapel each morning as well as Sunday, McCain was selected by the group to be their chaplain—a profound irony, considering the profanity that peppered his speech. McCain copied passages from the Bible before he returned it to the Vietnamese, and, on Christmas Day, the POWs were able to hold a church service during which scriptures from the Bible were read. "[T]he choir would sing a hymn, and then I would read from that part of the story of the actual birth of Christ," McCain later wrote. "The choir sang 'Silent Night.' I looked around that room and there these guys were with tears in their eyes. In some cases streaming down their cheeks. The tears were not of sorrow and homesickness. They were tears of joy that for the first time, in the case of some who had already been there seven years, we were able to celebrate Christmas together. It was one of the most, if not the most, remarkable experience of the time that I was in prison."

As McCain was enduring his fifty-sixth month of captivity, events in Hanoi, outside of the Hanoi Hilton, focused worldwide attention on the war and the plight of American POWs. On July 8, 1972, after establishing a reputation for being not only an accomplished actress but also a passionate social critic, Jane Fonda landed in Hanoi for a two-week visit as a guest of the North Vietnamese government. Only weeks before, she had won the Academy Award for Best Actress for her performance in *Klute,* so her supporters could not argue that she didn't know the power of the image. Therefore, it's hard to imagine she didn't understand what she was doing when, just days into her visit, as she was being given a tour of North Vietnamese military equipment, she was asked to pose in a tank and, strapping on a helmet, readily complied.

"The government guides took Miss Fonda on a tour of the environs of Hanoi and some of us reporters were allowed to accompany her," one Czech journalist would say years later, recalling the events of that day. "We stopped for lunch, where there were a lot of toasts in Russian wine and Hungarian *slivovitz.* Then they took her to an antiaircraft battery. She had this fixed smile on her face as they moved her toward one of the antiaircraft guns. They said that this was one of the heroic weapons that was protecting the city from the barbaric American air bombardment. Someone put a soldier's steel helmet on her head and she joked that this was just like a Hollywood publicity opportunity, except that her hair didn't look right. One of the guides, a woman, then fixed her hair so that it was arranged correctly around the edge of her helmet. They asked her to climb up into the gun mount, which she did, sitting in the gunner's seat. Everybody laughed, including Miss Fonda. I don't know whether or not she realized a camera crew was filming every moment of the incident."

When they were released by the North Vietnamese government, the pictures of Fonda, laughing as she cavorted in a Vietnamese tank, stunned the American public. Days later, what she had to *say* proved to be equally controversial. In a gesture that earned her a comparison to Tokyo Rose, Fonda delivered, on Hanoi Radio, an attack on President Nixon and a defense of the North Vietnamese. "Tonight, when you're alone, ask yourselves, 'What are you doing?'" Fonda said, in a direct address to the members of the American military in Vietnam. "[A]s human beings, can you justify what you are doing? Do you know why you are flying these missions, collecting extra pay on Sunday? . . . The people beneath your planes have done us no harm. They want to live in peace. They want to rebuild their country. They cannot understand what kind of people could fly over their heads and drop bombs down there. . . . I know that if you saw and if you knew the Vietnamese under peaceful conditions, you would hate the men who are sending you on bombing missions."

During her visit, Fonda toured homes, state buildings, and hospitals. She was shown the Red River delta, famous for its dikes. One day, she met with a group of seven captured American pilots. "The day before, these guys were cleaned up, given clean pajamas, haircuts, and all that good stuff," says William Haynes, then serving as a military pilot in Vietnam. "They were lined up and they knew they would be meeting Jane Fonda. So they got together and decided, 'Hey, we've got to do something. Some of our families don't even know we're here.' They came up with the scheme that they would have tiny little slips of paper with their Social Security numbers written on them. They figured they'd try to get them to Jane Fonda because they didn't believe she was really in support of North Vietnam. When she went down the line and shook their hands, they gave her these little slips of paper in the handshake, and she promptly palmed them. At the end of the whole thing—and this is all a photo-op, of course—when all of the cameras were off, she calmly walked over to the head of the North Vietnamese delegation, handed him the papers, and said, 'This is what these people did.' The POWs couldn't believe it. They absolutely couldn't believe it. They were beaten severely. The story I heard—and I was told this from guys who were present—is that one guy died from the beating."

On July 20, Fonda made a speech for which many members of the American military would never forgive her. "They are all in good health," she said about the pilots. "We exchanged ideas freely. They asked me to bring back to the American people their sense of disgust of the war and their shame for what they have been asked to do. . . . They all assured me that they are well cared for. They listen to the radio. They receive letters. They are in good health. . . . I'm sure that with the studying and reading they've been doing here, those pilots will go home better citizens than when they left."

The American POWs were horrified by Fonda's actions and comments. "We were absolutely dismayed when Jane Fonda showed up over there," Jack Van Loan says. "Because she went on Hanoi radio and told our young people in the South to lay down their arms and desert, she committed treason. That's what we thought. We knew right away when she was doing it too because they played Hanoi radio for us. The way she conducted herself was absolutely inexcusable."

One of the pilots Fonda had hoped to meet in Hanoi, before she left North Vietnam on July 22, was John McCain. Aware of the flood of propaganda that was sure to follow after a trip made by such a famous American, McCain refused to meet with her.

The years 1971 and 1972 were comparatively uneventful. Then, on December 18, 1972, the United States forces resumed their bombing of North Vietnam. Hanoi was a main target. "The bombs were dropping so close that the building would shake," McCain later wrote. "The SAMs were flying all over and the sirens were whining—it was really a wild scene. When a B-52 would get hit—they're up at more than 30,000 feet—it would light up the whole sky. There would be a red glow that almost made it like daylight, and it would last for a long time, because they'd fall a long way." With the bombing missions resumed, there was an influx of new POWs, who brought news from back home, a rare commodity in the Hanoi Hilton.

McCain learned a great deal about the war. At the end of October 1968, the month before Nixon's election to the presidency, Johnson ordered an end to the bombing of North Vietnam. Then, early in November 1969, Nixon announced what he called his policy of "Vietnamization," a plan that would turn over the fighting of the war to the South Vietnamese. That began the gradual withdrawal of American troops from Vietnam, a reduction process that continued during the next several months. In April 1970, Nixon announced that U.S. and South Vietnamese troops would invade Cambodia to keep North Vietnam from setting up supply bases there. When the reaction of the American public was negative, Nixon changed his position and declared that, from then on, the United States would provide only air cover to the South Vietnamese, who were continuing their ground assault.

In March 1972, the North Vietnamese began to attack installations in the demilitarized zone. On April 15, for the first time in four years, the United States resumed bombing Hanoi and the strategically important port city of Haiphong. In May, Nixon ordered the mining of Haiphong's harbor. On August 12, the last of the American troops left Vietnam by departing Da Nang, leaving some 43,500 troops in the country as a support force. The number was reduced to 16,000 by December, the month in which the United States began the worst bombing of the war. From December 18 until December 30, 1972, North Vietnam was subjected to relentless bombing. Finally, after 12 days, it was announced that the on-again-off-again peace talks would resume in Paris on January 8, 1973. Now, all sides were motivated to reach an agreement. With the possibility that a peace agreement could be reached, the POWs in North Vietnam began to sense they might be able to go home.

As this geopolitical drama unfolded, everyday life went on for the American POWs. "John is very competitive," Orson Swindle says. "He doesn't like to lose. In January, the guards were pretty much leaving us alone. We made a deck of cards out of some old cardboard so we could play bridge, and we had these little bridge games. One time, Bob Wagoner and John were playing together; Jimmy Bell and I were their opponents. In one hand, John was dealt a really poor hand to our seven no-trump. Jim and I just took our time playing each trick and harassing the living hell out of John. He was seething. We just kicked his butt. We just dragged it out. He pouted about it for a day or two. He would walk around the room, stiff-legged, and I would say, 'John, want to play a little bridge today?' We were merciless. He really scowled about this damn thing.

"Finally, the guards came around one night and told us to roll up and get ready to move. It became almost immediately apparent, by who they were calling, that this thing might be over. The bombing had stopped and there were lots of reasons to be optimistic. They separated us by date of shoot-down and told us to roll up and get out. I was in the first group so I went back and started rolling up my kit—rice mat and silly-looking pajamas. John ran up, grabbed me from behind and said, 'Orson, I have been a real prick. You know you're my best friend. I have really been acting foolish here. I am just really sorry, and I hate to see you go. We got to get together when we get home.' And I said, 'You little, shanty Irish bastard, I don't want to talk to you. You're such a poor loser.' John's jaw just dropped. He couldn't believe what I just said. I turned around and walked away, then I turned back, grinned, and said, 'I'll see you at home.' I left a few weeks later to be stationed in Jacksonville, Florida. When John arrived in Jacksonville himself, after I did, I was standing at the bottom of the stairs waiting for him as he got off the plane."

There were a few events that took place between Swindle telling McCain goodbye in Vietnam and greeting him in Florida. On January 20, 1973, McCain was moved from the Hanoi Hilton to The Plantation. For the first time, the POWs were hopeful that the war might be ending. On January 23, 1973, the peace accords were signed in Paris by Henry Kissinger and Le Duc Tho. President Nixon announced there would be "peace with honor," and a cease-fire would come as a preamble to withdrawal of U.S. troops and release of all POWs. "[A]fter I got back," McCain would write, "Henry Kissinger told me that when he was in Hanoi to sign the final agreements, the

North Vietnamese offered him one man that he could take back to Washington with him, and that was me. He, of course, refused, and I thanked him very much for that, because I did not want to go out of order."

After the accords were signed, American POWs knew it was a matter of time before they were released. Still, most did not allow themselves to become hopeful—not until they were told to get on an airplane that would fly them out of Hanoi. That day came for John McCain on March 14, 1973. Along with 106 pilots and one civilian, McCain was taken to Gia Lam Airport. When the Americans were lined up on the tarmac and ready to board the plane in order of their capture, The Rabbit was there to see them off. "When I read your name off," The Rabbit said, "you get on the plane and go home." Soon after McCain boarded, the plane, full of POWs, took off and headed away from Hanoi. McCain did not look back. For his service in Vietnam, McCain would be awarded the Legion of Merit, a Silver Star, a Bronze Star, a Purple Heart, the Distinguished Flying Cross, and the Vietnamese Legion of Honor.

McCain would struggle for years with what the Vietnam War had meant to him. "I think history will judge the Vietnam War in two perspectives," McCain says. "One is that it was the most divisive conflict, besides the Civil War, in our history and caused deep divisions within American society. We saw a tragic loss of thousands of young Americans. I think the second way it will be viewed concerns what we learned from that war. And we learned, hopefully, never to make those kinds of errors again—never, in other words, to find ourselves in a conflict without a clear, definable goal [or one] that doesn't have the support of the majority of the people. In short, there was a fundamental reform of the military—and our strategic thinking—as a result of the Vietnam War.

"Looking back, I am proud to have served my country in a cause that I believe was just—Vietnam. I am saddened by the way that it was conducted, which caused the tragic sacrifice of so many innocent young lives. I think the average age of those killed in Vietnam is nineteen and a half. That grieves me beyond description."

Chapter 4

Coming Home

"Other guys would have snapped," Richard Nixon would say, "but McCain never did. Those guys were really something. Everyone who served in Vietnam had guts. They could have ducked it; who wants their ass shot off? But McCain went, and once he became a POW—you know, the North really got a propaganda bonanza with him—he just never gave up."

That's how President Nixon described McCain years later. At the time of McCain's release, Nixon was happy the war was over and the POWs were returning home. Not long after McCain arrived in the United States, Nixon hosted a reception at the White House to honor the POWs. One picture taken on that occasion would become famous. In it, Nixon is extending a handshake to McCain who, crippled, on crutches, wearing his navy dress-white uniform, hobbles up to meet him.

"That night at the White House John looked so good," George Day says. "He had put on some weight. He was in a white uniform and had a haircut and a good shave. I was delighted to see how young he looked. He probably looked 10 years younger. He looked marvelous." Many of the POWs would remember the reception as being a highlight of their first months back. Of course, Nixon, himself under political fire, was cheered by the event as well. "Each of the POWs was invited along with a guest," Paul Galanti remembers. "We had the run of the White House. They even let people on the second floor. I mean, Nixon was ebullient. He was just bubbling. And he said: 'You want to go up and see the living quarters? Go ahead.' The Secret Service had a conniption, but he was the boss. So we went up."

After the tribute, McCain and the others had to readjust to civilian life in the United States. For McCain, it was easy. "It took me about 40 minutes to adjust to freedom," McCain says. "That was the time of the flight from Hanoi to get over the water. You see, I was 30 years old when I was shot down, so I was pretty well formed. The ones that suffered the most from the Vietnam War were the 18- and 19-year-old kids." By the time he was reunited with Carol and his children in Jacksonville, he was more than ready to resume the life they had enjoyed before he left for Vietnam.

But there was a new problem he had to deal with. At Christmastime in 1969, Carol was almost killed in a car crash. "Carol had taken the kids to her parents' house for the holidays," McCain later wrote. "After dinner on Christmas Eve, she drove to our friends, the Bookbinders, to exchange gifts. It had begun to snow by the time she started back to her parents, and the roads were icy. She skidded off the road, smashed into a telephone pole, and was thrown from the car. The police found her some time later in shock, both legs fractured in several places, her arm and pelvis broken, and bleeding internally.

"Several days passed before she was out of immediate danger. It would be six months and several operations before she was released from the hospital. Over the next two years, she would undergo many more operations to repair her injured legs. By the time the doctors were finished, she would be four inches shorter than she was before the accident. After a year of intense physical therapy, she was able to walk with the aid of crutches." Carol's new appearance was a shock for

McCain to deal with during his period of adjustment. Quite simply, Carol was a different person from the woman he left. Then again, Carol could say the same about him.

A first step McCain took to readjust to ordinary life was to write about his years in captivity. On May 14, 1973, two months after his release, McCain published a riveting account of his five and a half years in prison in Vietnam in *U.S. News & World Report*. Entitled "How the POWs Fought Back," McCain addressed the reception the POWs received on coming home, as well as his own future plans. "The outpouring on behalf of us who were prisoners of war is staggering," he wrote, "and a little embarrassing because basically we feel that we are just average American navy, marine, and air force pilots who got shot down. Anybody else in our place would have performed just as well. My own plans for the future are to remain in the navy, if I am able to return to flying status. That depends on whether the corrective surgery on my arms and my leg is successful. If I have to leave the navy, I hope to serve the Government in some capacity, preferably in Foreign Service for the State Department. I had a lot of time to think over there and came to the conclusion that one of the most important things in life—along with a man's family—is to make some contribution to his country."

First, McCain had to deal with his medical problems. Over the next several months, he underwent three operations; for six months he submitted himself to grueling physical therapy twice a week in an attempt to regain movement in his leg, since his shattered knee had left the leg frozen. "They said, 'You're never going to fly again,' " recalls Carl Smith, a navy pilot who was close friends with McCain. "He said, 'I can do it, I can do it.' He underwent ghastly physical therapy—where they just bent and pushed and stretched and stretched till he was ready to scream—in order to restore enough flexibility that he could fly. The problem was doing the brakes. You have got to be able to put your feet on the pedals and press up at the top of the pedals. Those are your toe brakes. He just didn't have the dexterity at that point because of the injuries. He said, 'No, whatever it takes I am going to do it.' And he kept at it until he finally *could* do it. So they put him back in there."

The operations and the physical therapy allowed him to return to the cockpit, but there were certain functions he would never be able to perform. Because of the injuries to his arms, he would not be able to type on a keyboard or tie his shoes. He could not raise his arms above his head to comb his hair, and he would never be able to throw a baseball or a football again. Naturally, even though he could fly, it was hard for him to work the gears in the cockpit. He also had trouble maneuvering the steering wheel. McCain knew if he could not regain his complete physical abilities, he would not advance to the higher ranks in the navy. He would most certainly never gain the rank of four-star admiral—a tradition that had been well established in his family.

During the academic year 1973–74, as he focused on getting the medical treatment he needed, McCain attended the National War College in Washington. At the end of 1973, he was featured in *U.S. News & World Report*, six months after he had written the article that had received tremendous notoriety. "The last two years that we were there the treatment was relatively mild," McCain was quoted as saying in the article published on December 31, 1973, as he discussed his readjustment to life in America. "If we had come out, say, in late 1969, the problems of readjustment would have been far more severe. Starting in 1971, the food improved considerably. We were allowed to be together more and set up educational programs, and work out some simple entertainment and do a lot of things for each other, to keep our minds active." According to McCain, he had had few problems adjusting to normal life. "The only thing that has been somewhat of an adjustment is the difference in the pace of living now, as compared to in prison. There, the big event of the day usually was when it came your turn to go out of your cell to bathe. I still seem not to have enough time to do all the things that I want to do—or have to do."

Finally, in the article, McCain discussed the major political story that had unfolded since his return: the Watergate scandal. "It has certainly made me sad that this situation should have arisen," McCain said about Nixon, the man who had welcomed him home only a few months earlier. "However, I feel that, in the context of history, Watergate will be a very minor item as compared with the other achievements of this Administration, particularly in the area of foreign affairs. I do hope that this country will get over Watergate and get going again on the very serious problems that we're facing today."

Because of his national reputation, McCain was approached for his opinion on issues important to veterans, especially those who had been in Vietnam. "During this period," says Senator John Warner, who was secretary of the navy from 1969 until 1974, "I had the extraordinary challenge of deciding how to dispose of allegations against several prisoners who allegedly, should we say, worked with the North Vietnamese in a manner that was detrimental to other prisoners and . . . in some cases, benefited themselves. I remember one case came to the point where we were about to file general court martial charges, and I sought John's advice as to the reaction of himself and other prisoners, were the case to go to full trial and be scrutinized publicly. His advice was very helpful to me. The record shows that the Department of the Navy made the decision to deal certain punishments to these individuals, short of bringing court martial."

McCain finished his year at the War College in August 1974, right around the time Nixon was forced to resign. The navy then officially approved McCain's return to pilot status. With his physical state now drastically improved, McCain undertook, in the late fall of 1974, a trip that he hoped would help him heal emotionally. He may have had few problems adjusting to life back home, but he was not sure how he felt about the world of Vietnam he had left behind. Nine months after he had left Hanoi, McCain joined a group of guests who flew to South Vietnam to celebrate what turned out to be the country's last National Day.

The American troops had left some time back, but the war between North and South Vietnam continued. When McCain arrived in South Vietnam, he was surprised to see protests raging against the government. Nguyen Van Thieu was in what became the final days of his presidency. While there, McCain attended a reception for former POWs, hosted by a Thieu aide. When he spoke to the group who had attended the reception, the aide said Vietnam could never repay the American POWs for what they had done for his country. If there was anything the government could do, the aide said—anything at all—they should let him know. Sitting among the others at the gathering, McCain raised his hand and suggested one way he could be repaid. "You can take me to Con Son," he said, referring to the most brutal facility in South Vietnam's prison system.

The aide was stunned by McCain's request; he was noncommittal about whether such a trip could be arranged. Finally, on the last day of his visit, McCain was taken to the island, 50 miles off the southern coast, where Con Son was located. It seemed to do McCain good. He reported later, to friends, that the South Vietnamese had prison facilities just as gruesome and inhumane as those of the North Vietnamese.

One veteran who joined McCain on the trip was Jim Thompson, the longest-held American POW in Vietnam. (He was captured by the Viet Cong in South Vietnam on March 26, 1964, and held until his release in 1973, when he would be described as a "skeleton with hair.") "I had heard legendary stories of Jim's fierce resistance to his captors," McCain would write about Thompson, "and of his heroic endurance under conditions that would have killed many men. Our trip together afforded me a welcome opportunity to get to know him. Never will I forget the love of country that accompanied his surviving the prison camps, his extraordinary test of patriotism, or the evident damage that years of concerted cruelty had done to this good and decent man."

After he returned to the United States, McCain reported to his new assignment in the navy: He was a member of Attack Squadron 174, stationed in Jacksonville, Florida. When he resumed active duty, he was named the executive officer of the squadron. (Many of the men who had been held as POWs were promoted to higher ranks, to make up for the service time they had lost in Vietnam.) While he went about his life at the base, McCain was fully aware of military and political events. He watched as, on April 30, 1975, the Vietnam War finally ended with the defeat of South Vietnam by North Vietnam. On March 4, 1976, two friends, James Stockdale and George ("Bud") Day, were awarded the Medal of Honor by President Gerald Ford at the White House. And as the country tore itself apart during the first presidential race ever to take place after a president had resigned from office, he watched Jimmy Carter defeat Gerald Ford. On July 1, 1976, McCain got good news: He was named commanding officer of the squadron.

"At the time, VA-174 was the largest aviation squadron in the navy, with 70-some aircraft," says Carl Smith, who served under McCain in Jacksonville. "The job of the squadron was to train the replacement pilots that were being assigned to the fleet. The whole squadron had become rather stagnant. It was at a time when, because of the post-Vietnam defense budgets, there really wasn't enough money to maintain the aircraft properly. As a result, a lot of practices were followed that were not optimal; cannibalization is the best example. You could routinely take from one airplane to keep another airplane flying. Realizing this was a bad practice, the navy implemented a policy that prohibited cannibalizing any airplane that had been down for 60 days or longer. Those were called SPINTAC aircraft.

"When McCain became the commanding officer, it was his squadron to run and he could put his mark on it. He immediately began making changes. He fired people, and he replaced people at the top, both senior officers and senior enlisted, whom he thought were not being as effective as he wanted them to be. He wanted real leadership. He wanted the squadron to come to life. It was an incredible transformation—what happened over the next six to nine months.

"We had at any given time one-third of our aircraft in that SPINTAC category. McCain said, 'All right, let's get these airplanes up and running.' The decision was reached that said McCain would write a letter to the authorities in AIRLANT in which he said, 'If you will give me permission to cannibalize the SPINTAC aircraft, then I will commit to getting every one of these aircraft up and flying, save two.' That was essentially putting his career on the line because there were a lot of guys back then who thought McCain was all show and no go.

"What we saw next was an example of leadership. McCain would say, 'You guys in the maintenance department, here's what I want you to do: I want you to get those airplanes up and flying. Give me a schedule and tell me how long it is going to take.' He was perfectly comfortable delegating. Now they had a goal and a challenge, and they had permission to do the cannibalization on the SPINTACs. They got that permission in response to McCain's letter. The enthusiasm in the maintenance department was magnificent after that.

"Let me just tell you what happened. What McCain would do was go around to each one of those shop spaces every day and motivate people. It was wonderful to see how he picked up the morale of the place that had just been dragging along. He would do it by giving his personal attention to individuals. Just by going there and talking to them, kidding with them, just showing them he knew what was going on. To cut to the chase: We finally got down to where we were approaching the change of command, and it was either the day before or the day of the change of command that we flew our last SPINTAC. And I mean our *last*. When he turned that squadron over, it was SPINTAC free. We didn't even have the two left. Every airplane in that squadron was off the SPINTAC list.

"We had had zero accidents. Six months after John left, the next commanding officer had a fatal accident. And the SPINTAC numbers came back. It was strictly a function of leadership—John's leadership. It was bad before him. It was bad after him. And it was great while he was there. As a result of his leadership, the squadron was awarded the navy's meritorious unit commendation for the first time in its history."

During the fall of 1977, in the wake of his success in Jacksonville, McCain was assigned to a Washington post his father had once held—the navy's liaison to the Senate. As soon as McCain got there, the liaison office changed. "The Senate Liaison Office had been a backwater office of no particular consequence before McCain arrived," says Carl Smith, who remained close to McCain even after he moved to Washington. "Suddenly, the electricity around the place was attracting people. It became alive. It became a center for people to come after-hours and just shoot the breeze with John McCain."

Specifically, it was McCain's job to be the face of the navy in dealings with the Senate. His job included planning trips abroad for senators—trips on which McCain often accompanied the Senate delegation. Another main function was dealing with lobbyists, a duty McCain sometimes found difficult to bear. "In the late 1970s," Carl Smith says, "Grumman, who manufactured the A-6, was aggressively lobbying to get some increased capabilities added to the A-6 at some expense, and Congress had expressed some misgiving about whether or not this program was really worthwhile. A retired admiral, who was a lobbyist for Grumman, once went to see McCain, and McCain was basically sticking to the navy line, which was not all that enthusiastic about the airplane and what Grumman was proposing to do. There this retired admiral was, leaning rather heavily on McCain, trying to get him to commit to supporting his project. Finally, the guy went too far, and McCain abruptly told him, 'Look, I don't work for Grumman in general, and I don't work for you in particular.' That was the end of the meeting."

McCain was asked to perform other duties. "Shortly after John came back to Washington, he came to a party at my house," says Ken Ringle, who had remained a friend of McCain since they were students together at Episcopal. "He told me that President Carter had been talking about opening up preliminary negotiations for establishing normal relations with North Vietnam. They were going to send a delegation from Congress. John said to me, 'They want me to go. Sometimes this country just asks too much of you. Can you believe that the navy expects me to go? Can you believe they would even ask me?' He was really bitter about this." McCain did not go to North Vietnam.

Mostly, in those years, he worked directly with the senators and their staffs. Among the senators who became good friends were John Tower of Texas (a Republican), William Cohen of Maine (a Republican), and Gary Hart of Colorado (a Democrat). "I think John went on two or three of those trips I was involved in," Gary Hart says, "and as you might expect, traveling together you begin to bond. Whereas he was always very respectful of us and our titles, being of roughly the same age, and observing the protocol of us being in the Senate and him being a navy officer, we nevertheless got to be friends. John had very strong opinions—and not only on military matters. He was not reticent. He was clearly a conservative, traditional Republican in many respects, but also clearly a free-thinker. When he did take a position, he wasn't just spouting a party line or an orthodox position. He would back up his views with his own arguments." In particular, Hart admired McCain's sense of humor. "It was a raucous, military, masculine, occasionally profane sense of humor. When talking about the navy, he would quote Churchill, who said of the navy, 'Rum, sodomy, and the lash!' So John would joke, 'I love the navy! Rum, sodomy, and the lash!' "

When he was not traveling, McCain was in his office in the Russell Senate Office Building. Since the office was down the hall from the suite of offices occupied by John Tower, McCain and Tower became good friends. "Tower took a natural liking to him for two reasons," says Carl Smith, who followed McCain to Washington and got a job on the Senate Armed Services Committee, thanks to McCain. "First, Tower was navy, but, second, Tower greatly respected intelligent people. He enjoyed being around intelligent people who were well informed, and John was—and is—extremely well informed. He has an incredible appetite for reading, and after Vietnam he had this need to read everything he could get his hands on—books, magazines, newspapers. Carol loved to read too. Every night, they would end the night by reading. McCain was truly a voracious reader. He once gave me a book to read. It was a very insightful book about the causes of the Chinese revolution. It was that interest, that facet of his intelligence, that made him so attractive to John Tower because Tower was truly a global and strategic thinker. McCain is the same."

While McCain was making new friends and connections, he and Carol were leading a busy life at home. "Their house in Alexandria was active with people coming and going," says Carl Smith, who lived with the McCains for four months after McCain had helped him to get the job on the Senate committee. "John and Carol were active socially. They probably had people over for dinner three or four nights out of the week, just as they had had in their house in Jacksonville. It was a meaningful procession that came through there too. There were all sorts of interesting people, not just from the navy or the government. It was all sorts of people."

Still, the main focus of McCain's life was working with the senators. He was able to get along with those who fit almost any political description, from left-leaning Democrats like Hart to Southern conservative Republicans like Thad Cochran. "As the Senate liaison for the navy, John took some trips with Howard Baker and me and Bill Cohen and a few other senators," Thad Cochran says. "We went to Europe. I got to know him and I developed a very strong feeling of affection for him. I had respect for him as a naval officer, although he was accident-prone. He said it didn't take a genius to get shot down. The real heroes were the great pilots who didn't get shot down. But he had already crashed at least one time before Vietnam. And he had been involved in the *Forrestal* fire. He could have gone overboard or gotten blown up in that explosion too. He had a lot of close calls."

In the spring of 1979, even though friends saw a rosy picture when they looked at John and Carol McCain's marriage from outside, privately the couple was having trouble. After years in captivity, McCain was not able to return to the life he had led with Carol before Vietnam.

As the marriage became rocky, McCain was unfaithful to Carol, or perhaps the marriage became rocky *because* McCain was unfaithful. Later, there would even be reports that he had, as the *Boston Globe* put it, "affairs with subordinate female personnel." The McCains had tried to achieve some semblance of a normal life—and, to a great extent, they had—but the problems continued. Years later, Carol would tell a reporter the main trouble was not complicated: McCain may have been 40, but he was acting like he was 25. The McCains separated. Then, McCain's life took a dramatic turn. The reason: a chance meeting in Hawaii.

McCain was escorting a Senate delegation on a trip that included a stopover in Hawaii. One night, at a reception for the senators hosted by the Pacific commander, he met a captivating young woman named Cindy Lou Hensley. Her demeanor was appropriate for what she was—a school teacher. She was quiet, soft-spoken, even bashful. She was 25 to McCain's 42. She had recently earned her master's degree from the University of Southern California, but she was born and raised in Arizona. Dignified and reserved, she had a strength of character and a resolve of will that came from growing up in the shadow of a powerful, successful father. For Cindy Hensley was no ordinary school teacher. Her father, James W. Hensley, owned one of the largest Anheuser-Busch beer franchises in the United States. This made him one of the most prominent businessmen in Arizona. He was a father who loved his daughter too; McCain could tell that right away when he met Hensley in Hawaii. Cindy's parents—her mother's name was Marguerite—had accompanied her there for spring break.

McCain was smitten with Cindy that night. They had dinner alone after the reception and agreed to stay in touch. In the coming months, McCain, separated from Carol, saw Cindy whenever he could. On August 1, 1979, he was promoted to captain as a reward for his excellent work for the navy in the Senate. During the fall of 1979 and into the spring of 1980, it became clear his marriage to Carol was over. The couple divorced on April 2, 1980. In the divorce, which Carol did not contest, McCain agreed to provide support for Carol and their three children.

During his courtship of Cindy, McCain learned about her family's business, Hensley & Co. "James Hensley," the *Arizona Republic* would one day write, "started in the business with his brother, Eugene, before World War II, in the heady days after Prohibition. At United Liquor Co. in Phoenix and United Distribution Co. in Tucson, the Hensleys worked with Kemper Marley Sr., a rancher and political fixer who years later would figure into the infamous car-bomb murder of *Arizona Republic* reporter Don Bolles. Marley died in 1990, but was never legally implicated."

Hensley had served as a bombardier in Europe during World War II and survived when his B-17 was shot down over the English Channel. "Returning to the liquor trade afterward," the *Republic* wrote, "he and his brother were convicted in 1948 of falsifying records to hide the illegal distribution of several hundred cases of liquor. Eugene went to jail for a year. Jim got a six-month suspended sentence. In 1953, Jim Hensley, Marley, and their company again were charged with falsifying records, but they were acquitted. The Hensley brothers soon bought into Ruidoso Downs horseracing track in New Mexico. Eugene stayed to run it. Jim returned to Phoenix, where, in 1955, he landed his Anheuser-Busch distributorship. It was long rumored that Marley had a hand in the deal." Hensley represented many different brands of beer until he was, according to the *Republic,* "approached by Anheuser-Busch with a deal: He could have the franchise for Maricopa County [in Arizona] if he agreed to sell only its brand." Hensley agreed. From then on, Hensley owned the franchise for the county, which became one of the fastest growing urban areas in the United States. It would make him and his family wealthy.

On May 17, 1980, six weeks after his divorce from Carol, McCain married Cindy Hensley in a ceremony in Phoenix. At the wedding, McCain's best men were Gary Hart and William Cohen. Throughout the rest of 1980, the year Ronald Reagan defeated Jimmy Carter, McCain served as Senate liaison. Then, on April 1, 1981, after he had been assigned as a commander of an aircraft carrier, a post he determined he could not hold because of his injuries, McCain reached the hard decision to retire from the navy. He had been in the service now for 22 years. The official reason for his discharge was "permanent physical disability."

There was another motivating factor in his decision to leave the navy. On March 22, as he was flying on a military aircraft while traveling in Europe, McCain's father died of heart failure. He had retired from the navy in 1972, when he gave up his command in the Pacific, and had led a comfortable life with Roberta. Part of that life included extensive travel, which Roberta loved. They were on yet another trip when Admiral McCain died suddenly—as his father had years before. As John McCain stood beside his father's grave on the day in March when he was buried in Arlington National Cemetery just as *his* father had been, he realized there was no overriding reason for him to remain in the navy.

Soon after he retired, McCain moved to Tempe and was named vice president of public relations for Hensley & Co. McCain worked through the remainder of 1981 and on into 1982. But early that year, he learned Congressman John Jacob Rhodes had decided not to run for reelection. Recently McCain had gone to Rhodes, then the leader of the Republican Party in the House, to ask his advice about running for public office. Rhodes told him he should go to Arizona and try for either the state legislature or a county board of supervisors. McCain told Rhodes he was not interested in either of those jobs. Now, in March, with Rhodes stepping down, McCain announced he was running for *his* seat.

Years later, McCain revealed what had motivated him to get into politics. "After Vietnam, I was hospitalized for a period of time," McCain says. "Then I went to the War College. Next I was able to go down and be the executive officer and then the commanding officer of an A-7 squadron. But finally I was sent up to Washington to be the navy liaison officer to the Senate, and that's where I first got very interested in politics. I became friends with people like Gary Hart and Bill Cohen. John Tower, I became very close to. When I saw, literally, a senator write an amendment on the back of an envelope that affected the military to a significant degree, I thought: 'Hey, this is something that should interest you.'"

Chapter 5

The Congressman
from Arizona

"When John married Cindy," says Senator Thad Cochran, "he changed his domicile to Arizona. One night, he invited Rose and me over to their house. They lived on one of those W streets in Alexandria. I could sense then he was beginning to think about running for Congress. That night, he mentioned that Barry Goldwater wasn't going to be in the Senate forever. And I figured it out. He had already set his sights on the Senate, not just the House. He would run for the House, but then the Senate. He had it all planned out ahead of time. It was quite amazing. He didn't say anything, by the way, about the White House."

Gary Hart also saw the growth of McCain's interest in politics. "I think something happened in the late 1970s where the navy let him know he wasn't going to get a star," Hart says. "That's when he decided to retire. Also, whenever you get to the Senate, one of the old-timers takes you aside, especially if you're young, and says, 'Young man, you will spend the first six months wondering how you got here, and years wondering how everybody else got here.' So I think McCain's exposure to us made him think, 'If these guys can be senators, *I* can be a senator.' I think that's exactly what happened. He looked around when he got there and realized all these guys put their pants on one leg at a time."

First, however, he had to win a seat in the House of Representatives. At the time McCain had first heard John Rhodes was going to retire from Congress, he and Cindy owned a house in a district other than the one Rhodes represented. The McCains quickly bought a house in Rhodes' district, the Arizona First. Naturally, McCain was greeted with charges of being a carpetbagger. In typical McCain fashion, he ignored the claims—his longest period of domicile in his entire life, he said, had been in Hanoi—and organized his campaign. Between the time he declared his candidacy in March and the primary election in September, it was his goal to meet as many of the voters in his district as possible, so McCain set out on an unbelievable odyssey: He walked from house to house, knocked on door after door, and talked to as many people as he could. By Election Day, he had worn out two pairs of shoes.

"John was a dark, dark horse in that primary," his political consultant, J. Brian Rhodes, later said. "No poll, including our own, had him finishing anywhere higher than third. But the great thing about John is: He can have a 3-in-10 shot and be thrilled." The hard work paid off. On September 14, in a four-way race among Republicans, McCain won. The final totals were McCain 15,363; Ray Russell 12,500; James A. ("Jim") Mack 10,675; and Donna Carlson-West 9,736.

Now the nominee of the Republican Party, McCain continued his walking tour of the district. From March to Election Day, he knocked on 20,000 doors. Because McCain's district was heavily Republican, he had little to worry about. The Democrats' candidate, William Hegarty, was able to mount only a less-than-lustrous campaign. On November 2, McCain received 89,116 votes to Hegarty's 41,261.

On January 3, 1983, McCain took the oath of office for the First Congressional District of Arizona and became a member of the 98th Congress. Ronald Reagan had been president for two years, and

McCain was more than happy to fall in line behind his party's leader. For the men who were POWs with him in Hanoi, McCain's entry into the House was especially pleasing. "We were both big fans of Felix the Cat," says Orson Swindle, who would hold a number of posts in the Reagan Administration, among them assistant secretary of commerce, before he became a federal trade commissioner, "the single-dimension, flat, no-depth cartoon character. We laughed about how, when Felix would get into trouble, he would always put his little paws up and rock back and forth with a sheepish grin on his face. When something went wrong among the group when we were prisoners, we would get pissed off at each other and start hollering and screaming. John and I would just look at each other, do the little hand signal, and bob back and forth grinning. I happened to be in Washington right after John was elected to Congress and sworn in. I found a Felix the Cat doll. He was just moving into his first congressional office when I walked in and said, 'I got a friend of yours here.' I gave him the doll and he just grinned. I said, 'I want you to put this somewhere where you can always see it and always remember—when you get too big for your britches—*always* remember where you came from.'"

During his first session as a congressman, McCain was assigned to the Committee on Interior Affairs and the Select Committee on Aging. He also became chairman of the Republican Task Force on Indian Affairs. As he settled into his new office and became familiar with his committee assignments, McCain again attracted the attention of *U.S. News & World Report,* which had been covering him since his return from Vietnam.

In late March 1983, the magazine ran a round-up piece called "A Return Visit With POWs—Ten Years Later." In the article, McCain was quoted as saying: "I spent three and a half years in solitary confinement. During that time, I lost a sense of personal ambition and gained a desire to spend my life serving my country." Later in the interview, he added: "Our role has changed. El Salvador is an example. We obviously have advisers there, but if it had not been for the Vietnam War, we might have had the 82nd Airborne there. I think there is a real reluctance on the part of the government to involve American troops again."

During the 98th Congress, McCain sponsored a number of bills, amendments, and resolutions. His work reflected two main areas of concern: Indian affairs and conservative issues important to his constituents back home. On Indian affairs, he sponsored, to quote from government records describing the proposed legislation, a bill "to add a representative of Indian tribal governments to the membership of the Advisory Commission on Intergovernmental Relations" (the proposal was made on April 13, 1983); a bill "to amend the Act of November 2, 1966 regarding leases and contracts affecting land within the Salt River Pima-Maricopa Indian Reservation" (May 4, 1983); a bill "to amend the Indian Tribal Government Tax Status Act of 1982 with respect to the tax status of Indian tribal governments" (November 18, 1983); and a bill "to provide for the administration and probate of certain estates under laws of the Salt River Pima-Maricopa Indian Community, and for other purposes" (May 22, 1984).

For the most part, the McCain-sponsored bills related to Indian matters got little support, although a few made their way successfully through the Congress. McCain's bill to amend the Act of November 2, 1966, progressed through each step in Congress and was signed into law by Reagan on November 22, 1983. That law, according to its abstract, "[a]uthorizes specified leases of trust or restricted lands on the Salt River Pima-Maricopa Indian Reservation (Arizona) to contain provisions for binding arbitration of disputes. [It also p]rovides that failure to submit to such arbitration or comply with the arbitration ruling shall be deemed a civil action arising under the Constitution, laws, or treaties of the United States."

In addition, McCain sponsored, as quoted from government documents: an amendment "to add that nothing in Title III (Operations and Maintenance) is to be construed to supersede or amend the War Powers Act" (submitted on May 24, 1984); a bill "to amend section 1201 of title 18 of the United States Code to provide a mandatory life sentence in the case of certain kidnappings of persons who have not attained the age of 18 years" (submitted on June 13, 1984)—a bill that, according to a government abstract, "amends the Federal criminal code to provide a mandatory life sentence for any person who kidnaps an individual under the age of 18 and [i]mposes the death penalty in any case where such a victim dies as the result of the kidnapping"; and a bill "to provide for the expansion and improvement of the National Cemetery System to better meet the needs of veterans" (submitted on June 29, 1984)—a bill that, according to a government abstract, "[d]irects the Administrator of Veterans Affairs to report to Congress a plan to expand the national cemetery system in at least ten areas with the greatest need."

By and large, during his first term, McCain supported President Reagan and his agenda. He concurred with Reagan on his hardline stands against the Soviet Union. He voted for Reagan's tax cuts, despite the fact that some critics of Reagan's economic policies, including Vice President George H. W. Bush, who had challenged Reagan for the Republican presidential nomination during the 1980 campaign, had called those policies "voodoo economics." McCain agreed with Reagan that the United States needed to take a firm stand in favor of democracy in Central America.

But, on one issue, McCain dramatically broke ranks with Reagan. In the early 1980s, Reagan had sent American servicemen, mostly marines, into Lebanon to serve as peacekeepers. McCain had been outspoken in his criticism of the decision. He said at the time: "I do not foresee obtainable objectives in Lebanon; I believe the longer we stay, the more difficult it will be to leave." Instead, he recommended, in no uncertain terms, "as rapid a withdrawal as possible." Reagan did not heed the advice. The marines stayed. Then, on October 23, 1983, a suicide bomber attacked an American military barracks in Beirut and killed 241 U.S. troops, almost all of them marines. In the wake of the horrific attack, Reagan decided to pull the troops out of Lebanon; some critics, McCain among them, pointed out that the move had come too late. Had Reagan made the decision earlier, the American servicemen could have been saved.

By supporting Reagan the way he did, McCain showed he was capable of being a team player. By opposing Reagan—and doing so vocally—on issues like sending U.S. troops into Lebanon, McCain signaled he was still his own man. In his first term in office, McCain became so popular that no other Republican challenged him in the primary when he ran for reelection in September 1984.

Then Cindy gave birth, on October 23, to the couple's first child, a daughter they named Meghan. In the general election on November 6, as Reagan crushed Walter Mondale, McCain destroyed *his* Democratic opponent, Harry W. Braun III. McCain got 162,418 votes; Braun 45,609. In his second term, he served on the Committee on Foreign Affairs, the Committee on Interior Affairs, and the Select Committee on the Aging.

In the 99th Congress, McCain continued to propose legislation. During the session, as House records show, he offered: a bill "to amend title 38, United States Code, to provide for annual reports to Congress to facilitate the orderly expansion of the National Cemetery System"; a bill that called for the Granite Reef Aqueduct of the Central Arizona Project to be renamed the "Hayden Rhodes Aqueduct"; a bill "to amend title 18, United States Code, with respect to offenses relating to the sexual exploitation of children, and for other purposes"; a bill "to authorize programs for the treatment and prevention of drug and alcohol abuse among Indian juveniles"; a bill "to provide for the settlement of certain claims respecting the San Carlos Apache Tribe of Arizona"; a bill "to recognize the organization known as the Red River Valley Fighter Pilots Association"; a bill "to provide for the proper administration of justice within the boundaries of the Salt River Pima-Maricopa Indian Community"; a bill "to amend the authority of the United States Geological Survey"; an amendment "dealing with the National Endowment for Democracy, making available to the public, upon request, all information regarding its organization, procedures, requirements, and activities, except those exempted by the Freedom of Information provisions of current law"; and an amendment "to set the per diem compensation rate for victims of terrorism at a minimum of $20 a day, adjusted by the Consumer Price Index."

One highlight of his second session in Congress occurred in February 1985. Between February 19 and 22, McCain returned to North Vietnam for the first time. The U.S. government, through the navy, had asked him to go there a decade before, but McCain was not yet emotionally ready. By 1985, he had a new perspective on his years in the Hanoi Hilton. Specifically, he traveled to North Vietnam to obtain information about Americans who were listed as missing in action but were still not accounted for. This effort would dominate much of his time in the coming years. One particularly memorable and emotional moment occurred during the trip when McCain returned to the spot in Hanoi where he had been shot down in October 1967. He discovered that the North Vietnamese had built a monument there—to him.

"There was one interesting episode at a monument to my capture built by a lake in downtown Hanoi," McCain told *U.S. News & World Report*. (The magazine published an article about his trip, which was also documented by Walter Cronkite for a CBS-TV special to commemorate the tenth anniversary of the fall of Saigon.) "This was the lake I parachuted into and was pulled out of on October 26, 1967. I still don't understand why they built this monument. They even have the wrong branch of service—air force instead of navy. Anyway, Walter Cronkite and I, and a film crew, went down there one day to the statue. A very large crowd of Vietnamese gathered, all pointing to me and repeating my name—'Mah-cain, Mah-cain.' It was perhaps the first time that someone was more recognized than Walter Cronkite."

To *U.S. News & World Report,* concerning his trip back, he added: "It certainly was an emotional experience for me—and not totally a pleasant one. But it was important to me, as one who did return, to do what I could for those who have not. I wanted to stress to the Vietnamese officials I talked to that the missing-in-action issue is still very large in the minds of millions of Americans. Until the Vietnamese show signs of making much greater efforts at a full accounting of those Americans still missing, there's very little prospect of improved relations with the United States. . . . It's my belief that for ten years Vietnam has used the MIAs in a most cynical fashion. They give back a few bodies every number of months to some visitors. Some of those bodies were of men we know were shot down, captured and photographed. To give their bodies back ten or so years later is the most cynical thing possible."

In particular, McCain wanted more of a good-faith effort from Vietnam, which was still, after all, a client state of the Soviet Union. McCain felt it was necessary for the Vietnamese to allow recovery teams from the United States to come into their country. "The fact," McCain said, "that they recently allowed one of our recovery teams into a plane crash site in Laos, where we think we recovered approximately 13 bodies, indicates that perhaps they're now realizing that their old policy probably wasn't the best way to go."

McCain also believed the Vietnamese desperately wanted to reestablish a relationship with the United States. "I got the distinct impression," McCain said, "that the Vietnamese do want better relations with the West, largely because their economy is in such terrible shape. I think it is fair to say that they won the war but lost the peace."

In the autumn of 1985, McCain introduced a congressional resolution "condemning the Government of the Soviet Union for the killing of Charles Thornton, an American journalist working in Afghanistan." For this resolution, dated October 10, McCain was joined by 58 cosponsors. As the fall passed, most of McCain's time and energy were occupied in probing the rumors that Barry Goldwater might not run for reelection. His Senate seat would be available if McCain wanted to run for it. McCain had one concern. The Washington gossip was: If Goldwater retired, Bruce Babbitt, Arizona's Democratic governor, might run for the seat. McCain believed he could defeat Babbitt, but he hoped his opponent would *not* be the state's popular governor.

On March 18, shortly after Goldwater had announced he was retiring, Babbitt said he would not seek the Democratic nomination for Goldwater's seat. On March 19, McCain held a news conference at the Hyatt Regency in Phoenix and declared he was a candidate. Apparently, Babbitt had made up his mind not to run for the Senate because he was convinced McCain *was* running, and he worried McCain was too strong a candidate. Instead, Babbitt decided to run for president.

On May 2, 1986, McCain celebrated the birth of his first son, whom he and Cindy named John Sidney McCain IV. Given this boy's name and pedigree, it seemed predetermined that, in 18 years, he would enter the Naval Academy as a preamble to joining the navy, as three generations of McCains had done before him. Meanwhile, John McCain III was busy achieving political successes. On September 9, he won the Republican nomination for the Senate. For the fall campaign, viable Democrats were unwilling to challenge McCain. It didn't hurt that the full force of the Republican Party was behind him. He even had as his campaign manager Barry Goldwater. "The night before the election," McCain recalled later, "[Barry] got a little nostalgic, and he said, 'You know, John, if I had been elected president in 1964 and had beaten Lyndon Johnson, you would have never spent all those years in a Vietnamese prison camp.' I said, 'You're right, Barry. It would have been a Chinese prison camp.' He was not amused by that."

On November 4, 1986, after an impressive campaign that featured a whistle-stop train trip that took him all across the state, McCain defeated Richard Kimball, the Democrat. McCain got 521,850 votes, Kimball 340,965. "It was a cakewalk," says Tim Meyer, the campaign manager for Jon Kyl, a Republican who was running for a seat in the House of Representatives from Arizona in 1986. "It was surprising. McCain had a very weak opponent. When you look back on it, in hindsight, McCain also ran a good campaign, a safe campaign. He ended up winning by a large margin." The race was so easy he had time to help out Kyl. "He made phone calls for us," Meyer says. "He made suggestions on the media. There were a couple of strategy sessions where we sat down and reviewed what our thoughts were, what our message was. I think McCain also helped with some behind-the-scenes introductions. I know I met with his campaign manager constantly, and we actually did a lot of get-out-the-vote efforts together. They allowed us to use their phone banks, and things like that. They were very, very helpful."

On January 3, 1987, McCain was sworn in by Vice President George H. W. Bush as a senator from Arizona serving in the 100th Congress. From the start of his Senate career, politically sophisticated observers studied McCain carefully. He would have a constant admirer in the man who had shaken his hand in 1973 and welcomed him home to the United States after his years in Vietnam. "President Nixon watched McCain operate in the Senate with a sense of bemused admiration," says Monica Crowley, Nixon's final aide. "He relished the fact that McCain was considered a maverick within his own party, a characterization Nixon often applied to himself." Nixon would one day say of McCain's Senate career: "Everything in him told him to fight. It was instinctual. The Senate is a different kind of battlefield, but McCain has it in him to do whatever it takes. He's scrappy. He's a fighter."

Chapter 6

One Hundred Kings

A t the start of 1987, John McCain became a member of the club that many people consider to be the most exclusive in the world: the United States Senate. The Senate's unique political force comes from the fact that each of its members wields immense autonomous power, which is why some observers describe the Senate as being made up of "one hundred kings." Throughout American history, it has not been uncommon for some senators—names like Claiborne Pell, Everett Dirksen, and Jacob Javits come to mind—to use the Senate to develop their own influential power bases. However, those same power bases have produced legislative improvements and social institutions that have had a profound effect on the country. In recent history, more than a few senators or former senators ran for the presidency, among them John Kennedy, Lyndon Johnson, Edmund Muskie, Robert Kennedy, Hubert Humphrey, George McGovern, Gary Hart, Walter Mondale, and Edward

Kennedy. Barry Goldwater, like McCain, was a Republican senator from Arizona when he ran for president against Lyndon Johnson in 1964.

In his early days as senator, McCain spent time acclimating himself to his new job, moving offices and shuffling his staff. He also began getting used to his new assignments on the Committee on Armed Services and the Committee on Commerce, Science, and Transportation.

On April 2, 1987, three months after he was sworn in, McCain attended the first of two meetings that would fundamentally alter his career. On that day, he joined fellow senators John Glenn of Ohio, Alan Cranston of California, and Dennis DeConcini of Arizona—all Democrats—in DeConcini's office for a meeting with Edwin Gray, the chairman of the Federal Home Loan Bank Board (FHLBB). The focus of the meeting was Charles Keating and his Lincoln Savings & Loan of Irvine, California, which was owned by American Continental Corporation of Phoenix. In the meeting, DeConcini, Gray later suggested, asked that Lincoln, then under investigation by the board, be given lenient treatment. In return, Lincoln would limit its high-risk investment and move into the home mortgage business.

A week later, on April 9 at six o'clock, the same four senators, along with Donald Riegle of Michigan, also a Democrat, met in DeConcini's office to discuss Lincoln. This time, four officials from the Federal Home Loan Bank of San Francisco were present. The five senators lobbied the officials to go soft with regulatory action about to be imposed on Lincoln. "We wanted to meet with you because we have determined that potential actions of yours could injure a constituent," DeConcini said to the officials; according to a transcript of the meeting later released to the *Wall Street Journal*. To show his willingness to get involved, Glenn said that Lincoln was an Ohio-based company, even though it wasn't. At another juncture, when one official commented that it was extremely odd to have five senators pressuring them about a case, DeConcini replied, "It's very unusual for us to have a company that could be put out of business by its regulators."

In short, DeConcini argued that the regulators should allow Lincoln to make some high-risk loans that could bring in big profits. But the tone of the proceedings changed when the four officials told the senators, in no uncertain terms, that Lincoln had been managed so badly its operators could be indicted on criminal charges by the

Department of Justice. In later testimony, Glenn, Riegle, and McCain claimed they departed as soon as they learned of this possibility. Cranston and DeConcini were then alone with the examiners. But the damage had been done. It was only a matter of time before these two meetings would become the impetus for what would be known as "the Keating Five scandal," an ordeal that had an acute effect on McCain. Much later, he acknowledged: "It will be on my tombstone, something that will always be with me, something that will always be in my biography. And deservedly so."

A t the time, McCain could not have estimated the political nightmare that would result from the two meetings he had attended on behalf of Charles Keating. For many years, the two men had been good friends. They met in 1981; then, each August, in 1984 through 1986, McCain and his family flew, aboard Keating's company jets, to Keating's home in Cat Cay in the Bahamas for a vacation. In all, McCain, or someone in his family, used Keating's jets for nine corporate or charter flights. In violation of congressional rules, McCain did not disclose the trips. He also failed to reimburse Keating's companies for the flights, which cost, it was later revealed, $13,433. What's more, Keating was generous with contributions to McCain, giving him some $100,000 over time.

Indeed, by 1986, the McCains' social and political bonds with Keating had become so strong Cindy and her father invested $359,100 in a shopping center named Fountain Square, which Keating was developing. Later, McCain revealed he knew about the investment but considered it legitimate because Cindy was a free agent apart from her husband and they even filed separate income tax returns. When the McCains married, Cindy had insisted on having a prenuptial agreement that allowed her to continue to maintain an independent financial status.

Apart from their business and political dealings, McCain and Keating liked each other. It was not unusual for them to pal around in Arizona, and they spoke on the telephone regularly. But all that changed just before the first meeting with regulators in April 1987. Desperate to have the regulators go easy on his struggling savings and loan, Keating wanted his friends in the Senate—including McCain—to represent him in the offices of Edwin Gray and the bank regulators in San Francisco.

McCain had even received a letter in which an accountant at Arthur Young and Company criticized the unusually long examination of Lincoln. The letter gave some credence to what Keating was asking McCain and others to do. Still, McCain refused to go to the offices of Edwin Gray or of the bank regulators based in San Francisco. When McCain let it be known he wouldn't travel to either office, Keating described him to DeConcini as a "wimp"—a remark that got back to McCain.

Keating met with McCain in McCain's Senate office on March 24, 1987. McCain told him what he would and would not do and what he thought of the "wimp" remark. "Keating came to my office," McCain later told the *Washington Post,* "and I said to him, a friend of mine, 'I have done all I can. Period.'" That was not good enough; Keating wanted McCain to take additional action on his behalf. When McCain told Keating he did not believe it would be prudent for him to do so, Keating got mad and called him a "wimp" to his face. Now angry, McCain gave Keating a "dressing down" in which he said, according to one of McCain's aides, he "had not spent five and a half years in a prisoner-of-war camp to have his courage or integrity questioned." As McCain put it, "[Keating] got angry and left, and we soon heard he called me a wimp"—yet again, when he met with a group of senators. "I," McCain would say, "never had any further dealings with him." As the aide put it: "The relationship clearly had come to a screeching halt."

So why did McCain go to the meetings? Because, as his counsel would later remark, "he also knew that he had a hell of a mess on his hands. He had a letter that stated in no uncertain terms that there was a very difficult problem here with this examination. . . . John McCain's staff determined that there was a legitimate reason to inquire about the length of the examination. . . . [A]t the beginning of the April 2, 1987, meeting, John McCain indicated that he did not want to do anything improper, and that he was only there to inquire. Mr. Gray replied that it was proper to ask questions."

In April 1987, McCain no doubt believed his dealings concerning Keating *were* legitimate. He had attended the meetings, which seemed innocent enough, after he had ended his friendship with Keating; now he intended to get on with his job of being the junior senator from Arizona. For the rest of the year, he did. In May, he traveled to West Germany to participate in the commemoration of the

750th anniversary of the city of Berlin. In June, he wrote a searing editorial about the Reagan Administration's decision to reflag Kuwaiti tankers so the United States could provide military protection for them, should they be attacked by Iran. Iranian officials had threatened to attack the Kuwaiti tankers because they were being used by Iraq, then at war with Iran, to ship Iraqi oil.

"The Reagan Administration plan to reflag and escort Kuwaiti oil tankers can be viewed as a dangerous overreaction in perhaps the most violent and unpredictable region of the world," McCain wrote in the *Arizona Republic* on June 21. "American citizens are again being asked to place themselves between warring Middle East factions, with no tangible allied support and no real plan on how to respond if the situation escalates." The plan's main point seemed to be to guarantee the "unimpeded flow of oil" in this part of the world—a noble but dangerous proposition. "In a real crisis, some of the burden of defending the energy lifeline must fall to our allies, who are much more dependent than the United States on Gulf oil. . . . What would happen if we do undertake the protection of Kuwaiti oil tankers? The United States will be defending the ships of a supposedly neutral nation that, in fact, serves as the conduit for Iraq's oil and most of Baghdad's imported war material. The Iranians have repeatedly stated their intention to attack Gulf tankers, regardless of who is escorting them."

In August, McCain took a very public position on the Gramm-Rudman bill, a piece of Senate legislation that required the United States government to balance its budget. "There is no doubt in my mind that Gramm-Rudman has motivated Congress for the first time to work seriously toward reducing budget deficits," McCain wrote on August 22 in another editorial in the *Arizona Republic.* "I do not support the approach of raising taxes without making significant spending cuts," he continued, referring to a recent proposal by the Democrats to balance the budget by increasing taxes in 1988. "Instead, we need to reprioritize our spending needs and cut out unnecessary programs before asking the American taxpayer to send an average of $200 more a year to the Treasury. . . . Clearly, reducing the deficit is the most important and difficult domestic challenge facing this nation. I believe that Congress and the president will need some procedural tools to assist in meeting this challenge. At the top of the list is the Gramm-Rudman effort."

Late in August, at the request of the Republican leadership in the Senate, McCain traveled to Honduras and Costa Rica for a three-day fact-finding trip. Between September 18 and 20, he toured El Salvador and Costa Rica. In late September, he revealed to the public what he had learned during these two trips about these countries and others in the region. "We must not let partisan divisions divert attention from Nicaraguan realities," he wrote. "We must assure that democratization is a fact, not another broken promise. . . . We must not trade our long-term security interests for a short-term political fix."

His opinions on foreign affairs, at least in this region of the world, had become revered by both parties' leadership in Congress, a not-inconsequential compliment for a first-year junior senator. He also had wonderful news in his personal life: Cindy was pregnant with their third child. Her due date was in May.

Near the end of March in 1988, McCain told the *Washington Post* it was time for the United States to begin a necessary process to "catalyze a resolution of outstanding political and humanitarian issues" with Vietnam. McCain now believed it was incumbent on the United States to find a way to develop a relationship with Vietnam that might eventually end the many years of conflict between the two nations. He was apparently offering forgiveness to the country that had once held him prisoner and brutalized him. His thinking on the issue of North Vietnam had come a long way, considering that, in the late 1970s, he had refused to go there, and when he *did* go back, in 1985, he called the experience "not totally a pleasant one."

In his personal life, McCain was thrilled when, on May 21, Cindy gave birth to their second son, whom they named James Hensley McCain.

The year 1988 was a presidential year, and in the Republican Party there had been some drama when Senator Robert Dole challenged George H. W. Bush, the sitting vice president, in the primaries. The feud got so heated that, at one point in a debate in New Hampshire, Dole snapped at Bush that he should "stop lying about my record." Dole crushed Bush in the New Hampshire primary, but on Super Tuesday Bush won all 17 contests, many of them in the South, and effectively wrapped up the nomination. From then until the Republican National Convention, scheduled to take place in the New Orleans Superdome in August, the speculation associated with the Bush campaign centered around whom Bush would choose as his running mate. At some stage of the process, McCain's name ended up on Bush's vice-presidential short list. In mid-July, McCain met with Bush at his home in Washington and, as he reported to the *New York Times,* "told him I am not interested in the job."

On Wednesday, July 22, McCain addressed the actions of Jane Fonda, a person toward whom he had harbored deep anger and resentment since her visit to Vietnam years before. Fonda had just made international news during an interview by Barbara Walters in which Fonda apologized for her actions during the Vietnam War. "I'm proud of most of what I did, and I'm sorry for *some* of what I did," Fonda told Walters. The interview was taped in the living room of Fonda's house in Santa Monica and aired on the ABC television network. "I'd like to say something not just to the veterans but to the men in Vietnam who I hurt, or whose pain I caused to deepen because of the things I said or did. I feel I owe them an apology. My intentions were never to hurt them or make their situation worse. It was the contrary. My intention was to help end the killing and the war. But there were times when I was thoughtless and careless about it, and I'm very sorry that I hurt them, and I want to apologize to them and their families." As for the picture in the tank, Fonda admitted: "It was a thoughtless and careless thing to have done. Being in a communications business, and knowing the power of images, it was thoughtless and cruel. I take full responsibility for having gotten on the gun. . . . I should have said no."

McCain could not resist responding to Fonda. "I would call upon Miss Fonda to join with me, with the VFW [Veterans of Foreign Wars], the Disabled American Veterans, the American Legion, the League of Families, and others who have spent these many years trying to resolve these issues," McCain said in a speech on the Senate floor. The issues to which McCain was referring were those involving POWs and men counted as missing in action, and McCain believed that Fonda could prove the sincerity of her apology by helping to resolve the POW/ MIA problem. Specifically, McCain was addressing the fact that over 2,000 POWs and MIAs could not be accounted for. "These issues,"

McCain said, "we know, will only be resolved when we can close this chapter of American history which has caused so much pain, suffering, and division within our country." When Vietnam officials said, soon afterward, that their country would not cooperate with an effort to account for missing United States military personnel—the men who had been the focus of a prolonged debate that had been raging between the countries since 1973—McCain said he would withdraw his support for legislation that would have set up limited diplomatic relations with Vietnam.

Then, at the Republican National Convention in New Orleans in August, McCain delivered a speech that made him a national political star almost overnight. At their convention in Atlanta, the Democrats had nominated Governor Michael Dukakis of Massachusetts, who then selected, as his running mate, a colleague of McCain—Senator Lloyd Bentsen of Texas. McCain may have made a trip to the vice president's house to tell him he was not interested in being *his* vice president, but McCain's name was still on George H. W. Bush's short list. Because Bush did not intend to reveal his choice of a running mate until the convention had started—it was one way to add drama to an otherwise lackluster proceeding—a heightened sense of anticipation surrounded the speech McCain was going to make on Monday, the first night of the convention.

For transportation to the convention, McCain chose a whistle-stop train tour, not unlike the one he used successfully in his Senate campaign in 1986. At seven o'clock on the morning of August 13, the McCains departed from Phoenix by train, en route to Louisiana. McCain was looking forward to resting up on the two-day trip, but, by the time he got to Houston on Sunday, the train was running so far behind that he decided to get off and fly the rest of the way. He arrived in New Orleans on Sunday night, just in time to have dinner with Katherine Graham, whose newspaper, the *Washington Post,* would run a glowing feature article about him the next day. Because his name was on Bush's vice-presidential short list, McCain's profile was elevated. A week before, in a fawning profile in the *New York Times,* he was described as "a young man in a hurry" who had "established himself not only as a key voice in the Senate on defense and foreign policy issues, but also a rising star in the post-Reagan Republican Party." The talk of his being a possible running mate with Bush intensified.

On August 14, the *Arizona Republic* ran an editorial McCain had written in reaction to Michael Dukakis's acceptance speech at the Democratic National Convention. Dukakis had taken shots at the accomplishments of the Reagan Administration and the weaknesses of Bush as a potential president. "I am proud," McCain wrote, "to be associated as a Republican senator with a Republican administration that has virtually ended inflation (that was double-digit when the administration took office) and slashed unemployment to its lowest level in many years. I am proud to be associated with an administration that has restored U.S. military strength while working diligently and successfully with the Soviet Union on agreements to reduce nuclear weapons. . . . To win in November, [Bush] needs to present not only a vision of the future but also how he plans to implement that vision."

When the day finally arrived for McCain to give his speech at *his* convention, he spent the morning rehearsing, and the rest of the day making the rounds of luncheons, receptions, and caucus appearances. He did a series of radio talk-show interviews as well. On Monday night, he headed for the Superdome. In the evening's lineup, there would be a five-minute video tribute to Barry Goldwater, who would watch from the VIP section, and both a tribute to First Lady Nancy Reagan and a farewell address by President Reagan. But before those events, three speeches would be delivered, addressing the topics of the economy, jobs, and national defense. McCain gave the speech on national defense.

At first, McCain's speech—12 minutes long and centered on the themes of "Duty, Honor, Country"—sounded as if it would be purely political. "Michael Dukakis," McCain said, a speck in the cavernous Superdome, "seems to believe that the Trident is a chewing gum, that the B-1 is a vitamin, and that the Midgetman is anyone shorter than he is." But then the speech turned personal as McCain narrated a story only he could tell.

He told the audience about Mike Christian of Selma, Alabama, one of his fellow POWs in the Hanoi Hilton. Using white and red cloth, Christian had sewn, with a bamboo needle, a replica of the American flag inside his blue shirt. The POWs would hang Christian's shirt on the wall and pledge their allegiance to the flag. "I know that saying the

Pledge of Allegiance may not seem the most important or meaningful part of our day now," McCain told the audience, "but I can assure you that, for those men in that stark prison cell, it was indeed the most important and meaningful event of our day." Then, one afternoon, the Vietnamese guards discovered the shirt. Confiscating it, they dragged Christian from the cell, and, out of sight from the other POWs but close enough for all of them to hear what was happening, they beat him.

Finally, Christian was returned to the cell. "He was not in good shape," McCain told the crowd. Moments later, McCain said, in the faint light of the cell, Christian had retrieved his bamboo needle and gotten a piece of red cloth, a piece of white cloth, and a shirt. "With his eyes almost shut from his beating," McCain said, his voice full of emotion, "he was making another flag."

Throughout the hall, delegates wept. In the wings, waiting to come on stage to make his farewell address, Ronald Reagan could be seen with tears in his eyes. When McCain finished, he was given a sustained, impassioned standing ovation.

On the second day of the convention, Bush announced he had chosen as his running mate Senator Dan Quayle of Indiana. The short list itself was leaked 20 minutes before Bush made his choice, and McCain's name was on it, despite the fact that no one from the Bush campaign had ever contacted McCain about a background check. On Tuesday, instead of being named as the party's vice-presidential candidate, McCain got the job of national chairman of an organization called Veterans for Bush.

No sooner had the name "Dan Quayle" come out of Bush's mouth than the choice looked like a disaster. The whole ordeal of Quayle's introduction to a national audience had an unsettling feel to it. As Bush brought him up before an audience at a staged event on the Mississippi River in New Orleans, the two men looked like cheerleaders at a high school pep rally, except that Bush was old enough to be Quayle's father. Then, because the nation had no idea who he was, Quayle got to make his first impression. It was unforgettable. With a goofy expression plastered on his face, Quayle delivered a speech so startlingly amateurish, he reminded onlookers of a giddy schoolboy running for a student-body presidency—not the American vice presidency. By the time Quayle finished, only sturdy Barbara Bush would refuse to admit her husband had jeopardized his chances of winning the presidency by picking this caricature of a politician.

Immediately, rumors started to circulate that Quayle might not survive as a member of the ticket. A controversy also emerged involving Quayle's service in the National Guard. Apparently, Quayle's family had pulled strings to get him into the National Guard, a way of avoiding Vietnam. Although there were few if any reports about it at the time, Bush had made phone calls to get his son, George W., into the National Guard as well. Many delegates openly called for Bush to rethink his choice of Quayle. McCain himself called the choice "a mistake." He also told the *Arizona Republic:* "Once you're burned like this, I think you're going to look at somebody like Dole or Simpson or one of those who clearly have been heavily screened. My God, it's one thing to make a mistake once." Still, McCain said he was unaware of any attempt to get him on the ticket to replace Quayle.

Bush refused to budge. On Thursday night, Quayle was nominated. When McCain was asked if Quayle was now acceptable simply because he had received the nomination, he said, "Oh, no, the issue has got to be resolved." Specifically, he was bothered by the flap over Quayle's National Guard service. "I think it's clearly serious," McCain said.

In early October, because of his position on English-only initiatives, McCain was one of 10 members of Congress honored by the National Council of La Raza, a nationwide coalition of Hispanic organizations. In a speech at a ceremony in Washington, before an audience of 500, McCain attacked English-only initiatives. "The building of our great nation is not the work of immigrants from one or two countries," McCain said. "It is the work of many cultures." McCain added: "I prefer to live in a bigger place. I prefer to live in a growing America, as proud of its diversity as it is of the ideas that unite us. . . . Our nation and the English language have done quite well with Chinese spoken in California, German in Pennsylvania, Italian in New York, Swedish in Minnesota, and Spanish throughout the Southwest. I fail to see the cause for alarm now."

Because this was the political season, McCain immersed himself in local and national politics. He was an honorary cochairman of the campaign of Keith DeGreen, the Republican candidate running against the Democratic incumbent, Senator Dennis DeConcini. An unwritten rule in the Senate forbids a sitting senator to campaign actively against another sitting senator; that practice is seen as demeaning the carefully maintained tone of the Senate as a government body. Under that rule, McCain should have sat out the campaign DeGreen was running against DeConcini, but, as would later be revealed, there was more than a little bad blood between McCain and DeConcini, so McCain decided not to remain as removed from the campaign as he could have been.

One gesture McCain made involved the Republican Senatorial Campaign Committee. As DeGreen surged in the polls toward the end of the campaign, the senatorial trust decided to give DeGreen $212,000, which DeGreen spent on a barrage of negative television ads attacking DeConcini. Furious, DeConcini accused McCain of being behind the effort to get the senatorial trust to give DeGreen the money. McCain denied that he had anything to do with the commercials and challenged DeConcini to provide documentation he had been involved—which, of course, DeConcini could not do. However, McCain could not deny that, toward the end of the campaign, he, along with other prominent Republican senators like Bob Dole, had become visible in their support of DeGreen over DeConcini—a tactic that also irked DeConcini.

On Election Night, McCain watched with pleasure—and, some surprise—as George H. W. Bush defeated Michael Dukakis in a landslide victory. Somehow, the choice of Dan Quayle had not torpedoed the campaign, although the effort was helped considerably by the brilliance of political strategist Lee Atwater. Using techniques like an ad that featured Willie Horton, a felon who committed murder while on early release in Massachusetts during Dukakis's watch as governor, Atwater painted Dukakis as an out-of-touch Massachusetts liberal.

In Arizona, by the end of Election Night, it was clear DeConcini had won reelection by a wide margin. In the final count, he got 57 percent of the vote to DeGreen's 41. On the day after the election, DeConcini held a press conference in which he criticized McCain and charged him with helping DeGreen get the money needed to pay for negative ads. "In politics," DeConcini said, "you find out who your friends are and who you can rely on, and you deal with a lot of people. I have no quarrel with Mr. McCain. I'm going to deal with him because it's good for Arizona, and we have had successes together in the past, and I see no reason we can't continue. Am I disappointed? You bet I am."

During the first days of the Bush Administration, McCain became embroiled in one of the ugliest fights of his political career. For the post of secretary of defense, Bush had nominated John Tower, the former Texas senator and a longtime friend of McCain. (Elected to the Senate from Texas in 1960 to fill the seat being vacated by Lyndon Johnson when he became vice president, Tower had resigned in January 1985.) In conducting its background search on Tower, the FBI had unearthed stories concerning Tower's character. In the 1970s, Tower apparently drank heavily and had engaged in questionable behavior such as womanizing—or so some reports implied. The Senate had to confirm Tower for the cabinet post, and many senators had had memorable experiences with him when he was drinking excessively. More than a handful of the senators were concerned that, though Tower said he now controlled his drinking, he still might have an addiction to alcohol. This could pose a severe problem, considering the cabinet post for which he had been nominated.

On Tuesday, February 21, it became apparent the rumors were going to delay the Senate's confirmation hearings. Fearful that this episode could turn into a debacle, Bush held a press conference in which he claimed that the extensive FBI investigation had "gunned down" any negative information on Tower. "What I got from [the report]," Bush said, "was that there has been a very unfair treatment of this man by rumor and innuendo, over and over again, rumors surfacing with no facts to back them up. I saw this [report] as a reaffirmation of what I've felt all along, and that is that John Tower is qualified to be secretary of defense."

The Senate postponed its vote on Tower's confirmation. Then, on Thursday, March 2, the *Washington Post* ran a story alleging that, between 1976 and 1978 on two trips to Bergstrom Air Force Base in Texas, Tower, drunk, had sexually harassed two women. These stunning charges, if true, would have fatally damaged not only his nomination as secretary of defense but also his standing in the Washington community. Furious about the character assassination, McCain went to the floor of the Senate on Thursday to attack a man named Robert Jackson, a retired air force sergeant, who was a key source for the *Post* article.

Armed with a letter written by a Pentagon official who quoted from Jackson's medical records (which McCain released to the press), McCain charged that Jackson, who had accused Tower of this inappropriate behavior, had been placed on temporary disability in 1977 because he "exhibited symptoms of a mixed personality disorder with antisocial themes and hysterical features." Because Jackson was not even present at Bergstrom in 1976 when Tower conducted his visit, McCain offered to produce a list of people who had witnessed Tower there and would swear he was not drunk and did not sexually harass any women.

To confuse the situation even more, Senator John Glenn was recognized to speak on the Senate floor and began to read from a confidential FBI report that contained damaging information about Tower. McCain shouted Glenn down and, in doing so, showed his willingness to get into a public squabble over the dual reports. Finally, Senator Sam Nunn, who was leading the effort to undermine the Tower confirmation process, suggested that the material should be discussed in a closed session. Next, Senator Phil Gramm spoke up for Tower and offered a weird, if accurate, defense: Great men like Ulysses S. Grant and Winston Churchill drank. As it happened, McCain's confrontation with Glenn was suggestive. Around this time, he had become so angered by what his colleagues were doing to a man he admired that he participated in a shouting match in an elevator with one senator and had a heated argument in a hearing room with another. McCain's temper, often written about but rarely witnessed by the writers, was clearly evident during the Tower confirmation hearings.

On Friday, the *Washington Post* printed a front-page story about McCain's spirited defense of Tower. That same day, Senators Nunn and Warner released more of Robert Jackson's medical records. One report said Jackson had been found to have a "personality trait disorder." The record, signed by Colonel Kenneth G. B. Joyce, ended with these comments: "Reliability may be a problem. . . . He also seems to have consistently fallen short in the area of bearing and behavior, in the judgment of his superiors." On Saturday, the *New York Times* published an article in which the accusations made against Tower by Jackson were described as "apparently false ones."

Ultimately, the efforts of McCain and others fell short. The allegations, whether false or otherwise, had done their damage. So when

Dennis DeConcini spoke from the Senate floor and said that he had witnessed Tower in the Senate chamber under the influence of alcohol, any hope of saving Tower vanished. On March 9, admitting defeat, Bush withdrew the nomination of John Tower to be secretary of defense. Bush substituted the name of Richard ("Dick") Cheney, the former congressman from Wyoming.

The internal squabbling had faded by April, and Congress got back to the workings of government. On Monday, April 17, McCain made a speech in the Senate in which he asked for the president to have what he called a super line-item veto. In introducing the "Anti-pork" Bill of 1989, a subject that was dear to him, McCain said: "The problem is that our current budget process doesn't require us to be thrifty and conscientious with money that is entrusted to us. We pick the taxpayer's pocket to play pork-barrel politics."

Two days later, when mass killings in Nicaragua and El Salvador were reported, McCain announced that in his capacity as cochairman of the Senate Central American Observer Group, he would be traveling to Honduras, El Salvador, and Nicaragua within the week. On his final stop, he said, he would meet with the Contras—who were being backed by the United States government—and with the Sandinista government. McCain headed a congressional delegation that included senators Bob Graham of Florida, Chuck Robb of Virginia, and Connie Mack of Florida. They met with the Contras in Nicaragua and determined that the civil war in El Salvador was growing because the Soviets were supplying the leftists with arms. They also predicted massive fraud in the May 7 election in Panama because Manuel Noriega had done everything within his power to ensure his reelection as that country's leader. When the four senators returned to Miami on Monday, April 24, they held a news conference during which McCain, the group leader, declared: "I believe the United States of America and all Latin American countries have an obligation to prevent this tragedy from being inflicted on the Panamanian people."

In April, while McCain was concentrating on foreign affairs within the hemisphere, another plot point in the Keating drama unfolded: The government took over the Lincoln Savings & Loan, a move with a potential cost to the taxpayers of as much as $3 billion—or more. But McCain tried to move beyond the potential Keating disaster. After all, he was part of a 13-member delegation the Bush Administration had chosen to observe the election in Panama. On May 6, the group arrived at Howard Air Force Base in the Panama Canal Zone, McCain's birthplace. On the previous day, the Senate had passed a resolution condemning Noriega's blatant attempts to fix the election. On the election day itself—Sunday, May 7—McCain witnessed, in his words, "a colossal fraud" in the form of gross voting irregularities. By Tuesday, May 9, the government, which had gathered all of the ballots cast in the country, had still not counted them. "Every objective observer from the church to the polls indicated the government would have lost by two to one," McCain said upon his return to Washington. If McCain had been undecided in the past, he was now convinced Bush should use military force to overthrow the government in Panama and remove Noriega from power.

In early August, McCain was again working on an issue that was vital to him: the line-item veto. In a meeting at the White House on Friday, August 4, McCain, along with three other Republican senators—Dan Coats of Indiana, Gordon Humphrey of New Hampshire, and William Armstrong of Colorado—presented Bush with a bill proposing that a Congressional majority vote would be required to overrule any line-item veto used by the president. Bush liked this version of the bill. After his meeting with the Republican senators, he commented that the bill would allow him to "do what the American people want . . . control spending."

On Sunday, October 8, a story broke that took a potentially dangerous scandal involving Charles Keating and his Lincoln Savings & Loan and, at least as far as McCain was concerned, placed it right on the front page. On that day, the *Arizona Republic* reported that McCain had failed to pay for the trips he and his family had taken in Keating's corporate jets, a bill totaling $13,433. Nine separate flights were involved, and McCain had not paid for any of them—or so it was charged. McCain had first learned in March that he had not paid for the flights, he said, when Keating's office had contacted him to say the IRS was going to force Keating to pay for the flights if McCain didn't. In May and June, McCain made payments, from his personal funds, totaling $13,433. In his mind, the matter had been resolved.

In an interview on October 11 for an article that appeared in the *Washington Post* the next day, McCain admitted his failure to pay for the flights "was a serious error," but he added, "it doesn't mean I did anything improper for Charles Keating." What he had done for Keating, and when, had now become exceedingly important. American Continental Corporation, Keating's company, had filed for bankruptcy in April, when the federal government took over his Lincoln Savings & Loan. The government was suing Keating for $1.1 billion, charging him with illegally transferring assets from his bank to his personal account and then making huge contributions to politicians.

The public disclosure of McCain's failure to pay for the flights came at a time when he was making a concerted effort to distance himself from the Keating scandal. But, on September 14, a senate staffer, according to an article in the *Arizona Republic,* charged that McCain had invited Donald Riegle to the second meeting. Since Riegle sat on the Senate Banking, Housing, and Urban Affairs Committee, this allegation implied McCain may have been more involved in trying to help Keating than he wanted reporters and members of Congress to believe.

For the record, McCain denied he had invited Riegle. Indeed, McCain said Riegle had invited *him* to come to his office and give him a briefing on what was going on with Keating and Lincoln Savings & Loan. However, Kevin Gottlieb, a Riegle aide, as the *Arizona Republic* reported, claimed McCain just showed up at Riegle's office without an appointment and invited Riegle to a meeting that was going to take place in DeConcini's office.

All of this was important because the Senate Ethics Committee had launched an investigation into the Keating matter. The committee wanted to determine what role, if any, the senators played in the failure of Lincoln Savings & Loan, the largest bank default in American history. Through meetings held on Keating's behalf, had the senators prevented federal bank officials from taking over Lincoln earlier, a move that would have saved the government—and American taxpayers—hundreds of millions, or maybe billions, of dollars?

In an effort to minimize his role in the meetings, McCain wrote a letter to Edwin Gray, the chairman of the Federal Home Loan Bank Board, requesting Gray to go on record as to whether McCain had done anything illegal or improper. Writing back to McCain, Gray said

McCain had done nothing wrong, but Gray did take the opportunity to criticize DeConcini. Indeed, an all-out war had broken out between DeConcini and McCain over Keating. The two men had certainly handled the situation differently. McCain had ended his relationship with Keating. DeConcini had stayed friendly with Keating and continued to fight for him. Then, once DeConcini realized he was in the middle of a controversy from which McCain had managed to distance himself, DeConcini insisted, "[McCain's] in it like I am," when, in fact, McCain was not. DeConcini's entanglement with Keating was disturbing, as evidenced by the revelation that DeConcini's campaign aides had reportedly gotten $50 million in loans from Lincoln Savings & Loan.

DeConcini had made a token gesture: He was willing to return $48,000 in campaign contributions he had received from Keating over the years. But that still left a lot unexplained, and the way DeConcini was being viewed in the Keating mess was not helped by another fact. In the past, he had been charged with investing heavily in land that was due to be bought by the federal government—an act that, if true, tended to show his willingness to push the boundaries of business arrangements.

In his personal life, in 1989, McCain saw Cindy enter the hospital to have surgery performed on her back. The resulting operation, instead of correcting her back problem, would leave her in chronic pain for years.

By September 1990, Robert Bennett, who had been named special counsel for the Senate Ethics Committee, had studied the Keating case and had met with the Senate committee. The committee was made up of three Republicans—Trent Lott, Jesse Helms, and Warren Rudman (vice chairman)—and three Democrats—David Pryor, Terry Sanford, and Howell Heflin (chairman). Bennett advised the committee to drop any investigation of Glenn and McCain but to continue pursuing Riegle, Cranston, and DeConcini. Bennett filed a formal recommendation with the committee on September 10. Heflin was not sure Glenn and McCain should be dismissed so quickly. Heflin wanted the committee to study the matter fully before it exonerated anyone. After all, Keating was now in a Los Angeles jail trying—so far, unsuccessfully—to come up with $5 million in bail.

Through the fall, the Keating controversy dragged on. In October, in an interview with the Ethics Committee, McCain described his relationship with Keating: "He was a supporter. I vacationed at his home in the Bahamas. He was one of the wealthiest men in the state of Arizona. He involved himself politically heavily in Arizona. That was the extent of my knowledge of his financial involvement in the state. And I was grateful for his support and his involvement in my political career. I had a friend. That friend wanted me to do something that was wrong. I refused to do so. That ended the friendship."

On Monday, October 22, McCain addressed the Senate. "I cannot accept a deliberate effort to withhold the truth and continued suspicion of a cover-up," he said, trying to force the Ethics Committee to be more forthcoming with the public. "I myself have served this nation for 35 years, always with honor and integrity. I do not deserve to be strung out week after week." He admitted he had been warned "that the remarks I am about to make may upset the very powerful Ethics Committee and could, in turn, cause me some political damage." But he made the speech anyway. "My concern is about my honor, my integrity, my reputation. There comes a time when you can no longer hold your tongue in the face of things that are wrong."

In November, the Ethics Committee began interviewing the senators and members of their staffs. During the first three days of hearings, the senators claimed, as a group, that by attending the meetings they had broken no Senate rules nor violated any laws. On November 16, John Dowd, counsel for McCain, defended McCain to the committee. His long prepared statement read in part: "Mr. Chairman, when you opened this hearing and this proceeding, you stated that many of our fellow citizens apparently believe that the services of these senators were bought. I tell you that there is no evidence that John McCain's services were bought. . . . John McCain placed integrity above friendship, and principle above political support. . . . In short, when John McCain was requested to go to Ed Gray's office, he said 'No.' . . . When John McCain was asked by Charles Keating to negotiate with the Bank Board for Lincoln Savings & Loan, he said 'No' to his longtime political friend and supporter. . . . When John McCain was invited to meet with Ed Gray, the Chairman of the Bank Board, he made it very clear that he was only going to inquire about two specific legitimate subjects."

By November 20, the proceedings had been reduced to squabbles over who asked whom to what meeting and—as strange as it may have seemed—who had been called a "wimp" by Keating: McCain alone or McCain and DeConcini. Specifically, McCain's side contended that DeConcini had lured McCain to the meetings because he wanted the proceedings to have a bipartisan image. DeConcini's lawyer, James Hamilton, responded that McCain had engaged in "pure speculation" and had been leaking negative stories about DeConcini to the press. Next, the McCain and DeConcini forces squared off over whether Keating had called *both* senators wimps. Aides for each side seemed to agree that Keating had indeed called McCain a wimp. DeConcini's side claimed Keating had also called DeConcini a wimp, although there was no evidence he had. Why was all, or any, of this important? "What it shows is," said Chris Koch, an assistant to McCain, "that John McCain had shown an unwillingness to do something that Charlie Keating wanted."

The day also featured an appearance by Gwendolyn Van Paasschen, the aide who dealt with McCain's banking issues. She argued that DeConcini wanted McCain in the meetings because "Senator McCain was a Republican and that would ensure that it was a bipartisan effort." Keating had raised money for both senators, so "if the press were to ever get a hold of it," Van Paasschen said, "it would be more embarrassing for Senator McCain than for Senator DeConcini." In fact, according to Van Paasschen, in mid-March, DeConcini tried to persuade McCain to go with him to Ed Gray's office or to the office of the California bank regulators, located in San Francisco. McCain wouldn't do it. "It was my view," Van Paasschen said to the committee, "and I told Senator McCain . . . that it was my view that what Senator DeConcini had suggested was inappropriate."

At the end of 1990, McCain continued to present the impression that he was conducting business as usual. In another editorial published in the *Arizona Republic,* he addressed the vital issue of Saddam Hussein and his recent aggression in the Persian Gulf. "As America and the world face Saddam Hussein's aggression," McCain wrote on December 9, "the Senate Armed Services Committee just completed a week of hearings that raised important questions about several dimensions of the Persian Gulf Crisis. Chief among these concerns were questions about the efficacy of economic sanctions, the timing and the use of force, Hussein's control of mass destruction weapons and whether to convene a special session of Congress to address these and other issues raised in the hearings. . . . What is ultimately at stake in the Persian Gulf is much more than the settling of yet another Middle East regional dispute. Saddam Hussein—the unwanted child of the Cold War—is a precursor of future challenges to global stability. . . . I enthusiastically support the president's decision to send Secretary of State James A. Baker III to Iraq. We must thoroughly explore every opportunity to resolve this crisis short of war. . . . Congress should pass a resolution authorizing the use of force if peaceful alternatives to such force fail. . . . The peace and security of the world for future generations [demand] that the world community act decisively to end the Gulf Crisis now, and to reduce the threat of new crises in years to come. The single most important aspect of this challenge is to limit or stop the proliferation of modern weapons technologies."

On January 4, 1991, the Keating Five senators began their closing remarks before the Ethics Committee. In his comments, McCain admitted that the senators had created "an appearance that something was improper." However, he said he had attended both meetings because they involved a constituent who employed a number of people in his home state. Heflin then asked McCain why it took so long for him to pay Keating for the trips he and his family had taken to Keating's home in the Bahamas. McCain responded he had been unaware Keating had not been fully paid and when Keating's office told him about the problem he promptly paid the money he owed. McCain acknowledged that failure to pay for the flights in a timely fashion had been "a mistake." In fact, McCain now believed he *had* paid for the trips, although there was no record of those payments being made, so he may actually have paid for the trips twice. Cindy was often responsible for paying for expenses related to the McCains' private life, including their family vacations. It was her recollection that monies had been paid to Keating, but, even though she had searched repeatedly over the years, she had not been able to find any documentation of those payments. That failure produced an untold amount of stress in her life, which only exasperated her emotional and physical states that were often bad because of her chronic back pain.

On January 15, John Dowd, McCain's attorney, told the Ethics Committee in his closing remarks that McCain had "conducted his public office with honesty, courage, and fidelity." He added: "The past fourteen months have been very painful and very difficult for John McCain, for he has been judged not by his conduct, but by his association with the conduct of others."

Finally, on the last day of February 1991, nearly four years after the two meetings that initiated the Keating Five scandal, the Senate Ethics Committee handed down its ruling. For his role in the scandal, McCain was found guilty of exhibiting "poor judgment" in attending the meetings. According to the report generated by Heflin's committee, only Cranston had been guilty of actual ethics rules violations. McCain, Glenn, DeConcini, and Riegle had not committed any violations. The committee did criticize McCain and Glenn for their judgment, and it said that DeConcini and Riegle had conducted themselves in ways that "gave the appearance of being improper." The actions of the senators, though not "improper" (except in the case of Cranston), *had,* the panel found, intimidated the regulators, who waited another two years before taking over the failing Lincoln Savings & Loan, a delay that cost the government $1 billion. For this, the committee gave DeConcini and Riegle a rebuke. Cranston received a formal reprimand.

For all intents and purposes, the panel absolved McCain of any improper or unethical behavior. At a press conference in Phoenix on March 1, McCain said he would return to the United States Treasury the $112,000 Keating had given to his campaigns between 1982 and 1986. Saying he hoped the committee's decision would "close the book" on the whole Keating nightmare, McCain vowed never to meet with another federal regulator. "Ever. Period."

Meanwhile, Saddam Hussein was taking actions in the Persian Gulf. On August 2, 1990, he had invaded Kuwait. Iraq had then positioned troops on the border with Saudi Arabia, a development that indicated Hussein's willingness to invade that country, which would have been unthinkable to the West. During the fall, Bush rallied world opinion against Hussein. He also sent 425,000 U.S. troops to the region, where they joined 118,000 troops sent by other countries. On November 29, the United Nations Security Council gave the allies permission "to use all necessary means" to force Iraq out of Kuwait, if Iraq had not withdrawn by January 15, 1991.

Four days before the cutoff date, McCain went to the floor of the Senate to argue that sanctions would not keep Hussein from carrying out "naked aggression of the most heinous and disgraceful kind." McCain said: "Who are the ones who would suffer as a result of sanctions? In my view, it is the innocent civilians, children and others that Saddam Hussein would view as nonessentials in his war efforts. Clearly, the American people do not seek a replay of that tragic chapter in our nation's history. I think you can make an argument: If we drag out this crisis and we don't at some time bring it to a successful resolution, we face a prospect of another Vietnam War."

The cutoff date came and went. Hussein did not pull his troops out of Kuwait. On Thursday, January 17, Bush requested Congress's permission to conduct military operations in the Persian Gulf. The Senate voted 99–0 to approve the president's request. Not only did McCain vote in favor of the request, but before the vote, he had proposed that the Congress should adopt a declaration of war—a move much more severe than simply committing troops to the region, as the president had requested. That day, January 17, the allied forces started bombing Baghdad. The air campaign, it was hoped, would make Hussein withdraw his troops.

On Sunday, January 27, McCain met at the Arizona Army National Guard headquarters with about 40 relatives of Arizonan service personnel fighting in the Persian Gulf. The war "will be over in a matter of weeks," McCain said, adding, "I would like to see Saddam Hussein dead. I don't know anyone who wouldn't." Noting that, under American law, Hussein could not be targeted, McCain said, "If he just happens to suffer death, it will not be to anyone's sorrow."

On Wednesday, February 13, McCain appeared at Phoenix College where he addressed the student body. "The world economy," McCain said, "is dependent on a free and unfettered flow of oil" from the Persian Gulf. "There is no doubt in my mind," he added, "that there are significant signs that the Iraqi morale is cracking, and that many of their troops, particularly the 17-year-old draftees and the over-50-year-olds that have been drafted by Saddam Hussein, are not happy where they are." Nine days later, speaking before 2,000 employees at McDonnell

Douglas, McCain revealed that the first shots of the Persian Gulf War were fired by eight Apache helicopters that attacked, among other targets, the early-warning radar facilities in Iraq. "The Iraqis [at the radar sites] did not know how they were being attacked," McCain said. He was speaking in the building where the Apaches were actually built, so when he showed a video of Hellfire missiles and 70-millimeter rockets hitting their targets, the audience erupted in wild applause.

In late February, after five weeks of bombing that had not forced Hussein to remove his troops, the allied forces began a ground attack. The 100-hour land battle, called "Desert Storm," ended on February 28 and resulted in the total destruction of Iraq's so-called million-man army.

In March, McCain and other senators—among them, Dennis DeConcini and John Kerry, the junior senator from Massachusetts—traveled to the Persian Gulf to survey the aftermath of the war. Much of Kuwait had been destroyed at the hands of the Iraqis. When Hussein realized that he was going to be defeated, he ordered his men to set the oil wells in Kuwait on fire and caused one of the worst acts of devastation the region had ever endured.

In 1991, McCain was able to advance his legislative agenda without the threat of the Keating scandal hovering over him. He introduced two bills concerning health care: The Private Long-Term Care Insurance and Accelerated Death Benefit Incentive Act of 1991, which would expand private long-term care, and The Long-Term Care Protection Act, which would, according to a McCain editorial in the *Arizona Republic* on November 10, "provide federal consumer protection in the long-term care insurance market."

As it happened, McCain had direct experience with the health care system in America at that very moment. In 1991, while she was on a mission to Bangladesh, Cindy had visited an orphanage in Dhaka run by Mother Teresa. At the clinic, Cindy found an infant girl born with a severe cleft palate. The child's mother had abandoned her; the child's father had either been killed or had abandoned her as well. The cleft palate was so bad that, had the condition been left untreated, the child would have died. Cindy carried the baby home to Phoenix for surgery and for adoption. The child, who would be named Bridget, was three months old when Cindy brought her to America. McCain went to the airport to meet Cindy, who presented the baby to her husband and said, "Meet your new daughter." Almost as soon as Cindy got her back to Arizona, Bridget would begin a total of a dozen operations.

During 1991, McCain also ended up at the center of another controversy. In early April, he returned to Vietnam at the request of the communist government; once again, he was there to help in the accounting of MIAs. In 1985, he had been in the country for the tenth anniversary of the fall of Saigon. On that trip, he had gone to the Hanoi Hilton and jokingly asked his tour guides not to close the door behind him. His 1991 visit would be much broader in scope. McCain left Washington en route to Bangkok and then to Hanoi for a two-day visit. Saying he was "struck by the amazing differences" in the country, compared to six years ago, McCain reported: "There are shops, stalls and little restaurants, and the people are profiting from this free-market economy." McCain had gotten guarantees from Nguyen Co Thach, the foreign minister, that the government would allow the United States to set up an office in Hanoi to help determine the fate of the 2,282 men still listed as missing in action. Of those, 1,665 were missing in Vietnam. The rest were missing in Laos, Cambodia, and China, which was why, following his stop in Vietnam, McCain proceeded on to Phnom Penh, the capital of Cambodia, and to Laos. On this trip, he had one goal: find out as much as he could about the fate of the MIAs.

In July, only weeks after his return to the United States, the mystery of the MIAs gained national attention. A *Newsweek* cover story featured a picture of three men, purported to be American POWs who were still being held against their will in Southeast Asia. The trio was given a nickname—"The Three Amigos"—and the picture was widely reprinted. There was only one problem. The picture was a hoax generated by people who wanted to perpetuate the myth that Americans were still being held captive in Southeast Asia. This image was important because, in numerous schemes concocted at the time, grieving American families were paying large sums of money to private investigators who promised to go to the region and make every effort to retrieve their loved ones.

The *Newsweek* cover story brought to a head an issue that had been alive in America, in one way or another, since U.S. troops had left Vietnam in the mid-1970s. Senator Bob Smith of New Hampshire now asked for a formal congressional investigation into the matter of MIAs and POWs, and John Kerry, himself a decorated navy veteran who had returned from Vietnam to help lead the protest against the war, was asked to chair the select committee. McCain joined the committee as well. For many years, McCain had held Kerry's actions against him because, while McCain was a POW in the Hanoi Hilton, Kerry was organizing veterans back home in the United States to protest the war. But, only weeks before, as the two senators flew to Kuwait to witness the aftermath of the Persian Gulf War, they sat next to each other on the airplane and, after a long—and, at times, emotional—conversation, they had finally put the past behind them.

Having survived the potentially career-ending debacle of the Keating scandal, McCain was ready to run for reelection in 1992. On the Democratic ticket, he would be opposed by Claire Sargeant, a civil rights activist who had no statewide political presence and no chance of winning. Evan Mecham was running as an Independent. A former car dealer from Glendale, Mecham had won the governorship in a three-way race in 1986. He was impeached and forced from office when the Arizona Senate found him guilty of obstructing justice. He allegedly tried to stop a state investigation into a threat said to have been made against a grand jury witness. He lent $80,000 from a protocol fund to his car dealership, which was illegal. In 1990, he tried to mount a comeback in a five-way race for governor, but Fife Symington won. McCain didn't support Mecham during the impeachment proceedings, and that angered Mecham. In the end, the Keating Five scandal did not sink McCain as a politician. On the first Tuesday in November, McCain got 55 percent of the vote, compared to 31 percent for Sargeant, 10 percent for Mecham.

Perhaps because he was up for reelection so soon after the Keating scandal, McCain had distanced himself from the presidential race. George H. W. Bush ran for reelection against Bill Clinton. So, on Election Night, as he rejoiced in his own victory, McCain watched as the national Republican ticket was defeated. The Bush loss was even more surprising because, a year or so before his defeat, Bush had enjoyed unprecedented approval ratings for his handling of the Persian Gulf War. That scenario, however, belonged to the past. The United States had a new Democrat as its president. Now that he was a member of the opposition party, McCain would suddenly become presidential material himself.

On January 13, 1993, just as Bill Clinton was becoming the new president, the select committee chaired by Kerry and featuring the work of McCain issued a 1,223-page report, the product of numerous trips to Vietnam by committee members, the examination of countless photographs and documents, and the declassification, by the Department of Defense, of more than a million pages of documents. The report concluded that "while the Committee has some evidence suggesting the possibility a POW may have survived to the present, and while some information remains yet to be investigated, there is, at this time, no compelling evidence that proves that any American remains alive in captivity in Southeast Asia."

The work of the committee that unfolded during 1991 and 1992 had not been without controversy. One battle concerned whether the Kerry committee would call Richard Nixon to testify concerning what he knew about the issue of MIAs and POWs. Some felt the testimony Henry Kissinger had provided was not complete. "By the end of 1992, Kerry had suggested publicly that he still might summon Nixon to testify," Monica Crowley later wrote, "and Nixon remained defiant: 'What the hell. I can't believe that after all this they're still at it. I'll just say that Kissinger testified and that I have nothing to add. I don't have anything to add. What are they going to do? They can't force me to say things I don't know. If I sit there with nothing to say, that will put an end to their questioning of me. That whole committee, with a few exceptions, are jackasses. And I know I've said this before, but very few of our people are any good. [Senators] John McCain and Hank Brown are okay: They're smart and tough, but I don't think they grasp what this means historically for Kissinger and me. Well, McCain probably does because he suffered through the goddamned war.'"

Eventually Kerry decided not to call Nixon as a witness. The committee reached its conclusions without the former president's direct input, and those conclusions were unanimously agreed upon by the committee. Even critics like Bob Smith, who repeatedly voiced skepticism about the motives and actions of the Vietnamese, signed on. In the end, though, all committee members had to acknowledge the findings of the committee, which, in time, proved to be historic.

"In the late 1980s and early 1990s," John McCain says, "there were a lot of things that came out of Vietnam that appeared to be hard evidence that Americans were still alive. There was the picture on the cover of *Newsweek* of three people, supposedly POWs alive in Southeast Asia, who turned out later to be Soviet farmers. There were these manufactured pictures, dog tags, et cetera. Many Americans, understandably, were absolutely convinced that we left Americans alive in Vietnam. So I came out on many occasions and said, 'Look, we don't have the evidence. I'm not saying they aren't there, but we've got to have the evidence.' When I did this, people were very disappointed in me, and then angered, because, obviously, I had been one of them. People felt that I betrayed those who I 'left behind.'

"Well, the select committee chaired by John Kerry met for over a year, and our conclusion—*unanimous* conclusion—was that there was no compelling evidence that Americans were alive in Vietnam. I've spent thousands of hours—on many trips to Vietnam—trying to get any evidence. I must say I think John Kerry and I and some others did play a role in getting the Vietnamese to agree to this full access to the records. But I also understand the feelings of someone who is the son or the wife or the brother of a man who's been listed as missing in Vietnam."

Chapter 7

The Senator from Arizona

During the Memorial Day holiday in 1993, McCain and John Kerry made yet another trip to Vietnam. The select committee had finished its work, but the two senators were still pursuing any avenue that might resolve the issue of MIA/POWs. In June, two weeks after their trip to Vietnam, McCain and Kerry met with Bill Clinton, at the White House, to lobby for an end to the economic embargo the United States still maintained against Vietnam. This topic was not popular with a large segment of McCain's party, especially the right wing.

Later that summer, McCain continued to redefine his political positions; this time, he focused on gay rights. The way he made his case was typical of McCain. He would go to an organization known for its antigay politics and make a speech about tolerance. He may suffer the wrath of gay groups for agreeing to speak to an antigay organization, but the larger victory would be more important: He would challenge the thinking of the antigay organization, and he would do it in person. This had become McCain's mode of operation: Create controversy while advancing an agenda.

The group he chose was the Oregon Citizens Alliance, an association known for its antigay politics. (It had been linked to a failed statewide ballot initiative that described homosexuality as "perverse.") McCain addressed the Alliance on August 30. The event was a fundraiser, and McCain had been invited to speak. His agreement to help the Alliance raise money angered some gay groups. A senator of McCain's stature, they argued, should not raise money for such an antigay organization; simply by being there—regardless of what he said—McCain would generate revenue.

Early in the speech, he quoted Abraham Lincoln's reminder, in an address to Union soldiers, that Americans have "this inestimable jewel," our birthright. "The 'inestimable jewel' to which Lincoln referred," McCain told his audience, "was the promise contained in our Declaration of Independence, in its sparse but eloquent affirmation of the rights of man: 'that all men are created equal; that they are endowed by their Creator with certain unalienable rights; that among these are life, liberty, and the pursuit of happiness.'" McCain went on: "In the exercise of these rights, some Americans will live their lives in ways that I would not choose for myself. They may pursue happiness in ways very different from my own pursuit of happiness. I may not approve of every way an individual chooses to exercise his or her rights as an American. . . . But I will not oppose them. . . . That, my friends, is the essence of tolerance."

During the fall, a controversy erupted on Capitol Hill concerning the universal health care plan proposed by the Clinton Administration under the direction of First Lady Hillary Rodham Clinton. McCain was opposed to the plan, although, in a break with many members of his party, he did believe all Americans should have access to the health care system. His concern with the Clinton plan was simple: He felt that socializing medicine would destroy America's health care system. "All Americans deserve the opportunity to obtain the health care coverage of their choice," McCain wrote in the *Arizona Republic* on October 13. "I hope that we will never see the day in which the government tells us which health care plan we may enroll in or who will provide the care. To socialize our health care system, as the Clinton reform plan would, will be to ruin it."

By the end of 1993, McCain himself had to depend on the health care system when on December 3 he underwent outpatient surgery to remove a malignant melanoma on his shoulder. Early periods of intense exposure to the sun are known to contribute to fair-skinned people's tendency to develop skin cancer in later years. McCain had often gotten sunburns during his youth from being outdoors. His personal doctor, Thomas Hudak, performed the procedure in his office—an indication that the melanoma, although malignant, did not require removal of a large section of the surrounding tissue. After the procedure, McCain's office released a statement indicating he would be "monitored occasionally in the future" to protect against any recurrence of the skin cancer.

Later in December, McCain headed for Russia to help monitor the country's first elections since the fall of the Soviet Union. The Russians voted on Sunday, December 12, to elect two houses of parliament and to ratify a new constitution. Boris Yeltsin had called for the elections back in September, and, for help in monitoring the event, he approached the United States Agency for International Development and the International Republican Institute, of which McCain was chairman. Along with McCain, a bipartisan delegation of 25 American politicians, including Vice President Al Gore, went to Russia. They used Moscow as a base from which to visit 12 other Russian cities during the elections.

In January 1994, McCain and Kerry offered a Senate resolution asking the president to end the embargo against Vietnam. In early February, Clinton dropped the 19-year embargo, setting up the possibility that the United States could normalize its diplomatic relations with Vietnam. That was the subject on which McCain and Kerry were going to work next.

In April, when the debate over health care was again a hot-button issue, McCain underscored his apprehension about a federal

government takeover of the medical establishment. "There are some
who have characterized opponents of the Clinton health reform bill as
political obstructionists who are not concerned with finding meaningful solutions," McCain wrote on April 21 in the *Arizona Republic.* "They
suggest that if you are not in favor of the Clinton plan, or some other
government-run takeover of the health care system, you are against
constructive health reform. Such claims are erroneous, simplistic and do
not help resolve the real national debate that we are having on health
reform."

That summer, McCain experienced an honor that reminded others
of the McCain family's rich tradition. On Saturday, July 2, McCain
attended a ceremony at the Bath Iron Works on the North Pier in
Bath, Maine, to witness former president George H. W. Bush commission a new 8,300-ton Burke class destroyer: the *USS John S. McCain.*
It was the second ship to have that name, the first having been part of
the fleet from 1953 until 1978. Before an audience of 1,000 civilians
and sailors, McCain summed up his feelings about the day, declaring,
"The navy is the world I know best and love most." Then he introduced Bush, himself a former naval aviator, who drew thunderous
applause from the audience when he defended the navy. "I don't like
to see the navy under constant attack from its antimilitary critics," he
said, adding that the "talking heads" with their "outrageous" attacks
based on the Tailhook scandal were "an embarrassment to the country."
Using Tailhook as an example of distortion was certainly an odd way to
defend the military, since much of the navy brass would say sexual har-
assment in a Las Vegas hotel—the claims behind the scandal—was certainly not the American military's finest hour. His remarks made, Bush
then performed the official duty of commissioning the ship that would
sail at once from Maine to Pearl Harbor, its future home port.

On August 22, 1994, Cindy McCain issued a prepared statement
about a problem she had been dealing with for years. From 1989
until 1992, she had used Percocet and Vicodin, two prescription pain-
killers. At the height of her use, she was taking between 15 and 20 pills
a day. She was getting the drugs, she said, "from several physicians, none
of whom knew that I was being treated by others. I occasionally sup-
plemented my supply by taking extra prescription drugs which were

obtained by the American Voluntary Medical Team [AVMT], a chari-
table organization of which I am president. Although my conduct did
not result in compromising any missions of AVMT, my actions were
wrong, and I regret them." With the release of the statement, Cindy
did a series of interviews with selected broadcast and print outlets to
discuss her drug problem. In these interviews, the *Arizona Republic*
reported, Cindy often became emotional, crying at times.

Her problem had begun in 1989 when she had back surgery twice
for ruptured discs. While she was in the hospital recovering, the Keating
Five scandal broke. Cindy had been the family bookkeeper during the
time the McCains vacationed at the Keating home in the Bahamas,
but she could not locate any records to show she had paid Keating's
company for the flights involved in those trips. During 1989, 1990, and
1991, as she dealt with her excruciating back pain and coped with the
stress she and McCain were living under because of the Keating scandal, she became addicted to prescription drugs. Finally, she began to use
her charity, AVMT, as a way to augment the drugs prescribed by her
personal doctors.

Cindy McCain had founded AVMT in 1988. Fulfilling its concept,
AVMT sent doctors around the world to provide emergency medical
care where it was needed. In its first years, teams of doctors, which she
often accompanied, had traveled to Vietnam, Micronesia, Bangladesh,
Nicaragua, El Salvador, and Kuwait, among other countries. Naturally,
as a medical organization, AVMT had access to prescription drugs.
AVMT only had to file a requisition order in triplicate and send one
copy to the Drug Enforcement Agency (DEA). When Cindy began
to use her charity as a way to get prescription drugs, she turned to
the company's chief physician, John ("Max") Johnson. Later, Johnson
claimed Cindy had him write prescriptions in the names of other company employees. Johnson wrote eight prescriptions under the names of
three employees—Kathy Walker, Tracy Orrick, and Thomas Gosinski (the
director of governmental and international affairs). The employees didn't
know their names were being used. Six prescriptions were for 100 pills
each; two were for either 400 or 500 pills each. Johnson also wrote three
prescriptions to Cindy, for her back pain and for a broken toe.

Gosinski had other dealings with Cindy McCain, or so he would
claim. Specifically, he would charge that, at the time the McCains

were trying to adopt Bridget, Cindy called him and asked whether he would testify that the baby's father had been killed in a rickshaw accident. Walker later told investigators that after Gosinski got off the phone with Cindy that day, he looked at Walker and said, "I can't believe she asked me to lie." Then Gosinski threatened, in Walker's presence, "I'm going to get her! I'm going to blackmail her if she ever fires me."

Apparently, the nuns from whom Cindy got Bridget in Bangladesh had told her that Bridget's father had been killed in a rickshaw accident, but there were no records to prove it. The adoption process would be easier for the McCains if Bridget had no parents, so Cindy needed testimony to confirm the absence of parents. In point of fact, in 1992, the McCains' adoption lawyer, Donald Gilbert, had told the court that Bridget's mother was dead and her father, who could not be found, was presumed dead as well.

Events turned ugly when Gosinski was fired from AVMT in January 1993—because of cutbacks, the company said. In April, Gosinski's lawyer, Stanley Lubin, wrote a letter to the McCains' lawyer, John Dowd, threatening to go public with damaging material about Cindy McCain by filing a lawsuit if his client was not paid $250,000. The suit did not use the word "drugs," but Lubin's letter offering a settlement did. "It is clear that you made it appear that Mr. Gosinski was ordering the drugs," Lubin wrote to Cindy through her attorney, "many of which were controlled narcotics, in an effort to hide your personal use of them." Gosinski "has done what he could to keep the sensitive matters from exposure." Dowd refused Lubin's request. In a letter to the Maricopa County Attorney's office, he charged that Gosinski's actions amounted to "a shakedown" and asked to have Gosinski investigated for alleged extortion of the McCains. Gosinski retaliated by tipping off the DEA to Cindy McCain's scheme involving AVMT and prescription drugs, about which he seemed to have firsthand knowledge. He then went forward with his lawsuit for wrongful termination. Gosinski had been asked "on numerous occasions," the suit said, to "engage in acts that were improper." The suit stated that Gosinski "was responsible for the maintenance of certain sensitive records and the overall operation and integrity of the organization." Gosinski also sued for libel and slander because Cindy

McCain, the suit charged, had bad-mouthed Gosinski when he tried to get another job.

Before long, AVMT was being investigated by the DEA and the U.S. Attorney's Office for the illegal prescriptions written by Johnson. By then, Cindy McCain no longer had a drug problem. In 1992, when she was confronted by her parents because her behavior was sometimes clearly influenced by drugs, she confessed to the problem and went "cold turkey." She simply stopped and somehow found a way to live with what had caused her to take the drugs in the first place—severe back pain. Then, in January 1993, her obstetrician discovered a medical problem that required her to undergo a hysterectomy. As soon as she had the operation, the pain she had been suffering for years suddenly ended. Now, she had a new problem: the various investigations into AVMT and her activities related to that company. She had never told her husband about the drug problem. In January 1994, given the possibility that the story was going public, she told him about her problem and the ongoing investigations.

Eventually, the DEA agreed not to prosecute Cindy McCain. She cut a deal that required her to do community service and join Narcotics Anonymous. She also agreed to pay for the cost of the various investigations into AVMT. In January 1995, John Johnson became the target of an investigation by the Arizona Board of Medical Examiners. Eventually, Johnson, who admitted to writing fraudulent prescriptions, was forced to relinquish his medical license.

Ultimately, the scandal was put into the context of Cindy McCain's life. She had no greater defender than her husband. "For anyone to imply that Cindy acted improperly in this matter is as despicable a falsehood as I have ever had the misfortune to observe," John McCain wrote on August 26, 1994, in response to a recent article in the *Phoenix Gazette*. "Cindy never asked Mr. Gosinski to lie about Bridget's adoption. The adoption was proper in every respect. The adoption court ruled that Bridget was an abandoned infant. There are no more relevant circumstances to this story than the facts which I have just provided— except this: The *Phoenix Gazette* decided to run a story without evidence to remotely prove its accuracy that has attempted to tarnish a story of kindness with the brush of scandal. I will accept a great deal in public life, but I cannot accept this."

In June 1994, McCain continued to define himself on the issue of gay rights, when he joined a movement in the Senate that said that, as employers, senators would not discriminate on the basis of sexual orientation. Specifically, 71 senators, McCain among them, signed a statement that pertained to hiring practices on Capitol Hill. Sexual orientation would not be, to quote from an announcement about the development issued by the Human Rights Campaign, a gay lobbying organization, "a consideration in the hiring, promoting, or terminating of employees in their offices."

McCain also focused on foreign affairs. One country that had concerned him for much of 1994 was North Korea. "Late in the year, McCain and I appeared together on Jim Lehrer's *News Hour* to discuss North Korea," says Congressman Gary Ackerman, a Democrat from New York. "My position was, we had to be very careful and walk them back from the nuclear precipice that they were in. We needed to do that through every available diplomatic means, including an international consortium. But McCain's position was pretty tough, which surprised me, because he was so reasonable as a Vietnam POW. He was so reasonable on Vietnam that he helped establish relations with the country. His position on North Korea was: 'Well, if they don't do what we want, we should basically blow them up.'"

One day in 1994, McCain picked up the phone and called Russell Feingold, the Democratic senator from Wisconsin. Feingold had the reputation of being an honest politician. During his campaign for the Senate in 1991, he ran a television ad that featured him giving a tour of his ranch house. In one sequence, he stopped at a closet, opened the door, and said to the camera, "No skeletons." So McCain knew what he was doing when he approached Feingold about working together to develop legislation that would bring campaign finance reform to the American political system. After McCain had seen what could happen to a politician in a scandal like the Keating debacle, he was determined to reform the system. The first step was to clean up the way campaigns were financed. Feingold jumped at the chance to work on the issue.

In the first half of 1995, McCain turned his attention to an issue that continued to dominate his thinking: normalization of relations between the United States and Vietnam. The effort had grown out of the work Kerry and McCain had done on the select committee and the end of the trade embargo. In April 1995, during an appearance at a symposium sponsored by the Discovery Channel, McCain said that the United States had to move beyond the Vietnam War and that the president should normalize relations with Vietnam. McCain also revealed that he and Kerry were prepared to cosponsor a Sense of the Senate resolution suggesting just that. McCain recognized that there were MIAs "who were lost at sea or in other circumstances which offer no hope of survival and little hope of recovery." Still, because of the lack of hope of recovering any more bodies, he felt it was time to resolve the issue of the MIAs once and for all. Normalizing relations with Vietnam would help accomplish that goal.

On May 23, McCain and Kerry met with Clinton in the White House and lobbied for normalization. Five days later, in the *Washington Post,* McCain stated his position in an editorial titled "Time to Open an Embassy in Vietnam." McCain wrote: "The issue involved in our relations of greatest importance to the American people is the accounting for our missing servicemen. Vietnam's cooperation with the United States on this issue is extensive and has increased since we lifted our trade embargo against Vietnam last year. . . . It is . . . absolutely to our national security interests to have an economically viable Vietnam strong enough to resist, in concert with its neighbors, the heavy-handed tactics of its great-power neighbor [China]."

The public campaign McCain had launched was working. In mid-June, the Vietnamese allowed an American recovery team to go into a Vietnamese military cemetery to look for remains of any U.S. POW or MIA. That gesture provided political clout for McCain to push for a treaty that would establish ties between the countries. To resolve what had happened in Vietnam, the United States had to find a way to deal with its former enemy. Only then would there be a kind of healing. Many of McCain's colleagues disagreed. When McCain was asked how he could break ranks with Phil Gramm, whom he had chosen to support in the upcoming 1996 presidential campaign, McCain said that Gramm "did not serve in Vietnam." When an NBC reporter confronted McCain and told him that Bob Dole opposed normalizing relations with Vietnam, McCain responded that Dole had "served in another war which has ended, and I would like for Senator Dole to let us end this one." On Tuesday, July 11, McCain joined up with an unlikely political ally, Bill Clinton, to endorse a normalization of relations. In a ceremony in the East Room of the White House, with McCain, John Kerry, Bob Kerrey, Chuck Robb, and others present, Clinton granted formal recognition to the Vietnamese government.

In his office in the Russell Senate Office Building on the morning before the ceremony, a reporter from the *Arizona Republic* had asked McCain how he felt about the historic development. "This is a time to heal," McCain said. "I experienced closure a long time ago—the day I left Vietnam in 1973. But others, they still need to heal." Following the ceremony, a reporter from another news outlet asked McCain if he believed he was being used by the Clinton Administration. "Maybe," McCain said, "but I'm just trying to do what's in the best interest of the country. . . . Do I trust them [the Vietnamese]? No, but I trust the history. They are meeting their commitments, and we should meet ours. It's a way of ending the war. It's time to move on."

There were, however, other Americans who couldn't move on. In July, the *U.S. Veteran Dispatch,* an underground publication circulated among a segment of the veteran population, called McCain "a fraud, a 'rhinestone hero' and a national security risk." The publication spoke for the portion of the veteran community that was angry at McCain because he would not accept their notion that a large number of POWs and MIAs were being held in Southeast Asia, particularly in Vietnam. The veterans were livid because McCain, whom they had considered to be one of their own, had modified the positions he had held in the past and now advocated—indeed, endorsed—resuming relations with Vietnam. "John McCain is no hero," the *Dispatch* said in its July edition. "He was never brutally tortured and, by his own admission, he collaborated with the communists." Without even attempting to justify how it could make such outrageous statements, the publication further undercut its credibility by claiming McCain was given "his own private affection nurse."

In July, decidedly more favorable press came to McCain in the form of Robert Timberg's highly praised book on the U.S. Naval Academy called *The Nightingale's Song.* Timberg had used Oliver North, James Webb, Robert McFarland, John Poindexter, and McCain as subjects for his examination of life before, during, and after Annapolis. Writing in the *New York Times Book Review,* Nicholas Proffitt had called the book "a significant contribution to our understanding of recent political and military history" and "a fascinating chronicle of the human element behind all history." Mark Shields declared in the *Washington Post:* "[The book] will help you understand why the unhealed wounds of the Vietnam War still pain and divide this American nation and shadow American politics. . . . Robert Timberg explains brilliantly the price paid by those who went, by those who didn't, and by the nation's leadership that failed them."

Autumn in 1995 was a season of disappointment and triumph. On a personal note, McCain was saddened by the spectacular fall from grace of a friend in the Senate, Robert Packwood of Oregon. Packwood had been the object of an Ethics Committee investigation based on allegations that he had made unwanted sexual advances toward 17 women. Through the long ordeal, Packwood defiantly made every legal and ethical move possible to keep himself in the Senate. But on Wednesday, September 6, the Ethics Committee unanimously voted to have Packwood expelled for sexual misconduct. Ultimately, there was too much evidence against him.

On Thursday morning, September 7, McCain and Alan Simpson, a Republican from Wyoming, met with Packwood in Bob Dole's Senate hideaway. "John and I sat there," Simpson remembers, "and said: 'What are we going to do for our friend?' He was getting torn to bits. It was going to be tough. He had no chance. Nobody was listening. The Ethics Committee was cutting him to ribbons, both parties. So we said, 'Bob, it may be time to go.' And he was heartbroken. He said, 'But I didn't do these things. I mean, I'm being crucified.' And, of course, the statute of limitations had expired on every one of them, in any other court."

Finally, McCain summed up the situation. "It's over," McCain said to Packwood. "You gotta go. I envision no scenario where the Senate would overrule a unanimous recommendation of the Ethics Committee." Packwood sat quietly, the weight of the moment bearing down on him. When Dole joined the meeting, the discussion shifted from *whether* Packwood should resign to *how* he would resign. "You should talk about how much you've achieved as a senator," McCain said, "and how much you love the Senate, and go out with grace."

In December, Dole and McCain teamed up to sponsor a resolution on Bosnia called Dole–McCain, a piece of legislation that would allow the president to commit U.S. troops to help the Bosnian Muslims in their ongoing struggle with Serbia. The resolution passed easily (77 to 22) but, within the process, which had far-reaching implications, a highly personal piece of information was revealed by Dole to McCain—a detail of history that brought the two good friends even closer.

"There was a debate in the Senate," McCain says, "and Bob Dole and I had joined together, against a lot of Republicans, in favor of sending troops into Bosnia. I had already spoken. Bob was to give the last speech before the vote, which is traditional for the majority leader. I was very interested in what he had to say because, on this issue, he had taken on the right wing. So I went down and sat in this little chair next to the podium, where the president of the Senate sits, so I could see him from that part of the Senate and watch him speak. He gave the speech, and in it he mentioned the fact that he'd worn my bracelet while I was in prison. He had never told me that he wore a bracelet with my name on it— until that speech. I was floored when he talked about it. After the speech, I went up to him and said, 'Bob, how come you never told me?' And he said something like, 'Well, I didn't think about it.' Something like that. And that was the way I found out that he wore a bracelet with my name on it while I was in prison in Vietnam."

For the presidential election of 1996, McCain supported Senator Phil Gramm of Texas. A staunch conservative, Gramm was much farther to the right than McCain on a number of issues. Even so, McCain was such a strong supporter, Gramm made him the national chairman of his presidential campaign. During the fall, McCain had worked hard for Gramm; he lobbied to get a number of elected officials in Arizona to support Gramm. But in the second week of February 1996, in the wake of a dismal showing in the New Hampshire primary, Gramm saw his campaign fall apart. The frontrunner in the party was McCain's friend Bob Dole, whom McCain endorsed on February 16, as soon as it was clear that the Gramm candidacy was finished.

In the late spring, after Dole had the nomination locked up, he decided to resign from the Senate so he could devote all of his energy to his campaign. One person who pushed strongly for him *not* to resign was McCain. In the end, Dole did not take McCain's advice. On

June 11, 1996, he delivered a speech and formally resigned from the body he had come to cherish. McCain was one of the many senators who offered testimonials to Dole. "Bob Dole [once] wore a bracelet that bore my name," McCain said. "I have never properly thanked him for the great honor he did me. I wish to do so now. For myself, for my comrades who came home with me, and for the many thousands who did not, thank you, Bob, for the honor of your concern and support for us. We fought in different wars, but we kept the same faith."

This was not the only time in the spring of 1996 McCain was willing to show his emotions. "I went to the funeral of David Ifshin," says Congressman Eliot Engel, a Democrat from New York, "a friend of mine who had been active in Clinton's first election. President Clinton came to the funeral and delivered one of the eulogies. The other person who delivered a eulogy was John McCain. I remember feeling very surprised, because Dave had been a radical left-winger on the Vietnam War, a real student activist who was even featured in magazines as a leader of the anti-war movement. And when John spoke he made a reference to it. Apparently, they first met each other almost as adversaries—John said he initially had disdain for him—but somehow they became acquaintances and then very close friends. When he got up and spoke, it was the first time I ever saw a side of John McCain that was more than what I thought he was: a right-wing reactionary Republican. That day, I saw the other side of McCain and I realized you can't put a mold on him. He spoke of David in glowing terms, this former adversary. He spoke with empathy, sensitivity, and heartfeltness."

On Wednesday night, March 27, 1996, the Senate voted for the line-item veto, a concept McCain had fought for for 10 years. He believed pork-barrel spending could be contained, at least in part, if the president was allowed to veto specific lines in the federal budget. Apparently, this idea's time had finally come: The bill establishing the line-item veto passed 69 to 31. To erase any doubt that Congress was ready to pass the bill into law, the House waited only 18 hours after the Senate vote and then passed the bill with a vote of 232 to 177.

On June 24, McCain took an action that further elevated his national profile, when, on the Senate floor, he introduced the product of his and Russell Feingold's efforts toward campaign finance reform.

The 1996 version of the bill banned political action committees and ended soft money—moves that caused Senator Mitch McConnell of Kentucky to call the proposed legislation "an unconstitutional, undemocratic, bureaucratic boondoggle." McCain saw the reform differently. "This bill will not cure public cynicism for politics," McCain said on the Senate floor, "but we believe it will prevent cynicism from becoming contempt and contempt from becoming alienation. . . .We know the consequences of failing to act are far more frightening than the consequences of involuntary retirement." Apparently, the Senate didn't agree. The next day, the Senate killed campaign finance reform on a procedural vote. McCain saw the defeat coming when he said to the body before the vote, "The people's will cannot be forever denied, no matter how well inoculated we are by the financial advantages we claim as incumbents. . . . The people will have this reform, if not by our work, then by the work of our replacements."

Through July and on into August, a political soap opera developed around whom Bob Dole would pick to be his running mate. This drama only heightened when Kenneth Duberstein, a well-placed Washington insider, had set up a luncheon at his home and invited Dole and Colin Powell for the express purpose of Powell's being offered the vice-presidential spot on the ticket. But Powell made it clear he was not interested, mostly because his wife, Alma, was strongly opposed to the idea. The soap opera continued into August. On August 1, McCain was added to Dole's list, and the FBI began a background check of McCain and his family. By August 8, other names had been leaked, among them Governor John Engler of Michigan, Senator Connie Mack of Florida, and a former governor, Carroll Campbell of South Carolina. Then, because Dole had decided to make, as the centerpiece of his campaign, a proposed across-the-board 15 percent tax cut, Jack Kemp, the former football quarterback and congressman from New York, was seen by some as an unusually appropriate pick. The plan that was finally put into place required Dole to make the announcement in his hometown of Russell, Kansas, on the Saturday before the start of the Republican National Convention.

"Ultimately, the short list was down to Connie Mack and Jack Kemp," says Joyce Campbell, the deputy press secretary for Dole for President. "Dole was literally sitting in a campaign trailer in Russell,

Kansas, trying to make his decision whether it would be Mack or Kemp. Finally, Senator Dole got on the phone with Jack Kemp for one last conversation, and that was when he made up his mind. Kemp was down in Texas, I believe, at the time, so Sheila Burke and Rod D'Arment were dispatched down to Texas on a private plane to pick him up."

Observers should have known the campaign was going to have problems when Dole arrived in San Diego and, as he made his opening informal remarks while standing near the city's beautiful picturesque bay, told the audience how happy he was to be in San Francisco. McCain was featured at the convention. It was he who actually delivered the nomination of Dole on August 14. But the convention was stolen by the candidate's wife, Elizabeth Dole, who gave a dramatic and poignant talk about her husband as she wandered about, Oprah-style, on the floor of the convention. Elizabeth Dole even upstaged her husband, whose schizophrenic acceptance speech—the sweeping, elegant passages were written by novelist Mark Helprin; the clunky info-speak parts were put together by a bevy of run-of-the-mill, work-for-hire speech writers— served as a preamble to a campaign that was, at best, disjointed.

"Before long, Dole was getting to the point where he was, while not going off message, having a hard time focusing on his stump speeches on the road," Joyce Campbell says. "So McCain was kind of called in to become a cheerleader." As they went from stop to stop on the campaign trail, McCain simply hung around Dole. He sat with him in Dole's private area on the plane and milled around with him back-stage at events. "Sometimes McCain would stand in the audience of some of the stump speeches or sit in the front row and prompt Dole to smile. I remember one or two occasions on which McCain drew a happy face on a legal pad and sort of flashed it at Dole—he'd hold it up so Dole could see it—to get Dole to smile at different moments during the speech. McCain was always very openly and physically kind toward Dole. He would pat him on the back, put his arm around him. It was kind of, like, here were two guys who had been through hell and back. I thought McCain was an extremely likable guy."

Maybe, but some campaign staffers saw what many people in Washington knew McCain had—a temper. "McCain was loyal to Dole, and we liked him for that," says someone who worked on the Dole campaign. "We all liked him because we thought he was honest and tough—and a very warm person. But he had a really bad temper. When he got mad, he'd use every expletive in the book. He had the mouth of a sailor, which should not have been surprising, since he *was* a sailor. He just had, I guess you'd say, a very feisty personality."

In November, on the night of the election, McCain watched as Dole lost to Clinton in a race that was never really competitive. Still, during the campaign, the two men had become close. "The common bond of their friendship," Campbell says, "was that they had been war veterans whose experiences in war had molded and defined their world views and their view of public service. Dole was almost killed; McCain was almost killed. They had this near-death experience in combat that they shared. They also both felt that they were American success stories—kind of up-by-your-boot-straps personalities. Finally, because McCain was of a different generation, he held Dole in enormously high esteem. He saw Dole as having leadership qualities, which was why he considered Dole a role model."

On November 12, McCain traveled to Phnom Penh, Cambodia, where he unveiled a plaque honoring American troops killed on the coast of Cambodia 21 years earlier in the final action of the Indochina War. Eighteen men from the marines, the air force, and the navy were killed by the Khmer Rouge as they attempted to rescue the crew of the *Mayaguez* on May 15, 1975. During this trip, McCain met, for the first time, Mai Van On, the man who had saved him years before. On, who still lived in Hanoi, was happy to meet the man he had saved. "We shook hands and hugged each other," On would one day tell the *Los Angeles Times.* "He sat next to me and asked me, 'I was your adversary; why did you rescue me?' I told him, 'You were about to die. Based on the humanitarian nature of the Vietnamese people, I rescued you.' "

When he returned to Arizona, McCain addressed an issue in which he was becoming more and more interested—the environment. "Have Republicans abandoned their roots," McCain wrote in the *Arizona Republic* on November 27, "as the party of Theodore Roosevelt, who maintained that government's most important task, with the exception of national security, is to leave posterity a land in better condition than they received it? The answer must be 'No.' . . . The estimable Morris Udall, the former Democrat representative from Arizona and a nation-ally recognized environmental leader, once taught me a valuable lesson. He reached across the aisle to enlist my help in his efforts to address the environmental problems of our state. We were able to place more than 3.5 billion acres of land into wilderness protection, increase the preser-vation of public lands and tackle complex environmental threats to the Grand Canyon."

In 1996, McCain had also made known his stand on the con-flict between Great Britain and Northern Ireland. "I was at the British Embassy when the new British ambassador invited a bunch of us to a formal dinner to discuss the Northern Irish situation," says Congressman Peter King of New York. "It was very elaborate, as only the British can do it. Among those attending were Chris Dodd, John McCain, Joe Kennedy, and some people from the White House. Well, I was convinced it was sort of a setup, because the ambassador had McCain sitting right opposite me. I didn't really know McCain at all, except that he was very pro-British on the whole Irish issue. During the course of the evening, McCain made some very pro-British state-ments, at which point I started to disagree with him. Within 30 or 40 seconds, we were going at each other across the table. Dodd said, 'Will you guys knock it off?' Then Kennedy said, 'No wonder nobody wants to invite the Irish anywhere.' We calmed down, but during the rest of the night I would see him occasionally looking over at me."

By the fall of 1997, McCain was ready to fight the next battle in campaign finance reform. On September 10, Russell Feingold announced that he and McCain were willing to force a fight in the Senate, if that's what it would take to get the issue discussed. Regardless of whether the bill passed during this session, McCain-Feingold was having a profound effect on McCain's career. Conservative advocacy groups, angered by McCain's attempt to push campaign finance reform through Congress, targeted McCain as a politician who needed to be eliminated from the national political scene. These groups, it seemed, believed campaign finance reform would affect their ability to be suc-cessful because it would limit the ways money could be raised and how it could be spent on issue-advertising. To get rid of McCain, one group, the National Right to Life Committee, decided to air a radio campaign attacking McCain in the key states of Arizona, New Hampshire, and Iowa. Discrediting him in his home state made sense, if the goal was to try to make him vulnerable in his next Senate race. But the idea of running negative ads in Iowa and New Hampshire meant that, even in 1997, some groups had identified McCain as a possible—or maybe even a probable—presidential candidate in 2000. The presidential rumors were so widespread that as recently as August McCain had been asked if he ever wanted to be president. His answer was flip but telling—pure McCain: "I prefer to be emperor."

McCain-Feingold died on February 26, 1998, when the Senate voted 51 to 48 to end a filibuster on the bill. In effect, the bill was nine votes shy of becoming law, because to pass in the Senate a bill actually needs 60 votes—the number required to end a filibuster. Soon after, McCain launched another crusade that was destined to generate controversy. On April 1, the Commerce Committee, which McCain chaired, passed a bill that, according to McCain, was designed to reduce the number of teenage smokers in the United States. The bill would raise the tax on a pack of cigarettes so high that teenagers would find smoking unaffordable. Much to the surprise of some political observers, the bill, which amounted to a hefty tax increase, had been passed, out of committee, by the overwhelming margin of 19 to 1. As soon as the committee passed the bill, the chairman of R. J. Reynolds, Steven Holdstone, who had been working closely with Washington until now, severed all relationships with both the White House and Congress.

By mid-May, McCain and the White House had reached an agreement on the amendments to McCain's tobacco bill. Most of the amendments dealt with civil lawsuit liabilities and the cigarette tax itself, which, if McCain and the White House got their way, would total $65 billion over five years. The Senate debate over the tobacco bill could now begin—as soon as possible. That debate raged throughout the rest of May and June.

Finally, there was a showdown over the tobacco bill. The Republican senators, most of whom opposed McCain's bill, had met for a luncheon during which the bill's opponents criticized the legislation. A flow chart was produced to show the cumbersome bureaucracy the bill would create, should it ever become law. McCain was incensed

John Sidney McCain III, in the arms of his grandfather in 1936. His father, John S. McCain Jr., is at left. (*Photo credit:* Corbis Sygma.)

Aboard the carrier *USS Forrestal,* Lt. Commander Robert Browning, Lt. Commander Kenneth McMillen, and Lt. Commander John S. McCain III survey the damage on July 30, 1967. Browning and McMillen, who were in their aircraft, were injured when the fire broke out. (*Photo credit:* Bettmann/Corbis.)

Freed from his years of captivity in Hanoi, Lt. Commander John S. McCain III smiles as he limps down the ramp and is welcomed at Clark Air Force Base in the Philippines, on March 14, 1973. (*Photo credit:* AP/Wide World Photos.)

Cindy and John S. McCain III were married on May 17, 1980. (*Photo credit: Corbis Sygma.*)

Senators John Glenn (D-OH), Dennis DeConcini (D-AZ), and John McCain (R-AZ) arrive at the Senate Ethics Committee hearing room on November 15, 1990. (*Photo credit:* AP/Wide World Photos.)

The McCains on vacation in Zebra Falls, Arizona, on August 1, 1999. Their children's ages were then: Meghan, 14; Bridget, 8; Jimmy, 11; and Jack, 13. Bridget was adopted from an orphanage in Bangladesh. (*Photo credit:* McGoon James/Corbis Sygma.)

Admiral ("Chuck") Larson, USN, CINCPAC, and Superintendent at the U.S. Naval Academy (Annapolis); Federal Trade Commissioner Orson Swindle, Lt. Colonel USMC; Colonel George E. ("Bud") Day, a Congressional Medal of Honor recipient; and John and Cindy McCain on day two of the Presidential Candidacy Announcement Tour, September 1999. (*Photo credit:* Angie Williams.)

McCain traveling on the Straight Talk Express, with reporters, December 20, 1999. "Mr. Anonymous," *Primary Colors* author Joe Klein, sits in the foreground. (*Photo credit:* Bergsaker Tore/Corbis Sygma.)

The Sacred Heart University, Fairfield, Connecticut, campaign event, March 3, 2000. (*Photo credit:* Ben Davol.)

Cindy McCain at the Sacred Heart University campaign event, March 3, 2000. (*Photo credit:* Ben Davol.)

In Sedona, Arizona, on March 9, 2000, with Cindy at his side, McCain announced that he was suspending his bid for the Republican presidential nomination. (*Photo credit:* AP/Wide World Photos.)

McCain, in his office on Capitol Hill, during the Senate debate of the McCain-Feingold campaign finance reform bill, March 23, 2001. (*Photo credit:* AP/Wide World Photos.)

In 2000, at the Fifth Avenue home of Republican power broker Georgette Mosbacher, national cochair for McCain's presidential campaign that year, with Ron Oehl, Dee Shepherd (Mosbacher's mother), Alexander Shustorovich, Mosbacher, and Naseer Hashim. (*Photo credit:* Property and Courtesy of Georgette Mosbacher.)

Bo Derek and John McCain at a *Newsweek* reception at the White House Correspondents' annual dinner, April 2000, at the Washington Hilton. (*Photo credit:* Marina Garnier.)

Russell Denson (President and CEO of Gruner + Jahr), John Byrne (Editor in Chief of Fast Company), and John and Cindy McCain posed in front of Elaine's restaurant on Sept. 2, 2004. Fast Company hosted the reception for McCain during the GOP convention in New York. (*Photo credit:* Marina Garnier.)

McCain on the Campaign Trail in 2008

over the flow chart. "That's a chicken-shit chart!" he snapped, much to the chagrin of the stately senators who had been badmouthing his bill. In the end, his pleas did no good. On June 17, after a four-week debate and much support from the White House and numerous public health groups, the bill—which would have called for a $1.10 tax on a pack of cigarettes to be phased in over five years as well as other restrictions on the tobacco industry—was killed when it failed to receive 60 votes on two separate roll-call votes. The first time, the bill was three votes shy; the second time, seven votes. It was a terrible defeat for McCain—especially since the bill had come out of committee with almost unanimous support—and an unqualified victory for the tobacco companies.

Coming off the defeat, McCain moved on to his next battle: reelection in Arizona. To run against him, the Democrats had found someone named Ed Ranger, a motorcycle enthusiast who owned a Harley-Davidson that was painted to look like the Arizona flag. The election in November was not close; McCain got almost 70 percent of the vote. He then decided to go forward with an idea he had been considering for a while. He set up a presidential exploratory committee. Officially, the committee was established on December 30, 1998, when aides went to the Federal Election Commission in Washington and filed papers that made him the first Republican to declare his intention of running for president in 2000.

In the first weeks of 1999, McCain cast one of his most important votes as a senator when he voted to convict President Bill Clinton in the impeachment trial that had come before the Senate. In August 1998, Clinton admitted, in a highly charged appearance on national television, that he had lied about having an affair with Monica Lewinsky while she was a White House intern. Because one of the occasions on which he had lied was a deposition he was required to give as a result of a lawsuit brought against him by Paula Jones, Clinton was now guilty of lying under oath. For that, the House of Representatives impeached him in late 1998. But unless the Senate voted to convict him, Clinton would not be removed from office. It didn't. Needing 60 votes to convict, the Senate vote was of 56 to 43, a number well short of the minimum. (One senator, Arlen Specter, a Republican from

Pennsylvania, voted "not proved.") After the ordeal, which left a profound scar on the national psyche, McCain sounded conciliatory. "It's time to move on," he was quoted as saying in the press. As evidence of that thinking, McCain urged Kenneth Starr, the special prosecutor who had investigated Clinton, not to indict the president.

In January, in his office on Capitol Hill, McCain held a meeting with his advisers, one of whom was a new addition to his staff. Having recently made overtures to McCain, who agreed to see him, Michael Murphy arrived in McCain's office with a plan for how McCain could win the Republican presidential nomination: Skip Iowa. Election after election, the tradition within both parties required starting one's presidential campaign by running in the Iowa caucus and the New Hampshire primary. The latter event presented a potential political land mine, since the New Hampshire voters were stridently independent and often did not foreshadow how people in other parts of the country would vote. But the Iowa caucus had its own—different—problem. Voters had to show up physically at various locations across the state on caucus night—places like public schools, civic centers, and town halls—where they sat in rooms and, when asked, voted for their candidates as a group. To do well in a caucus, a candidate had to have an extensive network of volunteer supporters, which meant that the candidate favored by the party usually performed well. That day, in McCain's office, Murphy told McCain he would not have the support of the vast majority of his party. Most Republicans would line up behind Governor George W. Bush of Texas, who was widely rumored to be thinking about running for president. Impressed, McCain retained Murphy as a consultant.

After announcing his intentions of running for president in April, McCain began to make campaign appearances in May. On August 14, in keeping with his intention of skipping Iowa, McCain did not participate in the straw poll. Instead, he called it a sham. In the poll, Dan Quayle and Lamar Alexander did so poorly they dropped out of the race. Still, the presidential field was more crowded than observers had predicted. In addition to McCain, George W. Bush had announced he was a candidate for president. With Bush as the front-runner and McCain as the dark horse, the rest of the Republican field included Elizabeth Dole (wife of Bob Dole), a former secretary of both labor and transportation; Steve

Forbes, the publisher of *Forbes;* Pat Buchanan, a conservative political commentator; Gary Bauer, a religious activist; Orrin Hatch, the senator from Utah; and Alan Keyes, an ultraconservative and former ambassador to the United Nations. During the coming months, Buchanan would leave the Republican Party to join the Reform Party, and Dole would drop out of the race, citing an inability to raise money. Six candidates held on for the primary season: Bush, McCain, Forbes, Bauer, Hatch, and Keyes.

The candidate to beat was Bush. In 1994, he had ended a long and lackluster business career that saw him drift from one failing oil-related venture to another, all the while drinking heavily (the record would never be clear on his cocaine use) until his fortieth birthday when his wife threatened to leave him if he didn't straighten up. He ended this earlier chapter of his life by running for governor of Texas against Ann Richards—and winning. Many political observers chalked up the win to a trio of advisers who came to be known as "the Iron Triangle": Joe Allbaugh, Karen Hughes, and Karl Rove.

Chapter 8

Presidential Politics

On Monday, September 27, 1999, a cloudy but warm fall day, John McCain greeted a crowd of 1,000 people packed into Greeley Park in Nashua, New Hampshire, and officially announced his candidacy for president. America was facing a "new patriotic challenge," McCain said, "a fight to take our government back from the power brokers and special interests and return it to the people. I run for president . . . so that Americans can believe once again that public service is a summons to duty and not a lifetime of privilege."

For the campaign, McCain assembled as his team: Rick Davis, campaign manager; Greg Stevens, media adviser; Mike Murphy, one of his political consultants; John Weaver, chief political adviser; Mark Salter, speech writer; and Howard Opinsky, press officer. In general, the team saw they had one asset beyond question: John McCain. Because McCain was barely tracking in the opinion polls, the team made an early decision.

To get the media coverage McCain now desperately needed, they would make him completely available to the press. So, the campaign featured a bus called the Straight Talk Express. Reporters could pile in, sit in the back with McCain as he held court in a red overstuffed captain's chair, and listen to him talk about any subject thrown at him. This level of access to a candidate had never before been seen in politics. It would become one of the hallmarks of McCain as a candidate and position him with the media in a way few candidates have enjoyed.

Throughout October and into November, McCain campaigned heavily. On November 16, McCain made clear his decision to use New Hampshire as the launching point of his national campaign. In a letter to Kayne Robinson of the Iowa Republican Party, he formally declared he did not intend to campaign in Iowa. "I will not conduct any organized campaign effort," McCain wrote. "Nor will my campaign be spending money on advertisements, staff, or organizational activities." He agreed to participate in debates to be held in Iowa on December 13 and January 15 (before the January 24 caucus), but he would make no other commitments. "My decision not to establish a campaign organization in Iowa," McCain said, "is based solely on the compressed nature of the primary schedule and the increasing influence of big money on the nominating process."

Another factor came into play. The New Hampshire race, which at first appeared as if it were going to be a blowout for Bush, was now tightening significantly. Some Washington observers began to sense that an organized whisper campaign had been started to smear McCain— in part to undercut McCain's growing popularity. Using "temper" as a code word, a group of Republican senators began to imply McCain was unstable. The line of reasoning went like this: The five and a half years McCain spent as a POW had damaged him mentally, and his outbursts of anger were evidence of emotional unsteadiness. On November 19, Elizabeth Drew, a journalist who had written about American politics for years, published an editorial in the *Washington Post* in which she claimed the whisper campaign against McCain was being conducted by Trent Lott, Don Nickles, Paul Coverdale, and Robert Bennett (the senator from Utah).

The whisper campaign was a stroke of genius for McCain's opponents. It took one of McCain's strongest assets as a candidate (not to mention as a person)—his years of military service, as represented so dramatically by his confinement in a prisoner-of-war camp—and turned that asset against him. It was a move worthy of Lee Atwater, perhaps one of the most heartless, if successful, operatives in the history of American politics. Candidate McCain was most proud of his military service. To negate that advantage, one had to single it out and imply that, because it contained lengthy periods of psychological torture that would have left almost anyone emotionally scarred, it disqualified him for the very office for which he was running.

Near the start of the whisper campaign, someone close to the Bush camp called James Stockdale, a retired navy admiral and a friend of McCain from the time they were both POWs in Vietnam. Stockdale had been Ross Perot's vice-presidential running mate in 1992. The caller, a friend of Stockdale, had approached him, to quote from a piece Stockdale published in the *New York Times* on Friday, November 26, "soliciting comments on Mr. McCain's weaknesses." The caller implied that one of McCain's weaknesses was a mental instability brought on by his imprisonment. "I think John McCain is solid as a rock," Stockdale told the caller. "And I consider it blasphemy to smudge [McCain's] straight-arrow prisoner-of-war record." On reflection, Stockdale decided to become even bolder in his defense of McCain. "The military psychiatrists who periodically examine former prisoners-of-war have found that the more resistant a man was to harsh treatment," Stockdale wrote in the *Times,* "the more emotionally stable he is likely to become later in life."

"His experience in Vietnam actually made McCain *more* balanced than he had ever been," Stockdale adds. "It was a building block. He had been brought up in a family of very high principles. He is a guy who can handle a crisis and not feel sorry for himself. He can keep his balance and not go off half-cocked." Others dismissed the entire issue of his temper as false. "There's a difference between anger and irritation," Senator Alan Simpson says. "And just because he's pretty feisty doesn't mean he's angry. He doesn't seethe; he's not a seether. He might say, 'Oh, that's just BS! That's nuts!' and steel his jaw. And then they see his jaw steeled and think he's angry. Well, there's a difference. With me, people say: 'Now what are you doing? Are you ranting?' I say: 'Ranting is a good thing.' It doesn't mean you want to stab anybody or spit at them. It just means you are saying: 'God, I'm tired of this crap! Tired of it!' "

As McCain headed for the primaries, the whisper campaign continued. McCain and his handlers then made a decision. McCain would deal with this controversy in the same way he had dealt with similar controversies in the past—he would address it publicly. On Saturday, December 4, McCain gave the Associated Press three three-inch-thick binders containing hundreds of pages of medical records. Their release to the general public came on Monday. The full and accurate account of McCain's medical history was an impressive presentation. The file contained general information: McCain had twice taken an intelligence quotient test; his IQ was established as 128 the first time, 133 at a later time. He had a slightly enlarged prostate gland, not unusual for a sixty-year-old man. He was also on a daily aspirin therapy.

But most impressive was the mental chronology established by the documents. Starting in 1973, McCain had taken a series of physical and mental tests at the Robert E. Mitchell Center for Prisoner of War Studies. Just 10 days after McCain's release from prison in 1973 one observer noted: "Patient's mental status has not been influenced by recent situational stress." That same year, when he was asked how he had withstood the ordeal of being a POW, McCain said, according to a note in the records, "Faith in country, United States Navy, family, and God." Indeed, one examiner wrote that the years McCain had spent as a POW taught him "to control his temper better, to not become angry over insignificant things." Three years later, another examiner drew an equally benign conclusion when he wrote: "There is no sign of emotional difficulty." In short, McCain's medical records proved he suffered no apparent psychological wounds from being a POW for five and a half years. The experience had left McCain with degenerative arthritis in his shoulders and right knee, which indicated that he might need joint replacements some day, but, psychologically, he was fine. "He had a very healthy way of dealing with his experiences," concluded Dr. Michael Ambrose, the director of the Center for Prisoner of War Studies. "There was never any mental illness."

In early December, delivering his first public speech in Connecticut, McCain stood before an overflow crowd in Silliman College on the campus of Yale University with neither a podium nor notes and spoke off-the-cuff. The event, a "master's tea," had previously hosted guests such as author Kurt Vonnegut and Supreme Court Justice Sandra Day O'Connor, but, to McCain, it was simply another stop on the campaign trail. He talked about social issues such as health insurance and prescription drugs, saying, "We have to address the fact that 11 million children are still without health insurance and many senior citizens can't afford prescription drugs." He touched on his signature issue when he noted: "Those lobbyists in Washington are scared to death; they know the status quo will not prevail if I'm president." On foreign affairs, he made comments that would prove to be prophetic. "Unless something changes," he told the Yale students, "it's likely one of those [rogue states] will acquire one of those weapons [of mass destruction] and a way to use it. I'd hate to see an American president held hostage." Finally, he turned to a subject he often included in his public addresses: patriotism. "During my time in prison I had the opportunity to fall in love with America," he said. "When I was deprived of her, I realized what a wonderful and noble experiment America is."

After his talk, McCain took questions from the audience. One student asked him about the "whisper campaign." "Do I get angry?" McCain fired back in jest. "Yes. I'll have a temper tantrum here for you if you want." Another student asked about Vietnam. "The shadow of Vietnam doesn't fall over everything I do or say," McCain offered, before he moved on to a sentiment he frequently delivered when asked to describe his time as a POW in Vietnam. "I was not a hero. My privilege was to serve in the company of heroes." Another student asked him to identify the biggest challenge he faced in the presidential race. "The biggest challenge I face?" McCain paused; then he became mischievous. "One, while we're having this meeting, Governor Bush is probably raising another $2 million or $3 million"—a reference to the painful reality that, so far, McCain had raised only $14 million compared to $65 million pulled in by the Bush campaign. "The biggest challenge I face is: going against the Republican establishment." And how worried was he about lagging behind in the fund-raising process? McCain could not resist an ironic response. Quoting Chinese Chairman Mao Tse-tung, he said dryly, "It's always darkest before it's totally black."

The next day, McCain and New Jersey Senator Bill Bradley, a Democrat, announced that, on the following Thursday morning, they would meet in Claremont, New Hampshire, to sign a mutual pledge that neither man would accept soft money from his party if he received his party's nomination. They chose to meet in Claremont because, in June 1995, President Bill Clinton and Speaker of the House Newt Gingrich had met there to shake hands on a vow to reform the campaign finance system. In retrospect, Claremont may have been a bad choice on the part of McCain and Bradley. The Clinton-Gingrich effort had died in Congress, and the two men ended up blaming each other for the failure.

On the day of their meeting, December 16, as a morning frost coated the ground in the mill town of Claremont, McCain and Bradley made their way to a worn wooden table on a hilltop near a senior citizens' home. Bundled up in overcoats and wearing gloves, the two men hunched over the table to put their signatures to this carefully worded agreement: "We pledge that as nominees for the Office of President of the United States we will not allow our political parties to spend soft money for our presidential campaigns, and we commit to working together toward genuine campaign finance reform." Bradley agreed to ban the use of soft money only if his Republican opponent did as well; McCain agreed to the soft-money ban outright.

Near where the two men met, a limestone bench bore the inscription, "Site of historic summit between President William Jefferson Clinton and House Speaker Newt Gingrich." Since the only thing that had come out of that summit was a photo opportunity for Clinton and Gingrich, Bradley and McCain, as they spoke to reporters at their pledge-signing, were careful to avoid discussing the previous ceremony that had taken place on this hilltop. But McCain couldn't help taking a swipe at Vice President Al Gore's fund-raising shenanigans. "The vice president of the United States asked monks and nuns to pay thousands of dollars to violate their vows of poverty so they could spiritually commune with him," McCain said, referring to a fund-raiser Gore had attended at the Hsi Lai Buddhist temple in Hacienda Heights, California, in April 1996. It had been one of the incidents that, later that year, forced Gore to claim he had "no controlling legal authority" to stop questionable fund-raising activities in the Clinton-Gore campaign. "If I'm elected president," McCain said, "I will be the controlling legal authority."

With the new year—2000—came heightened tension between the Bush and McCain camps. Before, civility had defined the way the two candidates talked about each other. Clearly, neither of them thought McCain really had a chance to be president. Bush had set every record imaginable for fund-raising, he had gotten all of the important endorsements within his party (and a vast number of endorsements that were not important, but he took them anyway), and, at least early on, it looked as if Bush would sail smoothly through the primary process and into the national convention in August. Then, McCain hit the campaign trail in New Hampshire, began his seemingly endless string of town hall meetings, and started to eat away at Bush's lead in the opinion polls in New Hampshire. Because the New Hampshire primary, now less than one month away, was shaping up to be competitive after all, Bush had to treat McCain more like a viable opponent who could actually beat him.

The first truly edgy exchange of words between the two campaigns occurred on January 4, the day Elizabeth Dole, who had dropped out of the race, endorsed Bush. In Bedford, New Hampshire, before an audience at the C. R. Sparks Center, she compared Bush to Reagan, in whose Cabinet she had served. "Today," she said, "we rally to another Western governor, just as bold in challenging the status quo, just as resolved to restore pride in our institutions, just as determined to be himself." In his speech, Bush took aim at McCain for gypping the middle class with the tax cut he was about to propose. Responding on the campaign trail, McCain argued that Bush's tax cut, which totaled $483 billion, would kill Social Security and help the rich. "Sixty percent of the benefits from Bush's tax cut go to the wealthiest 10 percent of Americans," McCain said, "and that's not the kind of tax relief that Americans need. . . . I'm not giving tax cuts to the rich."

The Dole endorsement was not without its history. "Senator Bob Dole had actually sent McCain a $1,000 check while Mrs. Dole was still a candidate," Joyce Campbell says. "After the press found out about the contribution, Dole kept saying, 'Elizabeth sent me to the doghouse.' But Dole saw McCain as having great potential. Some of Dole's past jealousy and animosity and all those tenuous feelings he had about Bush Senior were resurfacing a little bit too. Ultimately, though, Dole is a party man. There was a flirtation with McCain at the beginning"—maybe fueled by his former unpleasant encounters with George H. W. Bush—"but then the party won out. McCain had to know that the Doles had no choice but to do what was right for the party, especially since Mrs. Dole had been a candidate."

On January 5, McCain had to deal with another dilemma. The *Boston Globe* ran an article saying McCain, in his capacity as chairman of the Commerce Committee, had lobbied federal regulators to vote on a television license that had been applied for by Paxson Communications, a company that had been a major contributor to McCain's presidential campaign and had allowed him the use of its corporate jets. Over the next few days, as the story was picked up in the media, a fuller picture emerged. In the past few months, McCain had flown on Paxson corporate jets four times, and company executives had given his campaign $20,000. On December 9, as the *Washington Post* would report, McCain had flown on a Paxson company plane to West Palm Beach, Florida, where he attended a fund-raiser on a yacht. The very next day—supposedly at the request of Paxson's Washington lobbying firm, Alcalde & Fay—McCain sent a letter to the Federal Communications Commission (FCC), a government agency mindful of the influence of the Commerce Committee, to encourage a quick vote on Paxson's request to buy a television station in Pittsburgh. One week later, the FCC approved the sale. However, William Kennard, the FCC chairman, criticized McCain in a letter; McCain's request, he said, was "highly unusual." McCain had often fought with the FCC through the years because he believed the agency was slow and ineffectual. McCain had even told the *Globe,* when the paper first ran its story on the Paxson case, that he felt the FCC was "the least efficient, most bureaucratic, least responsive bureaucracy" in Washington.

Faced with the prospect that the Paxson matter could blow up into a full-scale scandal, McCain made the cautious move of canceling a fund-raiser that Lowell ("Bud") Paxson had scheduled for the coming weekend at his home. Sure enough, at a debate in Durham—an hour-long affair featuring all six Republican candidates and sponsored by New Hampshire Public Television, New England Cable Television, and the *Manchester Union Leader*—the first question from Tim Russert, the debate's moderator, concerned Paxson. Was the Paxson case an example of hypocrisy or of bad judgment? Neither, according to McCain.

"People deserve to know the answer," McCain said, meaning that companies with business before the FCC deserve to get prompt rulings. "I think that's appropriate in my role as chairman," McCain added, setting up the line of defense he would soon use. It centered around the notion that, as commerce chairman, he felt he had an obligation to prod regulators for action—not suggest decisions, only prod—regardless of whether the company involved was a contributor.

By Saturday of that first week of 2000, the Paxson matter had not gone away, so McCain made the decision to do what he had done to stop the whisper campaign: release a mountain of information. McCain took the unusual step of having his staff release to the media some 500 letters he had written to various government agencies on behalf of companies and individuals, some of whom were contributors to his political efforts. The strategy was simple: prove that the Paxson example was not suspect by showing that this approach to lobbying was not out of the ordinary. On Sunday, McCain returned to New Hampshire. At a press conference in Goffstown, he was asked by a reporter if he believed the Bush campaign was behind the original leak of the letter he had written on behalf of Paxson. "It doesn't matter," McCain said. "This campaign is very tough and it's getting more intense. The worst thing you can do is to get diverted by something like this, which causes you to get off your game."

As McCain was making these comments, newspapers, armed with this new batch of material, were preparing articles about McCain and Paxson. The *Hartford Courant,* for example, published a story that restated the facts but added new information. As chairman of the Commerce Committee, McCain had written not one but two letters during the fall—at the very time he was running for president—to the FCC commissioner. Each letter asked for a decision on a television license application made by Paxson Communications. For the record, McCain had reimbursed the company for the flights he had taken on its corporate jets, and when he had written to the FCC commissioner, he had not lobbied for any particular decision in either case. He had just implored the commissioner to reach a decision because the applications had been before the FCC for months.

All in all, the mass release of documents had the effect the McCain camp intended. After the new spate of stories based on the document dump came out, the controversy, such as it was, went away. McCain had clearly written similarly prodding letters on behalf of companies and individuals who had not given him any money. Here was the bottom line: McCain wrote the letters, in large part, because he was unhappy with the incompetency of the FCC, an organization over which he had some, but not complete, managing authority.

On Monday, January 17, while all of the other candidates were campaigning in Iowa in anticipation of the upcoming caucus, McCain was alone in New Hampshire, fighting the gusty winds, the ever-present snow, and the subzero temperatures. While he rode on the Straight Talk Express that day, McCain, seated in the big red captain's chair and surrounded by a pack of reporters, could not help but state the obvious. ";It's a very high-risk campaign we're running," he said. "I feel sometimes like the Wallendas" (the world-famous family of high-wire acrobats). To hedge those odds, he had a secret weapon for winning New Hampshire. He would campaign in the state more intensely than any other candidate. To that end, he had held town meeting after town meeting. On this day, as he wound his way through the state, McCain held town meetings numbers 93, 94, and 95. His approach—knocking on doors and talking to as many people as possible—had worked all those years ago in Arizona, at the beginning of his political career. He believed he would win this race only if he used the same dogged approach.

A week of nonstop campaigning followed. As of Monday, January 24, McCain's theme had become simple: "I am fully prepared to be the President of the United States." The line was meant to tie into a new ad that had just been launched. Called "Commander," the ad focused on national defense and foreign policy. In it, the narrator said: "There's only one man running for president who knows the military and understands the world: John McCain." Then the ad noted McCain's navy pilot experience and his years as a POW. The point was obvious. McCain was a war hero with extensive military experience; Bush was not. Nowhere did anyone in the McCain campaign mention publicly that, in 1968, at the height of the Vietnam War, Bush had allowed his father to pull strings to get him into a unit of the Texas Air National Guard so Bush could avoid active military duty.

But those were the facts. While McCain was being held in the Hanoi Hilton, Bush was living in an upscale "singles" apartment complex in the Galleria area in Houston, driving around in a sports car, and serving his country by flying practice runs as a member of the Texas Air National Guard.

As expected, Bush won the Iowa caucus on the 24th, but he beat Steve Forbes by only 11 points, a much slimmer margin than political observers had expected. When the final numbers came in, McCain finished fifth in a field of six. Orrin Hatch came in last, which spelled the end to his campaign. Because McCain had made his strategy of skipping Iowa so clear, he could use his poor showing to his advantage in New Hampshire. At the very time the Iowa caucus was being held on Monday night, McCain was holding a "First-in-the-Nation Primary" rally at Dartmouth College. "The eyes of the nation will be on the main event," he told the cheering crowd, meaning the primary in New Hampshire. "Iowa is the preliminary."

Bush did not echo that sentiment when he arrived in New Hampshire on Tuesday, fresh from his victory in Iowa. However, he could see from the internal tracking polls he was in trouble in New Hampshire. The Bush campaign was not yet ready to admit there was any way he could lose the state, but, just in case, Bush went out of his way to hedge his bets. "I'm in it for the long run," Bush said in an interview in New Hampshire on Tuesday afternoon. "I will be the last man standing."

That Wednesday night, the five remaining Republican candidates met in Manchester in a 90-minute debate sponsored by CNN and WMUR, the state's major television station. This last debate before the primary was moderated by Bernard Shaw of CNN and Karen Brown of WMUR. With Forbes, Bauer, and Keyes looking on, Bush and McCain fought, now more sharply than ever, over taxes, school vouchers, campaign finance reform, and government spending. At one point, Bush accused McCain of writing a tax proposal worthy of the Clinton-Gore Administration. Later, when Bush again compared a McCain position to that of the Clinton Administration, McCain looked at Bush and said, "George, if you're saying that I'm like Al Gore, then you're spinning like Bill Clinton."

Bush did not seem unduly insulted by the zinger. Nor did he later in the debate when McCain made yet another attempt to compare

Bush to Clinton and Gore by saying, "When I'm in the debate with Al Gore, I'm going to turn to Al Gore and I'm going to say, 'You and Bill Clinton debased the institutions of government in 1996. . . . And, George, when you're in that debate, you're going to stand there and you'll have nothing to say because you're defending the system."

"John," Bush said in return, "I don't appreciate the way you've characterized my position. I'm for reform. I sure am."

"The people of this country are suffering from Clinton fatigue," McCain said, "and it's because they want someone who will look them in the eye and tell them the truth."

On Thursday night, McCain held a rally at Timberlane Regional High School in Plaistow. There, he voiced what had now become a running theme in the campaign—his willingness to expand his conservatism to include more moderate votes. "My friends," McCain told the excited crowd, "I am a proud conservative Republican. I have a 17-year record as a conservative Republican. But Jack Kennedy and Ronald Reagan had something in common: They would inspire a crowd to causes greater than their own self-interest." These days, the crowds were cheering for McCain as if he were a famous actor or rock star. The response was much more visceral and highly charged than run-of-the-mill politicians got, even if they were running for president. The audiences and the opinion polls let McCain know he was making headway in New Hampshire. With Primary Day looming, some McCain insiders thought he might actually be able to win, a development that would certainly change the political landscape as it was then defined. McCain knew what this meant too. While he sat in his captain's chair on the Straight Talk Express that Thursday night, he answered a question the reporters sitting around him had not asked. "My question is," McCain said—prophetically, as it turned out—"will the Bush campaign go negative?" The question was rhetorical, for McCain knew the answer. He just wanted to lay down a marker with the reporters covering him. If he won New Hampshire, he knew what was going to happen next.

That Sunday, McCain appeared on *Meet the Press*. Then he went on to hold his 114th—and final—town hall meeting in New Hampshire. In Peterborough, 1,000 supporters showed up to cheer McCain on. "Whether we prevail or not," McCain told the excited crowd, "this has been one of the greatest experiences of my life." At the end of his appearance, confetti rained down on McCain and Cindy and music blared over the public address system as a band launched into the song "Play That Funky Music, White Boy."

This was where he had held the first town meeting back in July. How far he had come since then! Six months earlier, McCain had been a little-known senator from Arizona, someone perhaps best identified as being a POW in Vietnam or one of the senators involved in the Keating Five scandal. Now, he was a widely acknowledged challenger to Bush's lock on the Republican presidential nomination. He had done it with style, tenacity, and what had become his trademark sense of humor, as exemplified by the time a reporter asked him what he thought about a Bush ad that attacked McCain's tax-cut proposal. In an obvious attempt to poke fun at the image Bush surrogates had painted of him as having an out-of-control temper, McCain said, "That makes me want to punch him in the face." Then, deadpanning to the press corps, he told them to describe him when he made that remark as "quivering with rage."

By midafternoon on February 1, McCain had been told that, in all likelihood, he was going to win the New Hampshire primary. Superstitious as ever—he carried a lucky eagle feather, a lucky compass, a lucky penny and, occasionally, a lucky rock; an aide carried his lucky ink pen (a Zebra Jimnie Gel Rollerball, medium blue); he wore lucky shoes (L. L. Bean rubber-sole dress shoes); he ate barbecue on the day of each debate and on an election day; and he always made a point of going to a movie while the polls were open—McCain said he would wait until that evening, when the returns came in, before he became hopeful. He was superstitious about being too confident as well.

So McCain waited upstairs in his suite at the Crown Plaza Hotel in Nashua, the town where he had started his campaign in September 1999. Since then, McCain had traveled all over the state of New Hampshire; in all, by the time he had finished campaigning, observers would estimate he had shaken the hands of some 60,000 people in New Hampshire, roughly five percent of the state's population. As the hours went by, the mood in the hotel suite became more and more charged. "I went up to the suite," says Peter Rinfret, one of McCain's national finance cochairs. "He had a private function in his suite—for the senior campaign staff, senior campaign volunteers, the finance committee, and his family. Everybody was standing there. He was coming in and out of the living room, and they're letting certain press people in. And then came the official announcement—I think MSNBC broke it—that he had won by 21 points, some huge number. Brian Williams broke it. The place just turned into pandemonium. McCain threw his arms around Cindy and hugged her, and then he started hugging everybody. Everybody was hugging everybody. Everybody was screaming, yelling. Then all the networks started announcing. CNN. ABC. NBC. After that, it just sort of became a roller coaster."

As the night went on, McCain waited for Bush to give his concession speech so he could go downstairs and make his acceptance speech. For days, Bush had been saying he was going to win the primary, and he seemed to mean it. Now it was clear that not only did he not win, he was crushed. In a college auditorium, at what was supposed to be his victory celebration, Bush, appearing on stage with Laura and his two daughters, tried to put the best face on this disastrous loss. Saying McCain had run "a really good race," Bush added: "He spent more time in this great state than any of the other candidates, and it paid off. Tonight is his night and the night of his supporters. And we all congratulate him." Then he went on, "New Hampshire has long been known as a bump in the road for frontrunners. And this year is no exception. The road to the Republican nomination and the White House is a long road. Mine will go through all 50 states, and I intend it to end at 1600 Pennsylvania Avenue."

Not long after Bush finished, McCain headed downstairs to make his speech. In the descending elevator, McCain was surrounded by his top staff and advisers. At one point, he looked over at Peter Rinfret and said in a calm, stoic voice, "Well, now the toughest part is to come." Still, he was thrilled. "He was very pumped in the elevator," says Ben Davol, who had worked with the campaign. "He had that big grin on his face and he was very pumped, very determined. There was never a tinge of, 'God, I won this thing.' It was always, 'I'm glad we won. We were right to win. We need to win.' There is a difference there. Sometimes you go into a game and you think, 'I don't know if I am going to win.' It wasn't a matter of the senator winning because he wanted to win. He wanted to win because he felt it was right for him to win for the country. That he had the ideas, the thoughts, the background and the enthusiasm to really change Washington and change the culture."

Orson Swindle, the man who had slept next to McCain for 18 months in the Hanoi Hilton, was overwhelmed. "I am on that door where John is to come in on the right side," Swindle says. "Bud Day is there with several other former POWs. We are the first people John sees when he walks in, and he just has this stunned look on his face. We all got choked up. It was an emotional moment, an incredible moment. To think where we had been and the unlikely probability that we would ever be where we were. Just the leap—from the bad days in Hanoi to that moment."

McCain started his acceptance speech by saying, "Thank you. Thank you. Thank you. Thank you." The victory was by 18 percentage points, which represented a 40,000-vote advantage in a race that brought out 225,000 voters. McCain got 49 percent of the vote to Bush's 31 percent. (Forbes received 13 percent; Keyes, 6 percent; and Bauer, 1 percent.) "We have sent a powerful message to Washington that change is coming," McCain said. "This is a good thing. And it is the beginning of the end of the truth-twisting politics of Bill Clinton and Al Gore."

As McCain made his speech, many in the crowd still had trouble absorbing the moment. For McCain's family, the whole night had a surreal, fantasy-like quality. "I was standing, looking at the TV," Ben Davol says. "McCain's brother Joe was next to me looking the other way. His sister was on my other side. And then they flash across the screen 'McCain Wins!' I turned and I said, 'Mr. McCain, it looks like your brother is going to be President of the United States. Look at that.' Now the brother is really hyper. He's wild. He goes at, like, a million miles an hour. He looked at me and he said—I'll never forget, these were his exact words—'This, this is better than sex!' I said to him, 'Better than sex?' He said, 'Absolutely!'"

Following his victory speech and the myriad media appearances, McCain made his way to the airport where he, Cindy, his family, and his entourage boarded an airplane to fly to South Carolina.

The battle there was going to be so intense he decided to skip the upcoming Delaware primary, which was going to be held a week after the New Hampshire primary. If he won in South Carolina, that victory would set him up to win the next two primaries, in Michigan and Arizona. Should he then do well in the primaries in Virginia and Washington state, he would be a formidable power on the first real day of reckoning—March 7, Super Tuesday. But he had to win South Carolina. If he didn't, he could continue, but he would lack the red-hot momentum he needed to challenge the campaign of George W. Bush, not to mention the Republican Party establishment. So McCain felt hopeful when, at three o'clock in the morning, he landed in Greer, South Carolina, to discover the hangar where a rally had been planned was jam-packed with supporters, many of them students happily partying to the ear-splitting rock music pounding through the cavernous room. Then McCain told the cheering crowd: "We just came down from making history in New Hampshire!"

Chapter 9

"The Dirtiest Race
I've Ever Seen"

McCain may or may not have known it at the time, but the next 18 days of his life would determine his political future. His lopsided victory in the New Hampshire primary had stunned the Republican Party and confounded the Bush campaign. If he could pull off a victory—even a squeaker—in South Carolina, the damage to the Bush campaign would be enormous, perhaps lethal. That was exactly what Mike Murphy had said, all those months ago, when he met with McCain in his Capitol Hill office. So, as McCain prepared to spend 12 or 13 of the next 18 days in South Carolina, he felt hopeful he could take the message that had played so well in New Hampshire and sell it to the South. If he could appeal to Southern voters, there was no stopping him.

By Thursday, when a new poll conducted by John Zogby revealed that Bush was trailing McCain in South Carolina by five percentage points, 44 to 39, Bush was prepared to go negative. So, at a rally at the town courthouse in Sumter, Bush took his place on the steps beside a man with one of the most controversial reputations of anyone in the military. The chairman of the National Vietnam and Gulf War Veterans Coalition, J. Thomas Burch had made a name for himself by criticizing politicians from Ronald Reagan to George H. W. Bush to John McCain. On this day, as he stood surrounded by other veterans, some of them retired generals and Medal of Honor winners, Burch took aim squarely at McCain. In presenting what he considered an analysis of McCain's record on military issues, Burch told the crowd of 350 that McCain did not favor assistance for veterans who suffered from Agent Orange and Gulf War Syndrome and that McCain was "the leading opponent" of efforts to help veterans' families learn about MIAs in Vietnam. Saying that McCain "had the power to help the veterans," Burch summed up by uttering lines that would infuriate McCain, his friends, and his supporters. "Senator McCain has abandoned the veterans," Burch said as Bush stood silently beside him, a smile frozen on his face. "He came home from Vietnam and forgot us."

When Bush spoke that day, he didn't let up. He actually told the audience he—not McCain—would make the better commander-in-chief. He did not mention a detail from his youth—how he avoided active military duty by allowing his father to get him into the Texas Air National Guard. "We must have a commander-in-chief who understands the role of the military," Bush said. The audience and the traveling press corps were stunned by the display. Here Bush was coming to a state where 400,000 veterans lived—more veterans per capita than in any other state in the country—and he was challenging McCain, a Vietnam hero, on McCain's history on military issues. It was a stunning example of what is so hard to pull off in politics: damaging one's opponent by attacking his strength. To make sure this was what Bush was up to, reporters peppered him with questions at a press conference following the rally. 'Did Bush endorse Burch's comments?' one journalist asked. "These men have their opinion," Bush said, referring to Burch and the other veterans; "they have stated their opinion. The thing I respect is, they have chosen me to be their candidate."

That afternoon, the McCain campaign answered Burch's charges by distributing to reporters a document detailing some of McCain's accomplishments on veterans' issues. In 1991, he had cosponsored the Agent Orange Act, which provided disability benefits for veterans afflicted with the debilitating medical condition—a fact that disputed Burch's contention McCain had waffled on the subject of Agent Orange. In Arizona, McCain had helped found a Gulf War Syndrome support group—further proof McCain was sensitive to the medical needs of veterans. In 1997, McCain had sponsored a law that provided medical and dental care for retired and active military personnel suffering from Gulf War Syndrome. Later, the McCain camp, still furious, called Burch "a discredited trial lawyer" and demanded an apology. It never came.

On February 4, John Kerry, Max Cleland, Bob Kerrey, and Chuck Robb (all Democrats) and Chuck Hagel (a Republican) signed a letter to George W. Bush written on United States Senate stationery in which they said, "[W]e are writing to express our dismay at the misinformed accusations leveled by your surrogate, J. Thomas Burch Jr., regarding our colleague John McCain's commitment to our nation's veterans. These allegations are absolutely false. . . . Indeed, Mr. Burch was a leading critic of President Reagan's and your father's policies on POW/MIA." As for McCain, the five senators declared, "From his courageous efforts on POW/MIA affairs, to his most recent advocacy of decent living standards and adequate compensation for men and women serving in the military today, Senator McCain has earned recognition from his colleagues on both sides of the aisle as a real leader on veterans' issues in the United States Senate. . . . We are familiar with the intensity of political campaigns, but we believe it is inappropriate to associate yourself with those who would impugn John McCain's character and so maliciously distort his record on these critical issues. We hope you will publicly disassociate yourself from these efforts, and apologize to Senator McCain for Mr. Burch's misguided statement made on your behalf."

Fellow POWs who had served with McCain in prison in Vietnam were also offended by the Burch incident. "The first indication we got that things were about to get ugly came," Orson Swindle says, "when a guy I happen to know, Tom Burch—who, as Al Hunt says, claimed to be some titular head of some organization representing veterans—got up there with Bush. I heard what Burch said with his little Green

Beret hat on. I think if you looked into his Green Beret experience you might be shocked. When he got up and said in front of God and everybody, with George Bush standing beside him, that John McCain abandoned veterans, I just went berserk. It was just a blatant damn lie. He said McCain abandoned the Vietnam veterans, he abandoned the POWs and the guys left behind. That just infuriated me because I didn't know anybody left behind. None of us knew anybody left behind." Other POWs were just as angered. "What a farce Burch was," Everett Alvarez says. (Only Jim Thompson served longer than Alvarez as an American POW in Vietnam.) "I couldn't believe this guy was out there saying what he said. He was such an opportunist . . . and what a farce. It was all lies, what he was saying about John. I mean, I was there."

On Friday, McCain was scheduled to appear on *The Tonight Show with Jay Leno*. As he drove from the airport to the NBC studios in Burbank, California, accompanied in the limousine by his entourage, McCain, livid over the Burch appearance and the willingness of Bush and his surrogates to question McCain's integrity, resolved himself to the reality that it was time to strike back. The New Hampshire primary victory was quickly fading into memory; such was the nature of politics. If he did not hit Bush, he would look weak and defenseless. Therefore, McCain gave Mike Murphy a go-ahead to write a new commercial script, one that would get the Bush campaign's attention. His message to the Bush camp was this: Attack McCain and McCain will hit back—with a vengeance.

That night, in a hotel room in San Francisco, Murphy worked on a script for a new McCain commercial that was meant to draw blood. McCain already had a commercial ready to go; it included the line, "Do we really want another president in the White House America can't trust?" That question was meant to compare Bush to Clinton in the most divisive way possible. Still, asking a question was not as powerful as naming a name. As Murphy sat alone in the hotel room, hunched over his laptop computer, he decided he had no choice but to stop pulling punches. In an hour or so, he had finished a new script, this one with a tag line no one would forget any time soon. Murphy knew McCain was angry enough to name names and accuse Bush of "twisting the truth like Clinton."

On Sunday, February 6, Karl Rove appeared on *Face the Nation* and described McCain as a "17-year Washington insider whose accomplishments are few and far between" because he "cannot lead people and persuade them to back his agenda." On the other hand, Bush was "a successful governor of a big state." As for campaign finance reform, Rove said, "Senator McCain portrays himself as an advocate of campaign finance reform, as somebody who is cleaner than any-one else around the table, and yet he has accepted contributions and sought contributions from people with legislation pending before his committee." Meanwhile, Carroll Campbell, the former South Carolina governor who had endorsed Bush, attacked McCain on *Fox News Sunday,* saying, "The fact is that people parade before John McCain's committee and they give him money. He's been flying on some of their jets in the past. . . . [W]hat I see is a man that is talking literally out of both sides of his mouth." (Naturally, Campbell didn't note that Bush had taken twice as many flights on corporate jets as McCain and that some of those jets were owned by corporations that regularly did business with the state of Texas.) Finally, another Bush surrogate, Ralph Reed, hit the airwaves on a different Sunday morning show to say that McCain was "one of the most powerful men in Washington and he has little or nothing to show for it." His point was that McCain was not even successful at being a Washington insider.

Meanwhile, that Sunday, when he made a stop in his home state on his way to Michigan, McCain did not mention the orchestrated assault by the Bush surrogates. At a rally at the Sky Harbor International Airport in Phoenix, McCain told an audience of 250 that he was ready to fight. "We're still the underdog," McCain said. "We're still running an insurgency campaign. But I can't tell you how excited I am." He had reason to be, too. That day, an article in the *Arizona Republic* said early polls indicated McCain had a slight lead in South Carolina. Now, almost a full week into the South Carolina campaign, McCain was doing better than he thought he would. But the early polls did not reflect the full effect of the Bush campaign's new assault on McCain.

In their strategy sessions over the weekend, Karl Rove and the rest of the Bush staff—Karen Hughes, Joe Allbaugh, and others—had come up with another plan of attack. They unveiled it on Monday, February 7, as Bush made appearances in Delaware on the day before the primary in that state. (Bush had no intention of skipping Delaware, regardless of McCain's plans.) In Dover, as he stood before a big blue-and-white banner emblazoned with his new motto, "REFORMER WITH RESULTS," Bush proudly declared he was just what his new motto said he was—a "reformer with results." The slogan was a calcu-lated rip-off of the reform role in which McCain had cast himself from the start of his presidential campaign, but that did not seem to faze Bush one bit.

In fact, Bush had been flirting with the concept during the past few days. On Friday, as he campaigned in Michigan, Bush had begun toying with this new idea: He, not McCain, was the reformer. "I'm the person who has been a reformer," Bush said on the trail. "It's hard to be a reformer if you have spent your entire career in Washington, D.C., which [McCain] has done." Over the weekend, the Bush handlers completed the thought Bush had started to form on Friday. When they met, they decided Bush was not just a reformer, he was a reformer *with results!* But they weren't happy merely stealing McCain's mes-sage; they also felt a need to discredit McCain's ability to *claim* he was a reformer. They came up with this: McCain was not a reformer; he was a typical Washington politician who was willing to say anything to get elected. The reformer mantle he embraced was nothing more than a guise to make himself electable, a message he could sell to the public. The evidence they used against McCain was his willingness to accept campaign contributions from corporations that had busi-ness before the Commerce Committee, which he chaired. If he had been a *real* reformer, their line of reasoning went, he would not have taken money from companies like Paxson Communications. All dur-ing the day on Monday, as if he had been programmed over the week-end in coaching sessions, Bush repeatedly delivered his prepared line about McCain: "He says one thing and does another." When a reporter asked Bush if he was calling McCain a hypocrite, Bush replied, again as if he had been anticipating the fairly obvious question, "That's your word." Then what word would Bush use? the reporter wanted to know. "Washington," Bush said.

After hearing that Bush was calling himself a "reformer with results," McCain could not help responding to Bush's over-the-weekend con-version. "I understand Governor Bush is now a reformer," McCain told the reporters who were traveling with him in Michigan. "If so, it's his first day on the job. He should join me in going to the heart of what's wrong with the system today, and that's campaign finance reform." McCain had challenged Bush on this issue because he knew Bush had used the current fund-raising system to amass more money for his campaign than any politician in the history of the United States.

On Tuesday, McCain warned that he would hit Bush hard if Bush didn't stop his "character assassination" of him—that is, his determination to question McCain's honesty and integrity. "We're going to respond harder than we're hit," McCain said as he talked to reporters on the Straight Talk Express on a day when a new poll showed the South Carolina race was a dead heat. "That's an old tactic that we used in warfare." When the Bush campaign unleashed a new attack ad charging that "McCain solicits money from lobbyists with interests before his committee and pressures agencies on behalf of contributors," McCain, true to his warning, answered with two TV ads. The first one slammed Bush. "This is George Bush's ad promising America he'd run a positive campaign," the ad's narrator said as Bush's own voice came on to say, "A campaign that is hopeful and optimistic and very positive." Then the ad showed "The Handshake" in New Hampshire, when during a debate Bush and McCain agreed not to engage in negative campaigning. "This is George Bush shaking hands with John McCain," the narrator said, "promising not to run a negative campaign." Next the ad showed another clip, which the narrator explained by saying, "This is George Bush's new negative ad, attacking John McCain and distorting his position." Then came the tag line: "Do we really want another politician in the White House America can't trust?"

The allusion to Clinton was obvious. But on that Tuesday the McCain campaign wasn't finished. The second ad hit Bush even harder. McCain was now willing to run Murphy's ad naming names. The allusions to Clinton were gone. Instead, McCain directly compared his opponent to the one man, Clinton, currently most loathed by Republicans. "I guess it was bound to happen," McCain said in the ad. "Governor Bush's campaign is getting desperate with a negative ad campaign against me." Finally, McCain spoke directly into the camera and made the charge that Bush "twists the truth like Clinton. We're all pretty tired of that."

On February 8, as the contest in South Carolina became even uglier, Bush got a much-needed boost: He won the Delaware primary. There was, however, good news for McCain as well. He had not campaigned in Delaware at all, but he still got 25 percent of the vote. Steve Forbes, who campaigned heavily in a state where he had won the primary in 1996, mustered 20 percent of the vote—a showing that, only hours after the polls had closed, made him realize he had to rethink whether he should remain in the race. Bush got 51 percent of the vote, not an overwhelming result but good enough to win. Still, because McCain had not challenged him, the win somehow didn't count as much. South Carolina's Primary Day, February 19, became even more important.

On Wednesday, Forbes dropped out of the race. With Forbes gone, Bush and McCain focused on trying to woo any former Forbes supporters in South Carolina. The Bush campaign's inner circle, after deciding that this could be done best by tearing down McCain, released a new ad with a message not unlike McCain's "do we want someone in the White House we can't trust" ad. The new ad said that McCain "promised a clean campaign, then attacked Governor Bush with misleading ads. McCain says he's the only candidate who can beat Gore on campaign finance, but news investigations reveal McCain solicits money from lobbyists with interests before his committee and pressures agencies on behalf of contributors. He attacks special interests, but the *Wall Street Journal* reports, 'McCain's campaign is crawling with lobbyists.' "

This was not the only new attack ad directed at McCain that aired during the second week of the campaign in South Carolina. An anti-abortion lobby launched an ad that began by asking, "Who is Warren Rudman?" Most of the mainstream population of South Carolina didn't know that Rudman was a distinguished former senator from New Hampshire who was a cochair of the McCain presidential effort. That, of course, would have been one way to identify him. Instead, the ad said Rudman was someone in favor of abortion rights whom McCain wanted to name attorney general. "Don't vote for John McCain," the ad concluded with a directness that seemed harsh and brutal.

On Wednesday, the National Right to Life Committee endorsed Bush even as an antiabortion group called South Carolina Citizens for

Life put up an ad that said, "If you want a strong pro-life president, then don't vote for John McCain," and in one automated call, Pat Robertson, the founder of the Christian Coalition, warned voters they could "protect babies and restore religious freedom" by not supporting McCain. These ads were merely examples of a barrage of negative campaigning directed—sometimes personally, it seemed—at McCain. At McCain rallies, plants in the audience would walk up to supporters and whisper that McCain was no hero. Phone banks put out calls charging McCain was a traitor because he had wanted to normalize relations with Vietnam. Then there were the e-mails. One group even suggested McCain had fathered illegitimate children. "It was a black child," a McCain insider says. "They actually used the word *nigger*. The calls said McCain had a nigger baby. There were other push-calls that said McCain had given his wife venereal disease, which caused her to have to have a hysterectomy."

"In South Carolina," Frank Rich wrote in the *New York Times,* "Bush supporters—none of them affiliated with his campaign, we're told—circulated fliers calling Mr. McCain the 'fag candidate' even as Mr. Bush subtly reinforced that message by indicating he wouldn't hire openly gay people for his administration. A professor at Bob Jones University distributed email accusing Mr. McCain of choosing 'to sire children without marriage.' (The McCains have an adopted daughter from Bangladesh—from a Mother Teresa orphanage, no less.) Bob Jones IV wrote a cover story for a rag called *World* magazine slapping around the McCain family. Mr. Bush had nothing to do with this 'religio-political sleaze,' as William Safire described it, either, though *World* is edited by Marvin Olasky, the sometime Bush adviser who invented, if you please, 'compassionate conservatism.'"

On February 10, when a reporter asked Bush why he couldn't "state his positions . . . and just forget about McCain," Bush shot back, "Remember what happened in the past"—meaning New Hampshire. "I was defined as the insider. I learned my lesson."

It was Thursday morning, February 10, and the town hall meeting was proceeding like so many others McCain had had during his presidential campaign. This one was being held in the Fine Arts Center at the University of South Carolina. McCain had given a 20-minute talk on education before opening up the event to a question-and-answer period. Microphone in hand, he was answering questions when a woman, Donna Duren, stood up and told McCain what had happened to her 14-year-old son Chris the night before. "My son has found himself a hero," Duren said, meaning McCain. "But yesterday, [he] was push-polled. He was so upset. I don't know who called him. I don't know who's responsible. But he was so upset when he came upstairs and he said, 'Mom, someone told me that Senator McCain is a cheat and a liar and a fraud.' And he was almost in tears. I was so livid last night I couldn't sleep."

As the woman began to cry, McCain became furious. At first, his anger took over and he couldn't speak. Then he muttered, in a low, hushed voice, "The disillusionment of a young boy is something I think any of them, even as crass and as base as some of the people can get in this business, would be ashamed of." After a moment, he was able to regain his composure enough to complete the town hall meeting, but his heart wasn't in it. He had been shaken by Duren. As soon as he thanked the audience, McCain went over to talk to Duren and, embracing her, promised to phone her son that afternoon.

Outside, McCain called an impromptu news conference. He started by saying he was so rattled by what had happened he could not answer questions about education, which was supposed to have been the focus of the town meeting. Instead, he wanted to discuss negative campaigning and what he was going to do about it. "I'm calling on my good friend George Bush to stop this now," McCain said, clearly furious. "Stop this now! He comes from a good family. He knows better than this. He should stop it. I'll pull down every negative ad that I have. . . . Let's treat voters of South Carolina with some respect." He paused. "What's being done to the people of South Carolina is being done with disrespect. I've made my position clear. I'm making it very clear. Take down these ads. But most importantly as well, stop this sort of thing. We're not in the business of harming young people."

When the press conference ended, McCain boarded the Straight Talk Express. Thirty minutes later, he spoke by telephone with a reporter for the *Washington Post*. "Frankly, it's the first time in the campaign I've been a little rattled," McCain said, "because of the way the woman spoke about it and the harm it did to her son."

As the day wore on and McCain continued with his campaign stops, he thought about what he should do. He had many options, but the one with which he felt most comfortable was the one that was most risky. He would pull all of his negative ads, just as he had offered to, and he would challenge Bush to do the same. If Bush kept running his negative ads, the damage done to McCain could be enormous. On the other hand, McCain could get an unexpected boost by making an unconventional move and running only positive ads. By the end of the day, McCain had made up his mind. He would announce his decision that next day, in New York City. "I called a meeting last night and told my staff we can't be involved in this kind of thing," McCain said in a press conference at the Grand Hyatt following a fund-raiser. "I urge George Bush to do the same thing. I hope he will be able to recognize the damage this kind of thing does to the electorate." McCain admitted his move "defies a lot of conventional wisdom and I know that some may view this as not an intelligent approach to winning the primary. But the most important thing to me at the end of the campaign is that my kids, my children, would be proud of me." Finally, McCain unveiled the new ad he *would* be running in South Carolina. Entitled "Courage," it equated the struggle he endured as a POW with the battle he had waged in Washington to pass campaign finance reform.

Bush responded to McCain's move right away. "My reaction is," he told reporters in Charleston, "his ads trying to link me to Bill Clinton didn't work. The people of this state don't appreciate it and neither do I." His answer to McCain's challenge for him to pull his negative ads? "It's an old Washington trick. It's a bait-and-switch trick." In other words, no, Bush would not be pulling his attack ads. Just to prove it, he unveiled another one that day in South Carolina. In it, Bush looked straight into the camera and said in an unhappy but controlled voice, "When John McCain compared me to Bill Clinton and said I was untrustworthy, that was over the line. Disagree with me, fine, but do not challenge my integrity."

In the final days of campaigning in South Carolina, negative ads continued to appear on radio and television. Bush spent $6 million on his media buy in South Carolina—a staggering sum of money for a state primary. In one radio commercial, former governor Carroll Campbell implied McCain, to quote the *New York Times'* description of what he said, "is the tool of a Democratic plot." The former governor said: "Send the Clinton–Gore Democrats a message Saturday. Vote for the man they're desperately trying to stop: George W. Bush." In another ad paid for by an antiabortion group, McCain, it was implied, secretly supported abortion rights. The tag line: "So if you want a strong pro-life president, don't vote for John McCain."

The push-poll calls and mass mailings continued as well. The National Right to Life Committee sent out a mass mailing that claimed McCain "voted repeatedly to use tax dollars for experiments that use body parts from aborted babies." Beginning on February 14, the Bush campaign unveiled a phone call with a message taped by Congressman Henry Hyde of Illinois, a figure made popular by his involvement in the Clinton impeachment. Saying Bush had "a strong pro-life record in Texas," a state that now, thanks to Bush, had "a parental notification bill that is a model for the nation," Hyde declared, "It has been suggested that changes be made to the party platform on the life issue"—a shot at McCain, who had made just such a recommendation. Hyde concluded, "As president, [Bush] will be a defender of the unborn. He has my full support." Hyde's recorded message was also used by the Bush campaign in a 60-second radio commercial.

But what was impressive was the sheer volume of the ads being played on radio and television. In the last week of the campaign, it was all but impossible to turn on the radio or television and *not* hear an anti-McCain ad. Local call-in radio programs were also flooded with callers. Many of them were believed to be coordinated by the Bush campaign in the same way that whisperers at McCain rallies subtly suggested he was no hero. Even Rush Limbaugh, with his massive national audience, got into the act. Day after day in the weeks of the South Carolina primary campaign, Limbaugh pounded away on McCain, using talking points that were unusually similar to those of the Bush campaign.

On Wednesday, Gray Bauer, who had dropped out of the race, endorsed McCain. Standing alongside McCain at a rally at Furman University in Greenville, Bauer, whose conservative credentials—former adviser to Ronald Reagan and former head of the Family Research Council—made him extremely valuable to McCain in a state as conservative as South Carolina, said he had chosen to support McCain because "he is our best shot." Bauer may have said publicly he would work for McCain because he felt McCain, not Bush, could most easily win the White House in the fall, but his friend William Kristol, another authentic conservative, would tell the *Washington Post* that Bauer had decided to go for McCain because he had been offended when Ralph Reed and Pat Robertson had joined Bush's negative campaign against McCain. That, Bauer believed, sullied the reputation of the conservative religious movement.

The campaign to tarnish McCain's character had not stopped. At the very rally at Furman University where Bauer endorsed McCain, a man approached a woman in the crowd and told her that McCain was "no hero" and that "there are questions as to what he did in that POW camp." His words were overheard by Scotty Morgan, a retired naval aviator who had spent six months with McCain in "that POW camp." "I straightened that out in a hurry," Morgan said. He countered the anonymous man's unsubstantiated claims by telling a correspondent for the *Washington Post* about the incident. The woman who had been approached by the whisperer, according to the *Post,* "was upset."

On Friday, the candidates' last day for campaigning, the polls showed Bush was finally beginning to open up a lead on McCain—the apparent result of McCain's decision to pull his negative ads. By the end of the South Carolina primary campaign, McCain had seen it all—a flood of negative television and radio ads, push-poll phone calls, automated phone calls, a church flier describing him as the "fag candidate," a Bob Jones University professor's e-mail accusing him of fathering children out of wedlock, and on and on. Conservative religious leaders criticized him for his first marriage, his alleged affairs, his use of profane language, his willingness to meet with the Log Cabin Republicans, "his softness on gays."

"One of the entertaining vignettes from South Carolina," McCain says, "involved a professor at Bob Jones University who was blasting out mass e-mails saying that John McCain had fathered illegitimate children. Well, CNN tracked him down. It was Jonathan Karl, if I remember it right, and he finds this guy and he says, 'You've been saying that John McCain's fathered illegitimate children. Do you have any proof of that?' And this professor says, 'No.' So Karl says, 'Why are you doing it?' And he says, 'Well, it's up to John McCain to prove that he didn't.' And this was on CNN!"

On February 19, the polls would be open throughout the state from 7:00 in the morning until 7:00 at night—or at least they were supposed to be. From the start, polling irregularities developed. Specifically, a number of polling places didn't open in areas of the state where there was a large concentration of Independent or Democratic voters, particularly in African-American neighborhoods. Naturally, these were areas where McCain would have been expected to do well. When the morning dragged on and it became clear that these polling places were not going to open at all, J. Sam Daniels, the executive director of the Republican Party in South Carolina, was questioned about a development that hardly could be called coincidental. Daniels explained the situation by saying the polls had not opened because workers could not be hired to man the stations—a gross deficiency that should have been anticipated well before Primary Day. But Daniels had an excuse ready. Claiming voters were being sent from the closed polling places to those that were open, he reasoned, "Voters are just inconvenienced a little bit." Of the state's 1,752 polling places that opened in a general election, only 1,429 opened on February 19.

While this drama unfolded, McCain fulfilled the one campaign commitment he had scheduled for the day—a morning meeting with a veterans' group. As the day wore on, it became clear that 20 or more polling places in Greenville County alone—mostly in areas where the residents were black and Democratic—were going to remain closed or, as election officials called it, "consolidated" with other polling places. Kweisi Mfume actually got complaints at the NAACP on Saturday morning from people in South Carolina who said black polling places were closed. This meant confused voters had to go to alternative polling places, all the while being "inconvenienced a little bit." What's more, party officials revealed they knew on Friday that polling places would be unmanned, but they did nothing about the problem. Other irregularities also occurred across the state. Poll watchers were not being allowed into some polling places, and ballots with Bush's name already marked were being handed out at others. Matters were made worse by the fact that, on this day, a record number of people went to the polls and voted in the primary election in South Carolina. In all, over half a million people voted, compared to 276,000 four years before.

As he had in New Hampshire, Tim Russert called the McCain camp by early afternoon with the results of the exit polling. By the time McCain returned from the meeting with the veterans and was getting off his bus in the parking lot of his hotel in North Charleston, he knew the odds of his winning South Carolina were against him. At first, McCain thought the voting irregularities in the state might cause him to lose, but, soon after he had made his way upstairs to his suite, he realized that the numbers were going to break against him much more than he had imagined—and much more than the final polls had predicted. By early evening, when it was clear that he was not going to win, McCain took each of his children individually into a bedroom of the suite and told them he was going to lose. As she wandered about the suite, Cindy could not keep from crying.

After the polls closed, the early numbers looked grim. At about 7:10, McCain called Bush to congratulate him. It was a brief conversation. As he made his way down to the convention center next to the hotel, McCain realized what the final numbers would approach: Bush 53 percent, McCain 42 percent, Keyes 5 percent. The 11-point spread meant the results were not even going to be close. It also meant the negative campaign against McCain—"the dirtiest race I've ever seen," as a McCain insider later put it—had worked.

As McCain, Murphy, Weaver, Salter, and Davis had huddled upstairs in McCain's suite to decide the content of what would be called his "nonconcession concession speech," they had kept this fact in mind. So, while McCain stood in front of the cheering crowd, with Cindy and his family standing behind him on the stage, he delivered a speech, mostly written by Salter, that was anger-filled, defiant, and provocative. "My friends," he began, "you don't have to win every skirmish to win a war or a crusade, and although we fell a little short tonight our crusade goes stronger. . . . I'm going to fight with every ounce of strength I have, but I'm going to keep fighting clean, I'm going to keep fighting fair, and I'm going to keep fighting the battle of ideas. We are going to win. I will not take the low road to the highest office in this land. I want the presidency in the best way, not the worst way. The American people deserve to be treated with respect by those who seek to lead the nation. And I promise you, you will have my respect until my last day on earth. The greatest blessing of my life was to have been born an American, and I will never dishonor the nation I love by letting ambition overcome principle. Never. Never. Never."

The crowd erupted into loud applause. "My friends," McCain went on, "I say to you I am a uniter, not a divider. I don't just say it, I live it. I'm a real reformer. I'm a real reformer. I don't just say it, I live it. And I'm a fighter for this country, and I don't just say it, I live it. As this campaign moves forward, a clear choice will be offered, a choice between my optimistic and welcoming conservatism and the negative message of fear."

Chapter 10

The Best Man

By the time the two candidates arrived in Michigan for the primary on Tuesday, the battle between the camps in the media was well under way. Although the McCain campaign would not admit it at the time, it was telling voters, through automated calls, that Bush had stood beside Bob Jones administrators—which he *had,* at the start of the campaign in South Carolina—who had openly attacked the Pope and the Catholic Church. These "Catholic Voter Alert" calls charged that a past president of Bob Jones had described the Catholic Church as "a satanic cult" and implied that Bush supported such stands. "This is a Catholic voter alert," the voice on the phone said. "Governor George Bush has campaigned against Senator John McCain by seeking the support of Southern fundamentalists who have expressed anti-Catholic views. . . . Bob Jones has made strong anti-Catholic statements, including calling the Pope the anti-Christ and the Catholic Church a satanic cult. John McCain, a pro-life senator, has strongly condemned this anti-Catholic bigotry, while Governor Bush has stayed silent." The calls were designed to incite a state where one-fourth of the electorate was Catholic, but when Howard Opinsky, a campaign spokesman, was asked whether the McCain campaign was behind the calls, he said the campaign "is not making any such calls." Only later did the campaign admit it was behind the phone calls.

On Tuesday, as the exit polls began to come in, McCain realized he was going to win not only in Arizona, where he was expected to sweep Bush away in a landslide, but also in Michigan—by eight points, not even a close margin.

Next came Virginia and Washington state.

The setting for the speech had been chosen carefully: a high school in Virginia Beach, Virginia, the quiet Southern town that was home to Pat Robertson's Christian Coalition. The timing of the speech had been considered too: the day before Tuesday's primaries and caucus. McCain's traveling companion on that day would also be relevant: Gary Bauer, whose conservative Christian credentials were excellent. After he delivered the speech, McCain said that, since the South Carolina primary, he had been thinking about making a speech that his aides would describe as "a call to the grass roots," but he had decided to go through with it only recently. In fact, as late as Sunday, if he had backed out of the speech, no one within the McCain inner circle would have been surprised.

The speech was, simply, a no-holds-barred hit on the religious right and the Republican Party. Most of the speech was about, to quote McCain, "the fine members of the religious conservative community." In the speech, McCain said he was "proud to help build a bigger Republican Party, a party that can claim a governing majority for a generation or more by attracting new people to our cause with an appeal to the patriotism that unites us and the promise of a government we can be proud of again—and for that I have been accused of consorting with the wrong kind of people."

But McCain knew that the media covering the speech would focus on one passage that was unquestionably electric—and a shocking political gamble. "I am a Reagan Republican who will defeat Al Gore,"

McCain said at the start of the passage. "Unfortunately, Governor Bush is a Pat Robertson Republican who will lose to Al Gore. Neither party should be defined by pandering to the outer reaches of American politics and the agents of intolerance, whether they be Louis Farrakhan or Al Sharpton on the left, or Pat Robertson or Jerry Falwell on the right. We are the party of Ronald Reagan, not Pat Robertson."

As if this language was not inflammatory enough, McCain went on to say: "[W]e reject the practices of a few self-appointed leaders [who primarily hope] to preserve their own political power at all costs." Robertson and Falwell "distort my pro-life positions and smear the reputations of my supporters. Why? Because I don't pander to them, because I don't ascribe to their failed philosophy that money is our message. The union bosses who have subordinated the interests of the working families to their own ambitions, to their desire to pervert their own political power at all costs, are mirror images of Pat Robertson."

The media did indeed cover the speech, and the debate over whether McCain's rebuke of the religious right was a smart move started at once. Was it a stroke of genius that would, as his handlers hoped, motivate the grass roots, or was it a political blunder that would end up costing him any chance of winning the nomination? Some campaign staffers in Virginia had no doubt that it was a mistake. "They sent out a press release about the speech beforehand," Paul Galanti says, "and as soon as I saw it I said, 'Oh, my God! No, no, no, no, no, no, no! Don't do it.' And not because I particularly like Pat Robertson or Jerry Falwell, but it really wasn't appropriate for John to make the speech there. John had gotten hammered bad down in South Carolina—yes. Still, to come back and attack those guys was just not smart. I mean, nobody attacks Pat Robertson. That's like attacking Santa Claus. It cost John votes in Virginia."

As the Tuesday papers featured front-page stories about McCain's sojourn into the land of the religious right, McCain made comments that only pushed his attack on Robertson and Falwell further. On the Straight Talk Express on Tuesday, McCain said Robertson and Falwell were "an evil influence . . . over the Republican Party. . . . To stand up and take on the forces of evil—that's my job, and I can't steer the Republican Party if these two individuals have the influence that they have on the party today."

If McCain expected the speech to give him a bump in the voting on Tuesday, it didn't. Bush won the primaries in both Virginia and Washington. In Washington, the vote was too close to call on Tuesday night, so the Bush victory was not declared until Wednesday. But in Virginia, the state where McCain had made his controversial speech, it was not close at all. Bush won by nine percentage points, 53 to 44. To make matters worse for McCain, Bush won the North Dakota caucus by a huge margin, 76 to 19. At a rally in Cincinnati, Bush celebrated his victory: "Tonight, in an open primary by a solid margin . . . the voters of Virginia rejected the politics of pitting one religion against another. This campaign is winning, and we are doing it the right way. Tonight, we are one step closer to victory."

With these losses for McCain, there would be much debate about the Virginia Beach speech. "I think," Gary Hart says, "that John, given his refusal to kowtow to the religious right and their dominance in the party—and [given] his native independence—I think he had no choice but to challenge the party. Did he make a mistake in Virginia, giving a speech attacking the religious right? It depends on whether your view is pragmatic or cosmic. Pragmatically, yes; cosmically, no. I mean, his popularity had to do with his independence and his willingness to say things that nobody else would say."

One fact was certain. The dirty tricks in the race had not stopped after the South Carolina primary. In the days before Super Tuesday, another barrage of negative campaigning started up. Some of it duplicated what had been seen in South Carolina. For example, an organization called the National Right to Life PAC (political action committee) in Washington paid for a new spate of automated-message phone calls. One state targeted for the calls was Connecticut. The message there said that McCain "has made conflicting statements about abortion" and would not support reversing *Roe v. Wade*. In contrast, the message said, Bush "has maintained a strong and consistent pro-life position both as governor and throughout this campaign." The message did not point out that in 1978, when he was asked about the issue of abortion during his failed attempt to win a seat in the House of Representatives, Bush did not sound as equivocal, using language that was consistent with supporters of abortion rights. Instead, the automated message simply endorsed Bush and concluded: "For the children's sake, please vote George Bush for president."

Around the same time, in early March, another ad began running in the New York media market. It would become one of the most talked-about—and, for McCain, one of the most personally hurtful—ads in the campaign. The ad featured the voice of a woman named Geri Barish, who was the head of an organization called One in Nine, which was based in Baldwin, Long Island. The name One in Nine was a reference to the fact that, in some medical surveys, one in nine women on Long Island suffers from breast cancer—one of the highest per capita rates in the country. In the ad, Barish attacked McCain for not supporting federal funding for breast cancer research. "[I] had thought of supporting John McCain in next week's presidential primary," Barish said in the ad. "So I looked into his record. What I discovered was shocking. McCain opposes funding for vital breast cancer programs right here in New York." At the end of the ad, Barish said: "Next Tuesday, John McCain won't have my vote. We deserve a candidate with a record on women's issues we can trust." Then a voice-over said the ad was paid for by the Bush campaign.

The ad was stunning. It charged that McCain had a bad record on women's issues and was specifically opposed to breast cancer research when, in fact, McCain's record did not bear out those accusations at all. In 1991, McCain voted for increased funding for women's issues—breast cancer and osteoporosis—and $25 million was awarded to the National Cancer Institute. He also supported the general issue of breast cancer research, and he had voted, on various occasions, for federal funding of such research and of other health programs that benefited women. He did vote against legislation that would have earmarked millions of dollars for breast cancer research, but he did so because the funding for the programs—there were two of them—was contained in other spending proposals McCain opposed. A champion in the fight against "pork-barrel" spending, McCain had voted against funding that would have gone to a breast cancer program in the North Shore Long Island Jewish Health System because it was contained in an appropriations bill for the Department of Labor. He also voted against funding that would have gone to a women's cancer program at New York University because it was a part of an appropriations bill for the

Department of Energy. McCain opposed the two bills for procedural reasons; he was not against funding women's health programs or research into breast cancer. In fact, the issue of breast cancer was important to him: His sister, Sandy McCain Morgan—her given name was Jean but she went by Sandy—suffered from the disease. If there was any government official in Washington who wanted doctors to find a cure for breast cancer, it was John McCain.

While the breast cancer research ad continued to play, another ad started airing at the end of the final week before Super Tuesday. This one questioned McCain's record on environmental issues. When McCain learned of the details of the television ad, he was furious. At a noontime rally on Wall Street on Friday, he referred to the new ad when he told the crowd, "Two million has come into this campaign"— again, the Bush campaign—"from a source we don't know, alleging things that are untrue."

The television ad was produced by Rob Allyn, a political consultant based in Dallas. His firm had worked for Bush during his campaign against Ann Richards for the Texas governorship in 1994. Allyn also worked for the Texas Republican Party. The ad was credited to a group identified in the spot as Republicans for Clean Air. The ad, which was running in New York, Ohio, and California, attacked McCain for his record on environmental issues while it praised Bush. In the ad, a picture of McCain was superimposed over smokestacks that were billowing black smoke. A narrator then said that McCain had voted against solar and renewable energy and Bush had "clamped down" on coal-burning electronic plants. In fact, just the opposite was true. As governor, Bush fought to keep loopholes in place so Texas plants would not have to comply with the Clean Air Act. During Bush's time as governor, Houston even surpassed Los Angeles as the city with the worst air quality in the country—another fact not mentioned in the ad. Nor did the ad reveal that a group called Republicans for Clean Air did not actually exist. It was a made-up organization intended to be a front for the wealthy Wyly brothers of Texas, Sam and Charles. Specifically, the Wylys had spent $2.5 million to run the ads on television in three states. The Wyly brothers were careful not to use the words "vote for" or "vote against," so the ad could be classified as an "issue" ad, and, as such, not be covered by existing campaign finance laws. This was just one example of the questionable advertising McCain wanted to regulate through campaign finance reform.

"I was with McCain on a bus heading up from New York to Connecticut," Peter Rinfret says, "and they had the television on when the commercial came on about McCain being against breast cancer research. One senior staffer said, 'We're going to kill them, we're going to absolutely kill them.' Cindy McCain looked at John and he sort of went white. He just sort of went ashen as he was watching it. Cindy started talking and he said, 'It's going to be okay.' And he got very quiet. This is a man they say has a vile temper, but he did not budge one inch. On that bus everybody was in a rage, but not McCain."

On the Saturday before Super Tuesday, as he sat in the back of the Straight Talk Express, McCain was asked by a reporter what he would do if he lost on Tuesday. In his now-trademark tongue-planted-firmly-in-cheek style, he said, "Actually I would contemplate suicide. We have some razor blades stashed in the back room." He made a loud slashing sound as he pointed one finger at his wrist. "Orson Swindle and I are thinking, in fact, of going back and establishing residence in Hanoi. They know us there. They don't bother us there. Good food, three squares, and a flop. We're always under watchful care."

To be sure, McCain was doing all he could to win. On Saturday, he barnstormed New England in hopes of winning those states where polling indicated he was extremely competitive. On Saturday morning, 800 people came to a rally in Boston, where McCain attacked the ads being run against him in New York, Ohio, and California. "Where's the outrage?" he all but shouted at the crowd. "Are we going to allow Texas cronies of George W. Bush to hijack an election? Tell them to keep their dirty money in Texas, don't spread it all over New England and America." The audience, pumped up by McCain's inflated rhetoric, started chanting, "No New Texas! No New Texas!" Later in the day, during a television interview, McCain was asked if he still considered Bush a friend. Astonishingly, McCain allowed an agonizing 11 seconds to pass—*one, two, three, four, five, six, seven, eight, nine, ten, eleven*—before he said: "Yes."

On Sunday, campaigning from New York to Ohio to California, McCain kept up the offensive, at one point calling Bush's campaign

"Clintonesque." Obviously, McCain was furious over the Wyly ads. In a television interview on Sunday, McCain was as tough as he had ever been on Bush, who, he charged, was simply "not ready for prime time." Would McCain support Bush if McCain lost on Tuesday? "I expect Governor Bush to change," McCain said candidly. "I expect him to run an entirely different campaign than the kind that he's run in this primary. The scandal in Washington was the debasement of the institutions of government in 1996 by the Clinton-Gore campaign, which the Bush campaign is beginning to imitate right now as we speak. . . . It's so Clintonesque, it's scary. Raise the soft money. Run the attack ads. They're getting more and more like the Clinton campaign. They'll say anything."

As it turned out, Super Tuesday *was* decisive. Early in the day, as the results from exit polls began to come in from New York, Ohio, California, and other states, McCain and his staff saw the numbers were not going their way. It looked as if he would do well in New England, which was not surprising, but it began to appear he might not win any other states. McCain was in Los Angeles, holed up at the Beverly Hilton Hotel, but he was ready to give what he hoped would be a victory speech that night at the Pacific Design Center in West Hollywood. He spent the day doing a round of last-minute radio interviews by phone. Bush had returned to Texas; the media reported that he was happy to be back home in Austin. In the afternoon, before the polls had started to close, McCain made a remark that indicated how mean-spirited he felt the race had been. He ruled out the possibility that he would ever join a Bush ticket as the vice-presidential nominee. "Under no circumstances would I consider being vice president," McCain said. "I can serve the country and my family much better by being the Senator from Arizona."

By early evening, after the polls closed first on the East Coast and finally in California, McCain realized he was going to win four states: Connecticut, Massachusetts, Vermont, and Rhode Island. In the final analysis, McCain had needed to win more than these four states to have a mandate to continue his campaign. Of the 13 states holding primaries on Super Tuesday, Bush had won nine: New York, California, Ohio, Maryland, Maine, Georgia, Missouri, Minnesota, and American Samoa.

When it was obvious what the night's results were going to be, McCain placed a congratulatory phone call to Bush in Texas before he headed to a private reception where Cindy presented him with a replica of the Straight Talk Express. It was as if she knew this was the end of her husband's run for the White House. Next, McCain proceeded to West Hollywood to make his speech. Across the country, another group of supporters had gathered at the Roosevelt Hotel in New York (named in honor of McCain's hero, Teddy Roosevelt) to listen to what McCain had to say. Before an audience of 350 in the Pacific Design Center, with the television networks carrying his remarks live, McCain tried to put the best face he could on what had happened.

"We won a few and we lost a few today," McCain told his supporters, many of whom were crying. "And over the next few days, we will take some time to enjoy our victories and take stock of our losses. . . . Tomorrow, we will take a little time to reflect on the direction of our campaign. I want to assure you all that our crusade continues tonight, tomorrow, the next day, the day after that, and for as long as it takes to restore America's confidence and pride in our great institutions of democracy. . . . We will never give up this mission, my friends. I give you my word on that." Then, as confetti rained down from the ceiling, McCain and Cindy waved from the podium to a cheering crowd that did not want them to leave the stage.

McCain returned to Arizona the next morning and locked himself away in his cabin in Sedona with his family and staff. There, they debated what to do next. Much of their attention was focused on the future. At the moment, little energy was being spent on reliving the mistakes that had been made in the past. They had to decide what to do with a campaign that at one point looked like it could not be stopped. Only later would the questioning begin. When it did, one remark that seemed unusually pertinent came from the political consultant, Kieran Mahoney. "Looking back on it," Mahoney would say, "the day he'll rue in the campaign is when he went down and took on, in an inappropriate fashion, the Reverends Robertson and Falwell. If he had made those statements in sorrow and not in anger, it would have served him well. By being vitriolic, he raised more questions about himself than he did about them."

"I am no longer an active candidate for my party's nomination for president," John McCain said on Thursday, March 9, as he stood on top of a cliff near Sedona, against, as one newspaper would describe it, "a spectacular backdrop of red rocks, snowcapped ridges, and white clouds stacked against a huge blue sky." Standing outside in the state he loved, Arizona, in a tableau that was simply breathtaking in its beauty, he had to say the words he had never wanted to say—*no longer an active candidate.* "I hoped," he continued as Cindy stood beside him, "our campaign would be a source of change in the Republican Party, and I believe we have indeed set a course that will ultimately prevail in making our party as big as the country we serve."

McCain and his staff had debated throughout the day on Wednesday. Late in the afternoon, he had finally made up his mind, and his aides canceled McCain's travel plans to Colorado and Illinois. Leaving open the possibility that something strange might happen, McCain decided not to withdraw fully from the race. "I am suspending my campaign," McCain said. "A majority of Republican voters made clear their preference for president is Governor Bush. . . . I congratulate Governor Bush and wish him and his family well. He may very well become the next President of the United States. This is an honor accorded to very few, and it is such a great responsibility that he deserves the best wishes of every American. He certainly has mine." McCain was careful not to endorse Bush. Then again, since he was only suspending his campaign, it would not have been appropriate for him to offer any endorsement.

Finally, without taking questions from reporters, McCain left. He had arranged for his staff to join him back at the cabin where he would grill pork ribs for everyone. Mostly, McCain, his friends, and his staff drank beer and whiskey sours and ate as the music from McCain's favorite oldies rock station played in the background. At some point, Bush called McCain to acknowledge the announcement that he was suspending his campaign. "We hadn't told the Bush campaign we were making the announcement," one McCain staffer says. "So we were back at the cabin enjoying ourselves when the phone rang. Cindy answered it. It was Bush. And he said, 'Is John there?' She knew it was Bush, so she said 'Sure' and gave the phone to John Weaver. Weaver said 'Hello,' and Bush said, 'It was a very nice speech you gave; my family is very honored.' And Weaver said, 'Who is this?' And Bush said, 'Weaver, is that you?' And Weaver said, 'Hold on a sec.' Then he handed the phone to McCain."

On Thursday, April 13, after he and his family had taken a vacation, after he had returned to his job in the Senate, and after much negotiation between the two staffs, McCain and Bush announced they would meet face-to-face for the first time since the end of McCain's campaign. But that meeting, scheduled to take place in Pittsburgh, would not happen until May 9, and even then McCain would wait until his private meeting with Bush ended before he would decide whether to endorse Bush. Even so, Bush jumped at the chance to make a conciliatory gesture toward McCain. He told reporters in Austin: "I'm looking forward to it a lot."

Perhaps, but McCain would make him wait. On April 19, the day after Bush announced he might consider putting McCain on the ticket as his running mate and would bring up the matter during their meeting in May, McCain returned to South Carolina for the first time since he had lost the primary. In a 30-minute speech before a conservative organization called the South Carolina Policy Council, McCain made a stunning revelation. In short, he admitted he had misled the voters of South Carolina. Revealing that during the campaign he "feared that if I [spoke] honestly I could not win the South Carolina primary . . . so I chose to compromise my principles [and] I broke my promise to always tell the truth," McCain said he felt the Confederate flag "should be removed from your Capitol," adding, "I am encouraged that fair-minded people on both sides of the issues are working hard to define an honorable compromise." Two months before, McCain had said his ancestors had "fought honorably" for the Confederacy during the Civil War, but now, before the Policy Council, McCain declared his ancestors had "fought on the wrong side of American history." Still, the tone McCain struck that day was mollifying. "I am here," he said, "only to express my belated wish, my confidence, that you will resolve [the dispute] quickly."

Despite more-or-less constant tension between their staffs, Bush and McCain met in person on May 9. Joe Allbaugh, from Bush's staff, and John Weaver, from McCain's staff, had met for 45 minutes at the end of April to work out the details of the event. Bush had even phoned McCain on Sunday to say he was looking forward to their meeting on Tuesday.

So almost everything had been worked out and planned for when the two men met that May morning at the William Penn Hotel in Pittsburgh.

The first order of business was a private meeting between Bush and McCain in a fourth-floor conference room in the hotel. Bush sat on a green leather love seat; McCain sat across from him in a matching chair. In their 80-minute meeting, 10 minutes shorter than had been planned, the two discussed a range of issues, among them taxes, education, campaign finance reform, and Social Security. McCain told Bush, point-blank, that he didn't want to be considered as a running mate. Following the meeting came the event for which Bush had been waiting: the press conference, where they would be photographed together. Bush entered the press conference first, followed by McCain. Standing next to one another, they volleyed with the press. McCain said Bush had "the expertise" to lead the nation. But he added: "I want to emphasize one more time, I made it very clear to Governor Bush, I will continue to pursue the issue of reform. That is the agenda that drove me in my campaign and will drive me as long as I am in public service." McCain was asked if he would like a job in a Bush cabinet. "Secretary of Reform," McCain quipped.

When enough time had passed that it became obvious McCain was not going to say he endorsed Bush, a reporter asked the question.

"Are you endorsing the governor today?"

"Yes," McCain said.

"Aren't you avoiding the e-word?" the reporter went on.

"I endorse Governor Bush," McCain said.

Then, as if he were trying to undercut the endorsement he just made, McCain repeated his statement six times, not unlike a child reciting a nursery rhyme: *"I endorse Governor Bush, I endorse Governor Bush, I endorse Governor Bush, I endorse Governor Bush, I endorse Governor Bush, I endorse Governor Bush."*

Bush stood stiff as a rod next to McCain, no doubt furious at the flippant way McCain was performing the scene he had been brought here to play. But Bush was determined not to show his frustration. After several minutes passed and other subjects had been discussed, Bush offered, "By the way, I enthusiastically accept."

But the kicker to this awkward display was McCain's answer to the reporter's last leading question. Had McCain decided to "take the medicine now" and endorse Bush today instead of waiting until later? "I think your 'Take the medicine now' is probably a good description," McCain said, grinning.

Next came the Republican National Convention, held in August in Philadelphia. Between commitments there, McCain traveled to Bethesda Naval Hospital in Washington, where he was told by doctors he had two new skin cancers that had to be dealt with. He would do so following the convention. On Wednesday, August 16, he released a statement through his office. It read: "During a routine examination, two unrelated spots were discovered on Senator John McCain: One on his left temple, the other on his left arm. The spots were confirmed to be melanomas." The news put a different spin on a passage near the end of his speech at the convention where he talked about his own mortality and his youth, which was now in the distant past.

On Thursday, back in Phoenix, McCain underwent a battery of tests at the Mayo Clinic to determine how far the melanoma had spread. Besides a complete blood workup, he was given a chest x-ray, an electrocardiogram, an MRI, a CAT scan, and an echocardiogram. It was standard procedure for him to have these tests for this condition. When the tests were done, he consulted with his doctors, as he did again on Friday morning. On Thursday night, he had canceled an appearance at a fund-raiser for a local state senator; he also canceled a trip to Ohio. In the Friday morning meeting, which lasted for three hours, the doctors told him the test results were encouraging, though there had been a change in his condition. After a biopsy of his left temple in 1996, the results were negative. Now the skin cancer was malignant. Returning from the Mayo Clinic, McCain met with reporters at his house. There, he and Cindy took out to the reporters a wheelbarrow full of bottled water and a basket of sunscreen. When one reporter asked Cindy if she was scared, McCain took charge, saying, "I woke up late last night and I did see her thumbing through the insurance policies." That night, McCain and Cindy went to a baseball game at One Ballpark to see the Arizona Diamondbacks play the Chicago Cubs.

On Saturday, having checked into the Mayo Clinic early that morning, McCain was in surgery for five and a half hours, under a general anesthesia, to remove the malignant skin cancer from his left temple and left upper arm. Removal of the cancer from the arm required only a simple excision. However, the operation on the left temple was much more extensive; it included removal of lymph nodes from his face and his neck. Luckily for McCain, doctors determined that the cancer had not spread to the lymph nodes. If it had, his chances for survival would have been drastically reduced. Because doctors had caught the disease in time, McCain's prognosis was good. During recovery, when McCain was asked by his doctor, John Eckstein, if he wanted him to meet with the press and say anything on his behalf, McCain, able to muster his quick sarcastic wit, looked up at the doctor and said, "Call Trent Lott. I know he'll be on pins and needles." When the doctor did meet with reporters, he provided a straightforward description of McCain's status, noting that the cancer had not spread to the lymph nodes and declaring, "All melanoma was removed during the surgery." Speaking to reporters, Cindy was much more emotional. "I have said many prayers this week, as you can imagine," she said. "And all my prayers have been answered."

That fall, in one of the closest presidential elections in American history, George W. Bush defeated Al Gore when, after a 37-day legal dispute concerning the voting in Florida, the United States Supreme Court ruled in favor of Bush, who became president even though he had not won the popular vote. Throughout the fall campaign, despite their differences, McCain had campaigned for Bush, especially in battleground states where Independent voters could make the difference. Despite his help, McCain was still considered no friend of Bush, if he had ever wanted to be. In the early days of the Bush Administration, McCain would be treated like a political enemy, not a key Republican player who had helped him get elected. "I think we learned there is a compelling requirement for electoral reform," McCain says about the 2000 election. "Not just in Florida but all over America, their are groups of Americans who are underrepresented because their votes were not counted." Moving on, McCain would continue to advance the idea of reform. "He stayed true to his core beliefs," says Georgette Mosbacher, a national cochair for McCain's 2000 presidential campaign. "That's why he would be able to run again in the future."

Chapter 11

Man of the People

"**I** realized when we were about to organize for the new session," says Senator Thad Cochran, a Republican from Mississippi, "that John needed another vote for campaign finance reform. He had 59 votes to invoke closure to get the bill to the floor, to the motion to proceed to consider the bill, and I thought, 'If we are going to be able to write a bill that is fair to both parties and also the interests that are going to be reflected in the Congress, what better time than when you have 50 Republicans and 50 Democrats.' While I didn't agree with everything in McCain-Feingold, I did agree that we needed to start. So I walked up to John while we were at an organizational luncheon, sat down, and told him just what I thought. I could tell by the expression that he was ecstatic. He was really fired up over the fact that I would be willing to get on board."

This was all McCain needed. Bush had not even been sworn in as president when, on January 4, 2001, McCain and Feingold held a press conference on Capitol Hill—accompanied by their new supporter, Thad Cochran—to announce their intention to introduce McCain-Feingold on January 22, with Cochran as a cosponsor. The importance of the addition of Cochran was clear in the news conference; he represented the 60th vote, the number needed to prevent a filibuster.

With Feingold and Cochran at his side, McCain addressed the reason why he was not going to delay introducing his bill, a move in defiance of a number of Republicans who wanted him to wait to bring up campaign finance reform so as not to embarrass one of the main opponents of that reform, George W. Bush, the new president. "I promised millions of Americans, when I ran for President of the United States, that I would not give up on this crusade of reform, the gateway to which is campaign finance reform," McCain said. "I cannot and will not in good conscience give up on the effort."

On February 6, just days after Bush was inaugurated, McCain made a second move that angered Republicans. He joined with the Democrats to announce his cosponsorship of a patient's bill of rights. The bill was being sponsored in the Senate by one of the icons of American liberalism: Ted Kennedy. Lincoln Chaffee, the Republican senator from Rhode Island, intended to support the bill, as did Senator John Edwards of North Carolina, a Democrat. "What happened was," John Edwards says, "McCain and Kennedy and Tom Daschle—all three—stopped me one day and asked me to work on the bill with John. We had a series of meetings over several months, working on the bill, drafting the bill together. John McCain is a person of great strength and character. He stands up for what he believes in, whether it's popular or unpopular. He is a breath of fresh air to work with."

The White House was worried about the patient's bill of rights, so much so that on February 5 the Bush Administration had sent aides to meet with two key advocates of the bill in the House—Congressmen Charlie Norwood, a Republican from Georgia and a dentist, and Greg Ganske, a Republican from Iowa and a doctor—to persuade them not to advance the bill. It looked as if the White House was going to have luck with Norwood, if not Ganske. Norwood—a co-sponsor of the bill with John Dingell, a Democrat from Michigan—seemed to buckle from the pressure put on him over the weekend at a Republican congressional retreat. McCain's coming out publicly to support the bill in the Senate at the same time the White House was trying to kill it in the House was sending a signal to the Bush camp that, at least as far as McCain's legislative agenda was concerned, he could not be controlled.

In May, McCain continued his assault on the White House. On May 2, he criticized Bush for killing the Kyoto Treaty at the end of March. The treaty, endorsed by Vice President Al Gore in 1997, proposed to curb the global greenhouse effect by strictly controlling carbon dioxide emissions. "I wouldn't have done that," McCain said about Bush's decision to remove the United States from the list of nations that had agreed to sign it. "I don't agree with everything in the Kyoto Protocol, but I think it is a framework we could have continued to work with. We could have fixed it." The implication was all too apparent. Bush should have found a way to have the United States sign on to the treaty but didn't. The back story was implied: Because the treaty was championed by environmentalists and opposed by Big Oil, Bush caved in to pressure from the energy industry and came out against the treaty.

McCain's remarks about Kyoto were still fresh when on Tuesday, May 15, McCain and Senator Joseph Lieberman of Connecticut introduced a bill that would close the gun-show loophole. This was yet another piece of legislation the White House didn't want, so it was only a matter of time before rumors began to circulate that McCain was thinking about leaving the Republican Party. Bush set up a private dinner at the White House with McCain and their wives. It was supposed to take place on May 24, but McCain canceled at the last minute because he was working late in the Senate, trying to defeat the Bush tax cut— one more example of the ongoing conflict between Bush and McCain. Just two Republicans would vote against the Bush tax cut. McCain was one of them.

The gossip about McCain's leaving the Republican Party slacked off that same day, May 24, when, after a series of disagreements with Bush and his administration over its legislative agenda dating back to the first days of the Bush presidency, Senator James Jeffords of Vermont, a Republican, announced his decision to leave the party to become an Independent. When he made his move, the Senate was divided 50-50, with Vice President Dick Cheney serving to break the tie.

Jeffords's departure shifted control of the Senate to the Democrats. In the media firestorm following Jeffords's announcement, culminating with Jeffords's appearance on the cover of *Newsweek,* McCain released a statement that itself would attract attention for its biting tone toward his party: Republicans must learn "to respect honorable differences among us, learn to disagree without resorting to personal threats, and recognize that we are a party large enough to accommodate something short of strict unanimity on the issues of the day. Tolerance of dissent is the hallmark of a mature party, and it is well past time for the Republican Party to grow up."

Then, on the first weekend in June, rumors again began to circulate after Tom Daschle, a Democrat and the Senate majority leader, visited McCain at his vacation home in Sedona. McCain fueled the leaving-the-party rumors with comments like one he made to his friend, Senator Chuck Hagel of Nebraska: "Don't worry, Chuck, I'm going to do everything I can, but I can't guarantee that I can get Tom Daschle to switch parties." No doubt, such comments were behind Bush's insistence on McCain's having dinner at the White House, which finally took place on the evening of June 5. That dinner led McCain to make a number of jokes about the occasion. He made one joke over and over: *Yeah, Cindy and I had dinner at the White House with Laura, the president—and the two food tasters!* The dinner did not facilitate any rapprochement between the two men. Indeed, the feud between them was hard to miss. This fact was made undeniably clear when, on June 7, Congress passed Bush's tax cut, the one political victory Bush wanted more than any other, and, as expected, McCain voted against it.

One topic that must have come up at McCain's White House dinner, besides his opposition to the Bush tax cuts and rumors of his switching parties, was the patient's bill of rights. Bush was against it, but McCain and fellow supporters moved ahead with a bill that was passed by the Senate at the end of June. Despite Bush's threat of a veto, the final vote was 59 to 36. McCain played such a vital part in the bill's passage, Daschle said at the time: "We could not have done this without John McCain. John was extremely helpful and remarkably courageous."

By the first week in July, because rumors about his leaving the party would not stop, McCain wrote a four-page letter to the Republican precinct chairmen in Arizona, explaining his recent actions. To clarify why he voted against the Bush tax cut, he wrote: "I voted against the final bill, not because I suddenly stopped supporting tax cuts after a lifetime of support for lower taxes, but because those who needed it most were getting the least." McCain couldn't support the tax cut because it didn't help "the middle and lower classes." On the attention-grabbing visit Tom Daschle had recently made to Sedona, McCain wrote: "He is my friend. We don't agree on many issues, but someone very important to me taught me long ago that honorable political disagreement should not make personal enemies of people. I have many friends who are Democrats and many friends who are Republicans." In conclusion, McCain noted that "[d]espite occasional differences on some issues," he remained "a proud member of the party of Reagan, Goldwater, Roosevelt, and Lincoln."

On his 65th birthday, McCain checked into the Mayo Clinic to undergo surgery for an enlarged prostate gland. Under general anesthesia, he was operated on for 70 minutes in what turned out to be a routine procedure for a benign prostate enlargement, the kind that affects between 15 and 20 percent of men in this country. At the same time, doctors removed stones from his bladder, another common disorder. McCain stayed in the hospital for two nights, during which time Bush called to wish him well. In his self-deprecating style, McCain said of the operation, "It's a fairly routine thing for an old guy like me." McCain spent a weekend at home in Phoenix, then flew to Washington for the opening session of the Senate. It would not be too long afterward that tragedy struck—the terrorist attacks of September 11.

"I was in my office in Washington," McCain says about the morning of the attacks, "and I had the television set on. I saw it on television. My first thought [when the first plane hit] was, 'Maybe it's just an accident.' Then I began to think about it: 'That'd be very unusual for that kind of thing to happen.' Of course, all doubts were removed when the second plane hit. I felt shock, followed by anger. I concluded quickly that it was an act of terror. Then, obviously, I connected it with the embassy bombings in Africa, the attack on the USS Cole, and the other incidents, dating all the way back to the bombing of the marines in Beirut."

Later that day, McCain had clarified his thoughts. "These attacks clearly constitute an act of war," he said. " I mean unwarranted, unprovoked attacks against innocent American citizens is clearly an act of war, and one that requires that kind of national response and international response."

By the end of 2001, the United States treated the events of September 11, as McCain had described them, as an act of war and attacked Afghanistan, where the Taliban was believed to be harboring terrorists like Osama bin Laden, the mastermind behind September 11.

In the early morning hours of February 14, 2002, the House of Representatives voted into law Shays-Meehan, the House version of McCain-Feingold, by a margin of 240 to 189. The bill's cosponsors were Congressmen Christopher Shays of Connecticut, a Republican, and Martin Meehan of Massachusetts, a Democrat. It had been passed in the House in 1998 and 1999, but now there was an exact piece of legislation that had been passed by the Senate. The vote on March 20 was 60 to 40. This meant the bill could be submitted to the president and signed into law, and McCain would realize his dream of passing meaningful campaign finance reform. "We had pre-conferenced the bill," Christopher Shays says. "We had agreed to take up the same bill in the House and the Senate. This is what a lot of people didn't understand—the fact that we actually passed campaign finance reform without a conference. It's unheard of. So when it passed in the Senate, I was hopeful it would pass in the House, but we knew it was going to be nip and tuck because there's a hundred ways to kill it. If someone wanted to make one little change, that would mean our pre-conference would result in the bill's going to conference, where it would have been killed."

Right away, it was obvious the principals—McCain, Feingold, Shays, and Meehan—had produced legislation that could have a profound effect on the American political system. "I believe that you have to ask yourself," Shays said, "'What would happen if we didn't pass this legislation?' You can't say, 'Compare what it is today to what it will be.' You have to say, 'If it hadn't passed, what would it have become, compared to what it *has* become?' A few years ago, $10 million was a big fund-raiser—huge. Then it was $20 million. After that, $20 million became $30 million. Frankly, without campaign finance reform, you could have had a major soft-money fund-raiser that could have probably topped $50 million—and then ultimately $100 million. It's unbelievable."

As for working with McCain, Shays said: "When you've been locked up for five years in a North Vietnam prison, you can draw a line in the sand and not be so inclined to compromise. But we did good. We passed meaningful legislation. We did it as partners, and I'm pretty impressed with what we accomplished."

Almost six weeks later, on March 27, President Bush signed campaign finance reform legislation into law. He could have vetoed the bill, but a fight with Congress would have ensued, and at the moment, with the war in Afghanistan a dominant source of concern, Bush wanted to avoid unnecessary bickering with Congress. However, Bush revealed his true feelings about the bill by the way he signed it—just before eight o'clock in the morning, in the Oval Office, with no fanfare whatsoever. His audience was tiny: Vice President Cheney and Condoleezza Rice, his national security adviser. In the end, Bush may have also signed it because he and others felt the bill was unconstitutional and sure to be deemed so by the United States Supreme Court.

The White House announced the signing in a written statement. "The ceremony the White House chose," Ari Fleischer, White House press secretary, said, "is reflective of the president's thoughts on the legislation. It would be inconsistent to have a Rose Garden ceremony for a bill which on balance improves the system, but contains what the president views as several important flaws."

McCain learned that Bush had signed the bill when a midlevel White House staffer called him at home and told him. According to sources, McCain was furious at Bush for the way he handled the signing. The one-sentence statement McCain released through his office in Phoenix hinted at his anger: "I am pleased that President Bush signed campaign finance reform legislation into law." By the time he spoke to reporters that day, McCain had decided to handle Bush's snub with humor. "He didn't promise me a rose garden," McCain quipped.

The tension between Bush and McCain would continue when, in mid-June, McCain joined with the Democrats to defeat a Bush-endorsed plan to repeal the estate tax. The vote was not close: 54 to 44. But McCain was one of only two Republicans to break ranks and join with the Democrats.

On March 20, 2003, the Senate voted 52 to 48 against drilling for oil in the Artic National Wildlife Refuge in Alaska—a vote the *New York Times* called "a crippling blow to the central element of the Bush administration's energy plan." The vote did not fall along party lines. Five Democrats voted for the bill, eight Republicans against it. In keeping with his beliefs as an environmentalist, McCain voted against the bill. Members of the administration, especially Cheney, had lobbied Republicans strongly, although they knew the odds of winning over McCain were slim.

But the news of the vote was overshadowed by events in the Middle East, since March 20 marked the day the United States and a "coalition of the willing"—mostly Great Britain—invaded Iraq. The first wave of the invasion, described as "shock and awe," suggesting the deadly force the American military unleashed on a country whose military was drastically inferior, received saturated television coverage. Calling it a "real-time war," McCain said that "every ambush, explosion in Baghdad has an effect that it might not if it were taken in context." While McCain was in favor of the invasion of Iraq and would remain an advocate of the military action in the future, he was critical of the Bush administration's plan of attack, specifically Secretary of Defense Donald Rumsfeld's decision to use a relatively small force of 100,000 or so troops as opposed to a drastically larger troop deployment suggested by some American generals. Twelve days before the invasion, Cheney said the conflict would be over in "weeks rather than months." With the current "streamlined" deployment, there was no way Cheney's goal could be achieved, or so critics like McCain believed.

McCain maintained his opposition to the Bush Administration when, later in March, he voted against another round of Bush tax cuts. He was the only Republican to do so. When a different version of the plan was voted on in May, establishing this round of tax cuts at $350 billion over 10 years, he was joined by two other Republicans. By the summer, with the Bush tax cuts now a reality, attention was being paid to the cost of the war in Iraq, which was lasting longer than had been promised by Cheney in part because the resistance of nationalistic forces—the administration called them "insurgents"—were stronger than anticipated, and the allied fighting force had not been large enough to maintain order in the country after the initial wave of attack had toppled the government and army of Saddam Hussein. With a deployment now reaching 145,000 troops by July, the cost of the war had hit $3.9 billion a month—double the figure the administration had estimated before the invasion. The actual cost was still unclear. "I think," McCain said, "the American people need to be told, 'Look, we're going to be there for quite a while, and it's going to cost us a bit of money.' Americans will support the president, in my view, if he just talks straight to them and tells them what the challenges are we face."

McCain continued to work against the administration when, in November, he opposed the energy plan put forth by the White House and championed by the vice president.

Then, in January 2004, McCain finally found an initiative coming from the Bush Administration that he could support. In order to appeal to Hispanic voters in an election year, Bush was proposing legislation that would provide what one newspaper described as "a sweeping overhaul of the nation's immigration laws"—a proposal that "effectively amounts to an amnesty program for illegal immigrants." If passed, the legislation would allow undocumented workers to apply for the status of temporary worker that could last an unspecified length of time. As one member of the administration observed, it would "match willing workers with willing employers." The legislation would affect, according to the administration, between 8 million and 14 million people in the United States illegally. There was strong opposition to the proposal, especially from the right wing of the Republican Party, who felt the bill was unjust in bestowing amnesty on people who were in the country illegally, but McCain supported the bill. Perhaps he did because, to quote the *New York Times,* "Mr. Bush's proposal is closely modeled on legislation introduced last summer by Senator John McCain and Republicans Jim Kolbe and Jeff Flake, all Republicans from Arizona." It would have been hard for McCain to oppose his own bill, even if the Bush Administration had co-opted it from him.

In May 2004, the war in Iraq became an issue of contention after it was revealed that members of the American military were abusing and humiliating Iraqi prisoners, in particular at Abu Ghraib prison.

When the president tried to defuse the controversy—he apologized to King Abdullah II of Jordan, for some reason, in a meeting in the Oval Office—McCain would not comply. He and Chuck Hagel announced that they wanted to know more about the role played in the scandal by Donald Rumsfeld, whose resignation was now called for by some senators. The contentiousness became evident when McCain and Rumsfeld sparred at a Senate hearing over Abu Ghraib. When Rumsfeld dodged a question about the role private contractors were playing in Iraq, McCain snapped, "No, Secretary Rumsfeld, in all due respect, you've got to answer this question."

By August, a 171-page report had been generated by the U.S. Army concerning the abuse of Iraqi prisoners. The report dismissed the argument made by the Bush Administration that only a few police guards were responsible and placed the blame on the community of military intelligence soldiers and officers. McCain contended that the abuse happened because the allied force strength was too small; as many critics had said now since before the invasion, the United States did not make sure an adequate number of troops had carried out the military action. "One of the consequences of not addressing the postwar challenges is that there were not enough troops in Iraq, and many of those were untrained," McCain said after the report was released.

For over three years now, McCain had consistently opposed Bush on significant parts of his legislative agenda—tax cuts, the energy bill and specifically drilling in Alaska, and the patient's bill of rights. On the one development McCain supported the president on—invading Iraq—he was critical of the way the invasion was carried out. Because of the rumors about his dissatisfaction with the Republican Party around the time Jeffords departed, it should not have been surprising that a new series of rumors would spring up in the summer of 2004.

After it was clear John Kerry had secured the Democratic presidential nomination, word began to spread that he wanted John McCain to be his running mate. The notion was advanced aggressively by Kerry and members of his campaign. As the gossip began to surface in the media, operatives sympathetic to Kerry encouraged it with comments like the one Chris Lehane, an adviser who had worked for Kerry, made when he told the *New York Times,* "[It] would be the political equivalent of the Yankees signing A-Rod." For his part, McCain consistently contended that he never seriously considered Kerry's offer, but the rumors remained so prevalent that he eventually had to dismiss them publicly.

In fact, in time, McCain not only refused to join the Kerry ticket, he actively campaigned for Bush. The door for that to happen was opened when staffers for the two men, said to be Karl Rove for Bush and John Weaver for McCain, met privately to discuss a way for McCain to support Bush after opposing him so strongly for much of the first term. It was agreed, or so it would be said, that Rove assured Weaver that Bush would not attempt to derail McCain should he run for president in 2008 in exchange for McCain's fulfilling his obligation as a party loyalist and supporting the president. This agreed upon, McCain campaigned with Bush in the fall. McCain told audiences he could support the president because, in a time when national security was paramount, Bush had kept the country safe and deserved a second term. In a race that was so close the vote in Ohio proved to be the difference, McCain's support of Bush—his vouching for a president the public was growing increasingly leery of—may have made the difference.

The year 2005 saw McCain focus on the judiciary. For much of Bush's first term, there had been conflict over some of the appointments Bush made to the federal bench, and because federal judges who are appointed by the president have to be approved by the Senate, some of Bush's appellate appointments had been held up by a tactical procedure that kept them from being advanced to the Senate floor for a full vote. To end debate on a nominee so the nominee can proceed to a full vote, the nominee needs 60 votes instead of a simple majority, since in the Senate a filibuster can be used to hold up debate—and 60 votes are required to end a filibuster.

With the Republicans making gains in the Senate in the 2004 election—they now controlled the Senate 55 to 45—the administration realized there would never be a better time to force the issue of these federal judges being held up. Senator Bill Frist of Tennessee, the majority leader, threatened to lead an effort to do away with the Senate's ability to use the filibuster to block judicial nominees. This would have represented a profound change in the way the Senate operates, and some senators, such as Robert Byrd of West Virginia, warned that the very institution of the Senate would be altered if procedures such as the filibuster were ended, even in specific cases. So McCain gathered a group of 14 moderate senators who, meeting behind closed doors in his office, worked out a deal whereby the "Gang of 14," as they came to be called, would vote as a bloc with the Republican majority to allow three of the most controversial nominees—Janice Rogers Brown, William Pryor, and Priscilla R. Owen—to proceed to the floor for a full vote, while two others—Brett M. Kavanaugh and William J. Haynes—would not. The Gang of 14 also agreed not to use the filibuster to block judicial appointments except in "extraordinary circumstances." The Gang of 14, therefore, became the entity within the Senate that would dictate which nominees would and would not proceed to a full Senate vote in the future. It also maintained the existence of the filibuster, one of the defining features of the Senate. "We have kept the Republic," Byrd said of the compromise that protected the integrity of the Senate—and for that McCain was responsible.

All of this was a preamble to an expected showdown when, in the summer of 2005, Sandra Day O'Connor announced her plans to retire from the U.S. Supreme Court, and Bush nominated John Roberts as her replacement. The nomination met with enthusiasm from most senators, so when Chief Justice William Rehnquist died before Roberts could be confirmed, Bush renominated him to be chief justice, promising to nominate a replacement for O'Connor promptly. Once Roberts was confirmed, Bush nominated Samuel A. Alito to replace O'Connor. Much more conservative than Roberts, Alito generated deep concern from some Democratic senators, who viewed the nomination as provocative. There was talk of a fight in the Senate. But Senator Arlen Specter of Pennsylvania argued that the Alito nomination did not violate the spirit of the Gang of 14, and therefore it could not be deemed as coming under the provision for "extraordinary circumstances."

In the end, the Alito nomination was met with little resistance, since it had the support of McCain and the Gang of 14. Certainly, one could argue that the confirmation process would not have run so smoothly if the Gang of 14 had not been formed. In that way, McCain and his founding of an influence-wielding group of like-minded moderate senators had brought calm to a nomination process that could have ended up explosive, even outright divisive. "The agreement signed by the 14 senators noted that the Constitution expects the president to consult with the Senate about judicial nominees," the *New York Times* observed in an editorial, "something this White House has refused to do. If the senators who signed the agreement insist that the White House talk to them in advance about possible nominees, it could go a long way toward defusing the bitterness that has descended on the judicial nomination process."

In the fall, the Senate began to deal with a bill written by McCain that would ban the use of, quoting from the legislation, "cruel, inhumane, or degrading treatment or punishment" of anyone who had been taken into custody by an agency of the American government. The bill was a response to the incidents at Abu Ghraib. The administration, in the person of the vice president, strongly lobbied McCain to exempt the Central Intelligence Agency from the bill, but McCain refused. In October, the Senate showed its overwhelming support of the bill by voting in favor of it 90 to 9. Then, in early November, the Senate reconsidered the bill so it could be passed by a unanimous voice vote. When the Republican leadership in the House threatened to hold up sending its version to the full House for a vote because it was expected to pass easily, representing a blow to Bush and Cheney, McCain took to the Senate floor to issue a warning to the House.

"I would hope that no one seeks procedural maneuvers to thwart overwhelming majorities in both chambers," McCain said. "A bicameral, bipartisan majority in support of this amendment will prevail. Even if the will of the majority is thwarted this month, and thwarted next month, it will not be denied indefinitely. If necessary, and I sincerely hope it is not, I and the cosponsors of this amendment will seek to add it to every piece of important legislation voted on in the Senate until the will of a substantial bipartisan majority in both houses of Congress prevails."

In December, the House was finally allowed to vote on the bill and passed it by a wide margin: 308 to 122. Realizing he had been defeated on the matter, Bush tried to salvage some credibility on the issue and endorsed the legislation, going so far as to call McCain into the White House to give the senator a media moment—a gesture he did not offer him years earlier when he reluctantly signed McCain-Feingold into law. "We've sent a message to the world the United States is not like the terrorists," McCain said about the legislation as he sat in the Oval Office, the president looking on. It was an odd—and, for Bush, embarrassing—turn of events. "For Mr. Bush," one newspaper noted, "it was a stinging defeat, considering that his party controls both houses of Congress and both chambers had defied his threatened veto to support Mr. McCain's measure resoundingly. It was a particularly significant setback for Vice President Dick Cheney, who since July has led the administration's fight to defeat the amendment or at least exempt the Central Intelligence Agency from its provisions."

In the early months of 2006, Bush and McCain were looking for other areas on which they could find common ground. For some time, in the hope of not just appealing to the Hispanic community but appeasing his corporate donors, Bush had been in favor of comprehensive immigration reform. McCain teamed up with Ted Kennedy to draft legislation that would provide fundamental reform. At the same time, McCain was reclaiming the legislation, which had previously been taken over by Bush. In authoring McCain-Kennedy, McCain proposed immigration reform that would deal with illegal immigrants in the following manner: Illegal immigrants who had lived in the United States for five years, some seven million people, would be given citizenship, provided they remained employed. Those who had lived in the country between two and five years, some three million people, would be forced to apply for a temporary work visa. Any illegal immigrant who had been in the country less than a year, about a million people, would be required to leave.

The president supported McCain-Kennedy, but as of the spring, many Republicans were unwilling to endorse the bill unless it contained language demanding that, before the issue of illegal immigrants could be addressed, the United States borders had to be secured. The House had passed a security bill that required the securing of the borders. The general sense among the senators was that, unless a similar consideration could be added to the Senate version of immigration reform, it would fail. In April, when McCain attempted to get McCain-Kennedy to the Senate floor for debate, the bill got bogged down in parliamentary procedures. "The fact that we did not act tonight is a huge blow," McCain said about the events of April 6. He was right.

Comprehensive immigration reform would have to wait until later in the year, even to be considered.

But McCain and Bush had found an issue on which they could agree. There was another: the war in Iraq. As the years had passed and the war had become more unpopular, the president's approval ratings had suffered. Heading into the midterm elections of 2006, Bush looked to be so unpopular that some Republicans did not want him to campaign for them—a huge change from Bush's first midterm race when he actively campaigned for both House and Senate candidates, helping to assure the Republicans maintained control of the House as well as regaining control of the Senate. To help bolster the president, McCain began making regular trips to the White House to meet with Bush throughout the spring and into the summer. By early July, it had become apparent to the Washington press corps that the two former rivals had become less contentious than they had been in the past. They were trying to find a way to form a professional, if not personal, friendship.

Revealing that the president called him "Johnny Mac," McCain told a reporter at the time that their conversations about how to pass immigration reform had given way to pep talks where McCain was reassuring Bush that he was handling Iraq the best he could. "Look, hang on, things are bad," McCain said he had told the president. "I'm proud of the job you are doing, and I want you to know I will continue to do what I can to help." It was McCain's way of encouraging Bush, who was often down due to his dismal poll numbers, even though he was reluctant to admit it. In the fall, Bush would need further encouragement when, despite the best efforts of the White House, the Republican Party, and party luminaries like McCain, the Republicans lost control of both the House and the Senate in what was generally seen as a referendum against Bush and in particular his policies concerning the war in Iraq.

Heading into the midterm elections, McCain had more on his mind than winning or losing the Congress. He had already begun putting together the groundwork for a presidential bid in 2008. Relying on the core team of advisers who had been with him for years—John Weaver, Rick Davis, and Mark Salter—McCain had reached out to others in the Republican Party, even those who had been loyal to Bush. "Among the more prominent members of the Bush team who said they expected to play a role in Mr. McCain's candidacy, if he chooses to run," the *New York Times* reported in August, "are Mark McKinnon, a Texas political media consultant who has worked for Mr. Bush for years; Terry Nelson, political director of the Bush 2004 reelection campaign; Nicolle Wallace, that campaign's communications director; Wayne L. Berman, a Washington lobbyist, friend of Mr. Bush's, and prolific fund-raiser; and F. Philip Handy, chairman of Jeb Bush's two races for governor of Florida and a major supporter of the president." McKinnon said of the apparent thawing of relations between those loyal to Bush and those loyal to McCain: "I think a lot of people are surprised at the extent to which there has been rapprochement between the Bush and McCain worlds."

By late 2006, with a new Democratic majority heading into the Senate, there was a renewed effort to present McCain-Kennedy for possible passage early in the next Congress. Kennedy and McCain had met with their cosponsors in the House; the plan was to introduce their immigration reform bill as soon as the new Congress convened with a goal of voting on the bill in March. As for McCain, by then, he would be deep into his presidential campaign, for on an appearance on *The Late Show with David Letterman,* McCain had announced he was a candidate on president. As some expected, he had lined up Terry Nelson as his campaign manager and Mark McKinnon as his media consultant—both close Bush allies. From his 2000 race, McCain hired Davis and Weaver again, as was generally anticipated even though the two men had a history of feuding. McCain would also have the services of Charlie Black, a veteran strategist who had advised both Reagan and Bush Senior and who in his career had been associated with hard-hitting political operatives like Lee Atwater and Roger Stone.

Since Nelson was a product of the Bush style of campaigning, he attempted to recreate a similar campaign around McCain. "They tried to control McCain," says a source close to the campaign. "They tried to script him. Now the main asset of McCain as a candidate, the reason people think he's a maverick, is because you can't control and script him. He is his own man. He says what he believes. He does what he wants to do. That's why he is so popular with the people. That's why people will forgive him if he makes a mistake. People want a leader who is his own person, not someone who doesn't know what he thinks unless he is reading it from a script."

Besides handling McCain as if he were a more traditional candidate, Nelson and the McCain brain trust set about building a campaign structure that would be heavy on organization, with an army of consultants and handlers available for the candidate at any time. In addition to an impressive national headquarters in suburban northern Virginia, near Washington, the campaign would set up state and regional headquarters across the country. In short, instead of a lean campaign featuring a maverick candidate, such as the one that had worked well for McCain in 2000, this new version would resemble the sprawling, employee-rich campaigns that had gotten Bush elected twice. "I walked into the headquarters when they were getting started," says a source, "and I had never seen so many computers and Blackberries before. There were piles of them. I thought, 'Who is going to use all of these gadgets?' This does not look like a John McCain campaign.'"

To support such a massive operation, the campaign had projected that it needed to raise $25 million a quarter throughout 2007 to put it in a position to win the primary season, which would start with a caucus in Iowa in early January. After the nomination was secured in the spring, a whole new set of financial considerations would have to be met heading into the fall general election. That could not be determined until the early summer of 2008, when it would be clear who the Democratic nominee was and what kind of campaign would have to be run in order to win. But there was a problem. In the first months of 2007, money was coming in at roughly half the rate that had been projected.

There were reasons for the lackluster fund-raising. Historically, McCain had been a poor fund-raiser, as he hated to ask people for money and was often not the recipient of money from lobbying firms, a main source of campaign revenue, due to his long-standing war with lobbyists. At present, all Republican candidates were having trouble raising money because of a general malaise within the party brought on by Bush's poor standings in the national opinion polls. Finally, McCain was also suffering because when McCain-Kennedy had made its way for debate in the Senate during the spring, many Republicans ended up opposing the passage of the bill. Rank-and-file members of the Republican Party were unhappy with McCain for advancing a bill—with the liberal Ted Kennedy no less!—that they so disliked; these same Republicans were not about to give McCain money.

As a result, by the early summer, the campaign had a major problem. Even though money had been slow coming in, Nelson and the consultants had not adjusted spending, particularly on themselves. Raising $13 million in the first quarter and $11.2 million in the second—half of what they needed to bring in—the campaign had just $2 million as of the end of the second quarter. When key staff members met with McCain and Cindy at their home in Sedona in late June to tell them of the campaign's dire financial situation, the McCains were stunned and angry. McCain said he was shocked the campaign had spent the better part of $24 million, mostly on expensive travel and consultant fees, and they had not run a single television ad.

So, in private meetings, the McCains were forced to make some tough decisions. The campaign would have to let go about 80 of its 120 employees. Plus, the decision was made to ask for the resignations of Nelson and Weaver. "In effect, they were fired," says a source. Firing Nelson was not hard, since he was relatively new to McCain's political life, but the decision to fire Weaver was much more difficult. McCain and Weaver were not only close friends, but Weaver had been one of McCain's closest advisers for the better part of the decade, enduring many hardships together—McCain's defeat in 2000 and Weaver's subsequent successful battle with leukemia. Davis would become the campaign manager; Black, Salter, and McKinnon would remain as advisers. With a stripped-down staff and no travel budget, McCain would get back to the kind of campaign he was good at. He would again become the underdog trying to advance his message of reform and returning the government to the people.

Not surprisingly, as soon as word of the massive staff shake-up surfaced, word began to spread that McCain was dropping out. He was going to be out of the race before it had even gotten started. "No, no, no, no," McCain said to reporters when they asked him if his campaign was on the verge of collapse. "I'm very happy with it."

As it turned out, he should have been. After losing the Iowa caucus to Mike Huckabee, the former governor of Arkansas, as he had expected he would because of his continued opposition to ethanol, McCain went on to New Hampshire, a state that proved to be his political salvation once again, just as it had in 2000. By chalking up an impressive win in New Hampshire, McCain put himself back into the presidential race. In six months, McCain had gone from being a candidate who in the summer looked as if he were all but finished, to the likely Republican frontrunner for president. It was, quite simply, one of the most remarkable turnarounds in American political history. "My friends," McCain told the audience that night at his celebration rally in New Hampshire, "you know I'm past the age when I can claim the noun 'kid,' no matter what adjective precedes it. But tonight, we sure showed them what a comeback looks like."

"John McCain came back," says Orson Swindle, McCain's best friend and an adviser to his campaign, "because John McCain was allowed to be John McCain. Whenever he is allowed to be himself, the public will respond to him every time because he is such a likeable guy and because he tells it like it is, the way he sees things. People respond to that. People want a leader who is comfortable with himself."

Then, in a departure from 2000, McCain headed for the primary in South Carolina, and instead of meeting a smear campaign, the likes of which most political observers had never seen, he encountered a state where many voters felt sorry for the way he had been treated eight years before. As he was campaigning, it was not unusual for people to walk up to him and apologize for that treatment in 2000. For good measure, McCain had formed what he called "truth squads," whose mission was to answer charges about him or his family as soon as they were made. Any attempt at mounting a smear campaign would be stopped before it even got started, but because the South Carolina primary of 2008 was marked by the absence of Karl Rove there was little, if any, attempt to smear McCain. On Election Night, in a field that included as his main rivals Huckabee, former Tennessee senator Fred Thompson, former New York mayor Rudy Giuliani, and former Massachusetts governor Mitt Romney, McCain did not have to wait until late before he realized he would win by a comfortable margin of five percentage points.

The victory set up a showdown in late January in Florida, and in part because McCain enjoyed such support within the Hispanic community, specifically the Cubans of Miami, because of his efforts to pass comprehensive immigration reform, he won the state handily, defeating his remaining opponents—Romney, Giuliani, and Huckabee. (Thompson had dropped out after South Carolina.) McCain received 36 percent of the vote compared to Romney's 31, Giuliani's 15, and Huckabee's 14. Giuliani's dismal showing forced him out of the race. Then, on Super Tuesday, McCain became the prohibitive front-runner for the Republican presidential nomination by winning an array of states, including New York, California, Illinois, New Jersey, Connecticut, and Delaware. While Huckabee won his share of states—four Southern states plus West Virginia—as did Romney—six altogether, the largest of which was Massachusetts—McCain won the states with the most impressive delegate counts. This led to Romney's withdrawal from the race, leaving only Huckabee. When McCain defeated him soundly in Texas and Ohio in early March, he sealed the nomination, forcing Huckabee out.

"Now we begin the most important part of our campaign," McCain said that night in a victory speech in Dallas, "to make a respectful, determined, and convincing case to the American people that our campaign and my election as president, given the alternatives presented by our friends in the other party, are in the best interests of the country we love. I will leave it to my opponent to propose returning to the failed, big-government mandates of the 1960s and 1970s to address problems such as the lack of health care insurance for some Americans. I will campaign to make health care more accessible to more Americans with reforms that will bring down costs in the health care industry without ruining the quality of the world's best medical care."

"That's John McCain for you," Orson Swindle says. "He's not doing what he's doing for himself. That's one of his mantras: We must devote ourselves to a cause greater than our own self-interests. John McCain's doing what he's doing because he cares about people. God, Country, and the American people." Georgette Mosbacher adds: "John McCain's life is one of the most memorable in American presidential politics. It is my honest belief that the last chapter of that life, still unwritten, will be the most memorable yet."

Notes

Prologue

Page xi "'When I was five years old' . . ." This quote comes from a speech given by John McCain at the Los Angeles World Affairs Council on March 26, 2008. Other quotes in the Prologue referencing comments made in Los Angeles by McCain come from the same speech.

Page xii "In describing McCain's approach . . ." This and the following paragraph reference and quote from David Brooks, "Tested Over Time," *New York Times*, March 28, 2008.

Page xiii "'I cannot in good conscience support' . . ." Pat Toomey, "The McCain Record," the *Wall Street Journal*, March 13, 2007.

Page xiii "'The tax cut is not appropriate' . . ." Ibid.

Page xiv "'In a 1999 interview, McCain said' . . ." James Kirchick, "Why John McCain Isn't So Bad," *The Advocate*, March 20, 2008.

Page xv "'The First Amendment is an important safeguard' . . ." Pat Toomey, "The McCain Record," *Wall Street Journal,* March 13, 2007.

Admiral McCain

Page 1 "He had commanded . . ." The official biography of John Sidney McCain was supplied to me by the Department of the Navy.

Page 2 "Task Force 38's motto . . ." Some details in this paragraph come from *John McCain: An Essay in Military and Political History* by Jack Karaagac (Landham, Maryland: Lexington Books, 2000).

Page 2 "In the last six months of the war . . ." From the official naval biography of John Sidney McCain.

Page 2 "That same day, he made his point . . ." The information in this paragraph comes from "War Strain Kills Adm. McCain as He Gets Home," *New York Herald Tribune,* September 8, 1945.

Page 2 "The last year of the war . . ." The information in this and the next two paragraphs concerning the typhoons comes from the *USA Today* Web site.

Page 3 "He was born on August 9, 1884 . . ." From the official naval biography of John Sidney McCain.

Page 3 "When he graduated on February 12, 1906 . . ." The yearbook citation of John Sidney McCain was supplied to me by the U.S. Naval Academy.

Page 4 "The couple had three children . . ." The official naval biography of John Sidney McCain Jr. was supplied to me by the Department of the Navy.

Page 4 "In 1918, the year World War I ended . . ." The information in this paragraph comes from John Sidney McCain's official naval biography. The quote comes from an interview with John Sidney McCain Jr. conducted by John T. Mason Jr. on January 6, 1975, for the U.S. Naval Institute. The interview,

"The Reminiscences of Admiral John S. McCain Jr., U.S. Navy (Retired)," was published in phamplet form by the Naval Institute in December 1999.

Page 4   "'My father,' he would say, 'was a great leader' . . ." The quote comes from the Naval Institute interview with John Sidney McCain Jr. conducted by John T. Mason Jr.

Page 4   "In September 1927 . . ."The information in this paragraph comes from the naval biography of John Sidney McCain Jr.; the quotes come from the Naval Institute interview with John Sidney McCain Jr. conducted by John T. Mason Jr.

Page 5   "When he graduated on May 1, 1931 . . ." The yearbook citation for John Sidney McCain Jr. was supplied to me by the U.S. Naval Academy.

Page 5   "'The only thing I say to you' . . ." The quote comes from the Naval Institute interview with John Sidney McCain Jr. conducted by John T Mason Jr.

Page 5   "Roberta and her twin sister . . ." The information in this paragraph comes from *Faith of My Fathers* by John McCain with Mark Salter (New York: Random House, 1999) and "McCain's Chiefs of Distaff; Think 'Auntie Mame' Rolled into Two, and You'll Get the Picture" by Ken Ringle, *Washington Post,* March 6, 2000.

Page 6   "In July 1933 . . ."The information in this paragraph comes from the naval biography of John Sidney McCain Jr. as well as "McCain's Chiefs of Distaff" by Ken Ringle.

Page 6   "Slew McCain remained . . ." From the naval biography of John Sidney McCain.

Page 7   "During World War II . . ." From the naval biography of John Sidney McCain Jr.

Page 7   "As for Slew, he served . . ." From the naval biography of John Sidney McCain.

Page 8   "Admiral Charles Lockwood gave the luncheon . . ." From the Naval Institute interview with John Sidney McCain Jr. conducted by John T. Mason Jr.

Page 8   "McCain's body was flown . . ." The information in this
paragraph comes from the obituaries of John Sidney
McCain published in the *New York Times* and the *New York
Herald Tribune*. Certain facts were also confirmed with the
Office of Senator John McCain in Washington, D.C.

Page 9   "'They brought me back and put me in charge' . . ." From
the Naval Institute interview with John Sidney McCain Jr.
conducted by John T. Mason Jr.

Page 9   "McCain held that post . . ." From the naval biography of
John Sidney McCain Jr.

Page 9   "'We were all steeped in the tradition' . . ." This unpublished quote comes from my interview with Thad Cochran,
June 2002.

Anchors Away

Page 12   "As a young boy, Johnny exhibited . . ." The information
about John McCain's temper emerging at an early age comes
from *Faith of My Fathers* by John McCain with Mark Salter.

Page 12   "In the early years of his life, Johnny's parents . . ." The
information in this paragraph comes from my interview
with John McCain, August 2001.

Page 12   "The first demonstrative move . . ." The information about
St. Stephen's comes from documents supplied to me by
the school and from my interview with Charles Hooff,
March 2002.

Page 13   "'Episcopal was one of the better prep schools' . . ." This
unpublished quote comes from my interview with Dick
Thomsen, March 2002.

Page 13   "Jack and Roberta were enrolling Johnny . . ." The information in this and the next two paragraphs comes from
various documents supplied to me by the Episcopal High
School.

Page 14   "'In a word, it was brutal' . . ." This unpublished quote
comes from my interview with Charles Hooff, March 2002.

Page 14   "'We lived in curtained alcoves' . . .'" This quote comes from "The School with a Southern Accent" by Ken Ringle, *Washington Post,* November 11, 1989.

Page 14   "'It had been used by the Union' . . .'" This unpublished quote comes from my interview with Ken Ringle, June 2002.

Page 15   "Before long, the brash . . ." This information comes from documents supplied to me by Episcopal. The unpublished quote comes from my interview with Ken Ringle, June 2002.

Page 15   "'As headmaster, I actually saw' . . .'" This unpublished quote comes from my interview with Dick Thomsen, March 2002.

Page 15   "'That was another subculture, being a waiter' . . .'" This unpublished quote comes from my interview with Ken Ringle, June 2002.

Page 16   "By his senior year, McCain had gotten in line . . ." Senior yearbook entries were supplied to me by Episcopal.

Page 16   "'William Ravenel was a leader' . . ." This unpublished quote comes from my interview with Robert Whittle, March 2002.

Page 16   "'It was three fateful years ago' . . ." The senior yearbook citation of John McCain.

Page 17   "'Following his first summer at the Naval Academy' . . .'" The incident in which McCain returned to Episcopal from the Naval Academy was told to me by Dick Thomsen when I interviewed him in March 2002.

Page 17   "'I was basically told when I was young' . . ." This unpublished quote comes from my interview with John McCain, August 2001.

Page 18   "'He had a little bit of internal conflict' . . ." The quote by Frank Gamboa comes from the *Boston Globe,* January 23, 2000.

Page 18   "'The plebe will be barked at' . . ." This quote comes from *John McCain: An Essay in Military and Political History* by John Karaagac.

Page 19   "'The next four days'. . ." This quote comes from *John McCain: An American Odyssey* by Robert Timberg (New York: Touchstone Books, 1999), page 52. This book was taken, for the most part, from *The Nightingale's Song* by Robert Timberg (New York: Simon and Schuster, 1995).

Page 19   "'John, better known' . . ." The yearbook citation was supplied to me by the U.S. Naval Academy.

Page 20   "For the next two-and-a-half years . . ." The incident of the airplane crash comes from *American Odyssey* by Robert Timberg.

Page 20   "McCain continued to fly himself . . ." The incident of the airplane crash comes from *American Odyssey* by Robert Timberg.

Page 21   "On November 9, 1958, McCain's father . . ." From the naval biography of John Sidney McCain Jr.

Page 21   "'When Admiral McCain was commander' . . ." This unpublished quote comes from my interview with Tom Arrasmith, June 2002.

Page 22   "On May 1, 1967, Jack McCain was named . . ." From the naval biography of John Sidney McCain Jr.

Vietnam

Page 23   "For Lieutenant Commander John McCain . . ." The description of the *Forrestal* episode comes from articles that appeared in the *New York Times* in July and August 1967.

Page 26   "'The ship went back' . . ." This quote comes from an essay written by John McCain included in *The Soldiers' Story* edited by Ron Steinman (New York: TV Books, 1999).

Page 26   "'It was dumb the way we were doing it' . . ." This unpublished quote comes from my interview with Robert W. Smith, June 2002.

Page 27   "On the morning of October 26 . . ." John McCain first wrote about his shoot-down over Hanoi in his article

"Inside Story: How the POWs Fought Back," *U.S. News & World Report,* May 14, 1973.

Page 29 "Carrying a bamboo pole ..." The description of and quotes about the rescue of John McCain by Mai Van On come from "McCain's Vietnam Rescuer Recalls 32-Year-Old Event," an Associated Press article that appeared in, among other newspapers, the *Los Angeles Times* on February 24, 2000.

Page 29 "Once On and Lua had pulled McCain ..." "Inside Story" by John McCain, *U.S. News & World Report.*

Page 30 "'I was taken into a cell' ..." John McCain first described the incident with an interrogator and a Vietnamese doctor in "Inside Story" in *U.S. News & World Report* and his essay in *The Soldiers' Story.*

Page 31 "Men soon came and took ..." "Inside Story" by John McCain, *U.S. News & World Report.*

Page 31 "McCain was rolled ..." Ibid.

Page 32 "On Saturday, November 11 ..." "Hanoi Says McCain's Son Terms U.S. 'Isolated,'" *New York Times,* November 11, 1967.

Page 32 "Two weeks after the surgery on his right arm ..." From "Inside Story" by John McCain, *U.S. News & World Report.*

Page 32 "That night, McCain was taken ..." The facts in the rest of this paragraph come from "Inside Story" by John McCain, *U.S. News & World Report,* and McCain's essay in *The Soldiers' Story.*

Page 33 "'My first thought' ..." This unpublished quote comes from my interview with George ("Bud") Day, July 2002.

Page 33 "'When Overly left, John and I were alone' ..." Ibid.

Page 33 "One day in mid-June, McCain was taken ..." John McCain first described the episodes involving the Vietnamese's attempt to release him in "Inside Story" in *U.S. News & World Report.*

Page 34 "'I was in a cell that was catty-corner' ..." This unpublished quote comes from my interview with Jack Van Loan, July 2002.

Page 34   "Three days after the previous meeting . . ." "Inside Story,"
U.S. News & World Report.

Page 35   "One night in August . . ." Ibid.

Page 36   "In August of that year, Navy Lieutenant Robert
F. Frishman . . ." "Ex-POWs Charge Hanoi with Torture,"
New York Times, September 3, 1969.

Page 37   "One morning during Christmastime, the guards came . . ."
The description of the episode at Christmas 1969 comes
from the essay by John McCain in *The Soldiers' Story.*

Page 37   "'the hotel where they didn't leave a mint' . . ." John McCain
often made this remark during his speeches on the cam-
paign trail during his run for the presidency.

Page 37   "'He had landed in that Ho Chi Minh pond' . . ." This
unpublished quote comes from my interview with James
Stockdale, June 2002.

Page 38   "'My first encounter with John McCain' . . ." This unpublished quote comes from my interview with Orson Swindle,
June 2002.

Page 38   "At the time, the Hanoi Hilton . . ." The description of
the prison comes in part from *P.O.W.* by John G. Hubbell
(New York: McGraw Hill, 1976).

Page 39   "'In late 1970,' McCain later wrote, 'there was a
change' . . ." This quote comes from the essay by John
McCain in *The Soldiers' Story.*

Page 39   "'I called it Skid Row' . . ." This unpublished quote comes
from my interview with Orson Swindle, June 2002.

Page 40   "'Finally' Swindle says, 'in November 1971' . . ." Ibid.

Page 40   "'Believe it or not,' McCain would write . . ." *The Soldiers'
Story.*

Page 40   "'We had hours upon hours of time' . . ." This unpublished
quote comes from my interview with Orson Swindle,
June 2002.

Page 41   "In 1971, the POWs were finally able to have a proper
church service . . ." *The Soldiers' Story.*

Page 41 "As McCain was enduring his fifty-sixth month . . ." The description of Jane Fonda's trip to North Vietnam comes from *Jane Fonda: An Intimate Biography* by Bill Davidson (New York: Dutton, 1990).

Page 42 "'The day before, these guys were cleaned up' . . ." This unpublished quote comes from my interview with William Haynes, April 2002.

Page 43 "'We were absolutely dismayed' . . ." This unpublished quote comes from my interview with Jack Van Loan, July 2002.

Page 43 "The years 1971 and 1972 . . ." "Inside Story," *U.S. News & World Report*.

Page 44 "'John is very competitive' . . ." The episode about the bridge game comes from my interview with Orson Swindle, June 2002.

Page 45 "'[A]fter I got back,' McCain would write . . ." "Inside Story," *U.S. News & World Report*.

Page 46 "'When I read your name off' . . ." Ibid.

Page 46 "'I think history will judge the Vietnam War' . . ." This unpublished quote comes from my interview with John McCain, August 2001.

Coming Home

Page 47 "'Other guys would have snapped' . . ." This unpublished quote from Richard Nixon was provided to me by Monica Crowley who interviewed Nixon repeatedly during the four years prior to his death when she worked as his aide.

Page 48 "'That night at the White House' . . ." This unpublished quote comes from my interview with George ("Bud") Day, July 2002.

Page 48 "Paul Galanti remembers . . ." This unpublished quote comes from my interview with Paul Galanti, July 2002.

Page 48   "'It took me about 40 minutes to adjust'..."This unpublished quote comes from my interview with John McCain, August 2001.

Page 48   "'Carol had taken the kids to her parents' house'..." *Faith of My Fathers.*

Page 49   "'The outpouring on behalf of us'..." "Inside Story," *U.S. News & World Report.*

Page 49   "'They said, "You're never going to fly again" '..." This unpublished quote comes from my interview with Carl Smith, June 2002.

Page 50   "At the end of 1973..."The quote and facts in this paragraph come from "One POWs Fresh Appraisal of U.S.: Interview with Cdr. John S. McCain III," *U.S. News & World Report,* December 31, 1973, pp. 47–48.

Page 50   "Finally, in the article..." Ibid.

Page 51   "'During this period,' says Senator John Warner..."This unpublished quote comes from my interview with John Warner, June 2002.

Page 52   "'I had heard legendary stories'..." This quote comes from the foreword John McCain wrote to *Glory Denied: The Saga of Jim Thompson, America's Longest-Held Prisoner of War* by Tom Philpott (New York: W.W. Norton, 2001).

Page 52   "'At the time, VA-174'..." This unpublished quote comes from my interview with Carl Smith, June 2002.

Page 54   "'The Senate Liaison Office had been a backwater office'..."This unpublished quote comes from my interview with Carl Smith, June 2002. Certain facts about the Senate liaison office contained in this section of the chapter were confirmed by the Office of John McCain.

Page 54   "'In the late 1970s,' Carl Smith says..." Ibid.

Page 55   "McCain was asked to perform..."The facts and quotes in the paragraph come from my interview with Ken Ringle, June 2002.

Page 55   "Mostly, in those years..."The facts and quote in this paragraph come from my interview with Gary Hart, June 2002.

Page 55   "When he was not traveling . . ." The facts and quote in this paragraph come from my interview with Carl Smith, June 2002.

Page 56   "While McCain was making new friends . . ." Ibid.

Page 56   "'As the senate liaison for the navy' . . ." This unpublished quote comes from my interview with Thad Cochran, June 2002.

Page 57   "During his courtship of Cindy . . ." The information and quotes about the Hensley family in this paragraph come from "Beer Baron Father-in-Law Key McCain Funds Source" by Pat Flannery, the *Arizona Republic,* February 17, 2000.

Page 58   "Hensley had served as a bombardier in Europe . . ." Ibid.

Page 59   "Years later, McCain revealed . . ." The unpublished quote in this paragraph comes from my interview with John McCain, August 2001.

The Congressman from Arizona

Page 61   "'When John married Cindy' . . ." This unpublished quote comes from my interview with Thad Cochran, June 2002.

Page 61   "'I think something happened in the late 1970s' . . ." This unpublished quote comes from my interview with Gary Hart, June 2002.

Page 62   "'John was a dark, dark horse' . . ." "McCain's Complex Quest: Campaign Must Deal with Many Paradoxes" by David Broder, the *Washington Post,* May 23, 1999.

Page 63   "'We were both big fans of Felix the Cat' . . ." This unpublished quote comes from my interview with Orson Swindle, June 2002.

Page 64   "During the 98th Congress . . ." All facts and quotations in this and the next two paragraphs come from the official Congressional record.

Page 65   "But, on one issue . . ." Details in this paragraph were confirmed in my interview with John McCain, August 2002.

Page 66   "In the 99th Congress . . ." All facts and quotations in this
paragraph come from the official Congressional record.

Page 66   "One highlight of his second session in Congress . . ." Facts
and quotations about McCain's trip to Vietnam included
in this and the next four paragraphs come from "Inside
Vietnam: What a Former POW Found," *U.S. News & World
Report,* March 11, 1985.

Page 68   "In the autumn of 1985 . . ." The information in this paragraph about legislation comes from the official Congressional
record.

Page 68   "On May 2, 1986 . . ." Certain biographical facts about
McCain and his family were confirmed by the Office of
John McCain.

Page 68   "'The night before the election' . . ." McCain often told this
anecdote about Barry Goldwater during stump speeches
while on the campaign trail as he ran for the presidency in
1999 and 2000.

Page 69   "'It was a cakewalk' . . ." This unpublished quote comes
from my interview with Tim Meyer, August 2002.

Page 69   "'President Nixon watched McCain' . . ." This unpublished
quote comes from my interview with Monica Crowley,
June 2002.

Page 69   "'Everything in him told him to fight' . . ." This unpublished
quote from Richard Nixon was provided to me by Monica
Crowley who interviewed Nixon repeatedly during the
four years prior to his death when she worked as his aide.

One Hundred Kings

A general note: Through a source, I approached Dennis DeConcini
in mid-2002 on two separate occasions and asked him to give me an
interview for this book; the conversation could have been conducted
either on or off the record, at his discretion. DeConcini declined.

Page 72   "A week later, on April 9 . . ." the *Arizona Republic,* July 7,
1989.

Page 72   "In short, DeConcini argued . . ." Ibid.

Page 74   "Keating came to my office . . ." "McCain Repays Keating Firm for Trips," the *Washington Post*, October 12, 1989.

Page 75   "'The Reagan Administration plan to reflag' . . ." the *Arizona Republic*, June 21, 1987.

Page 75   "'There is no doubt in my mind' . . ." the *Arizona Republic*, August 22, 1987.

Page 76   "We must not let partisan divisions . . ." the *Arizona Republic*, September 27, 1987.

Page 76   "The year 1988 . . ." Certain facts in this paragraph were confirmed with Joyce Campbell.

Page 77   "In mid-July, McCain met with Bush . . ." the *New York Times*, July 22, 1988.

Page 77   "On Wednesday, July 22, McCain addressed . . ." In this and the next paragraph, the comments made by Jane Fonda were taken from *Jane Fonda* by Bill Davidson. The comments made by McCain were taken from the *Congressional Record*.

Page 79   "On August 14, the *Arizona Republic* ran . . ." the *Arizona Republic*, August 14, 1988.

Page 80   "No sooner had the name 'Dan Quayle' . . ." Certain facts in this paragraph were confimed with John Batchelor, the author of *Ain't You Glad You Joined the Republicans?*, a history of the Republican Party.

Page 81   "Immediately, rumors started to circulate . . ." Information about the military records of George W. Bush and Lloyd Bentsen Jr. comes from my article "All Hat, No Cattle," *Rolling Stone*, July 1999.

Page 81   "McCain himself called the choice . . ." the *Arizona Republic*, August 19, 1988.

Page 81   "In early October . . ." the *Arizona Republic*, October 6, 1988.

Page 82   "In Arizona" the *Arizona Republic*, November 14, 1988.

Page 89   "Through the fall . . ." The quotes from this and the following four paragraphs are available in the *Congressional Record*.

Page 90   "At the end of 1990, McCain . . ." the *Arizona Republic*, December 9, 1990.

Page 91   "On January 4, 1991 . . ." The quotes from this paragraph are available in the *Congressional Record.* The events were also covered by the major daily newspapers, including the *Washington Post,* the *Los Angeles Times,* and the *New York Times.*

Page 93   "Four days before the cutoff date . . ." The comments made by McCain were taken from the *Congressional Record.*

Page 95   "In July, only weeks after his return . . ." Information in this and the following paragraph was supplied to me by John McCain; I also used "A Friendship That Ended the War" by James Carroll, *The New Yorker,* October 21, 1996.

Page 97   "On January 13, 1993, just as Bill Clinton . . ." The information in this paragraph comes from my interviews with John McCain and John Kerry as well as "A Friendship That Ended the War" by James Carroll.

Page 97   "'By the end of 1992, Kerry had suggested' . . ." This passage was taken from *Nixon in Winter* by Monica Crowley (New York: Random House, 1998).

Page 98   "'In the late 1980s and early 1990s' . . ." This quote comes from my interview with John McCain, November 2001.

The Senator from Arizona

Page 100   "The group he chose was the Oregon Citizens Alliance . . ." The description of the event and the quotes from McCain's speech come from the *Arizona Republic,* September 5, 1993.

Page 100   "'All Americans deserve the opportunity' . . ." the *Arizona Republic,* October 13, 1993.

Page 102   "'There are some who have characterized' . . ." the *Arizona Republic,* April 21, 1994.

Page 102   "That summer, McCain experienced . . ." *Arizona Republic,* July 3, 1994.

Page 102   "On August 22, 1994, Cindy McCain . . ." The information in the section dealing with Cindy McCain's addiction to prescription drugs comes mainly from the reporting of the *Arizona Republic* (and *Phoenix Gazette,* its sister publication), particuarly articles published by John Kolbe on August 22, 1994, Bill Hart on August 24, 1994, and Martin Van Der Werf and Susan Leonard on August 23, 1994. I also used information from the Stanton Peele Addiction Web site and an article called "The Next First Lady?" by Toby Harnden, which appeared on the Web site The Age, February 25, 2000. "How Cindy McCain Was Outed for Drug Addiction" by Amy Silverman, which appeared on October 18, 1999, on Salon.com, was helpful as well.

Page 106   "'Late in the year, McCain and I appeared' . . ." This unpublished quote comes from my interview with Gary Ackerman, June 2002.

Page 107   "On May 23, McCain and Kerry . . ." "Time to Open an Embassy in Vietnam" by John McCain, the *Washington Post,* May 23, 1995.

Page 108   "On Tuesday, July 11, McCain joined up . . ." "A Friendship That Ended the War" by James Carroll.

Page 108   "There were, however, other Americans . . ." The *U.S. Veteran Dispatch* has a Web site with the address usvet@ icomnet.com; the home base of the publication is located in Kinston, North Carolina.

Page 109   "On Thursday morning, September 7, McCain and Alan Simpson . . ." The information in this and the following paragraph comes from articles published in the *Washington Post;* the unpublished quote comes from my interview with Alan Simpson, July 2002.

Page 110   "'There was a debate in the Senate' . . ." This unpublished quote comes from my interview with John McCain, August 2001.

Page 111   "'Bob Dole [once] wore' . . ." This quote by John McCain comes from the *Congressional Record.*

Page 111   "'I went to the funeral' . . ." This unpublished quote comes from my interview with Eliot Engel, July 2002.

Page 112   "'This bill will not cure public cynicism' . . ." This quote by John McCain comes from the *Congressional Record.*

Page 112   "'Ultimately the short list' . . ." This unpublished quote comes from my interview with Joyce Campbell, April 2002.

Page 113   "'Before long, Dole was getting' . . ." Ibid.

Page 113   "'McCain was loyal to Dole' . . ." This unpublished quote comes from an anonymous source.

Page 114   "'The common bond of their friendship' . . ." This unpublished quote comes from my interview with Joyce Campbell, August 2002.

Page 114   "During this trip, McCain met . . ." The Associated Press article that appeared in, among other places, the *Los Angeles Times,* February 24, 2000.

Page 114   "'Have Republicans abandoned their roots' . . ." the *Arizona Republic,* November 27, 1996.

Page 115   "'I was at the British Embassy' . . ." This unpublished quote comes from my interview with Peter King, June 2002.

Page 117   "In the first weeks of 1999, McCain cast . . ." McCain's vote on the impeachment of Bill Clinton is documented in the *Congressional Record.* Certain facts in this paragraph were confirmed with John Batchelor.

Page 118   "In January, in his office on Capitol Hill, McCain . . ." Details about McCain's meeting with Mike Murphy included in this and the next two paragraphs were confirmed in my interview with John Weaver, June 2002.

Presidential Politics

Page 121   "On Monday, September 27, 1999 . . ." McCain's announcement was covered by the major daily newspapers; certain details about the event were confimed with Peter Rinfret.

Page 123   "Near the start of the whisper campaign . . ." Details about the editorial published in the *New York Times* on November 26, 1999, as well as his unpublished quote about the matter come from my interview with James Stockdale conducted in June 2002.

Page 123   "'There's a difference between anger and irritation' . . ." This unpublished quote comes from my interview with Alan Simpson, July 2002.

Page 127   "The Dole endorsement . . ." This unpublished quote comes from my interview with Joyce Campbell, August 2002.

Page 133   "By midafternoon on February 1 . . ." Details in this and the following paragraph were confirmed with an anonymous source as well as the Office of John McCain.

Page 133   "'I went up to the suite' . . ." This unpublished quote comes from my interview with Peter Rinfret, February 2002.

Page 134   "Not long after Bush finished . . ." The comment made by McCain to Peter Rinfret was confirmed by Rinfret.

Page 134   "'He was very pumped in the elevator' . . ." This unpublished quote comes from my interview with Ben Davol, February 2002.

Page 135   "'I am on that door where John is to come in' . . ." This unpublished quote comes from my interview with Orson Swindle, June 2002.

Page 135   "'I was standing, looking at the TV' . . ." This unpublished quote comes from my interview with Ben Davol, February 2002.

"The Dirtiest Race I've Ever Seen"

Page 139   "On February 4, John Kerry, Max Cleland . . ." The letter organized by John Kerry was supplied to me by the Office of John Kerry.

Page 139   "'The first indication we got that things' . . ." This unpublished quote comes from my interview with Orson Swindle, June 2002. In his quote Swindle refers to "John McCain and Russell Feingold" by Albert R. Hunt, *Profiles in Courage for Our Time,* edited by Caroline Kennedy (New York: Hyperion, 2002).

Page 140   "'What a farce Burch was' . . ." This unpublished quote comes from my interview with Everett Alvarez, August 2002.

Page 145 "'It was a black child' . . ." This unpublished quote comes from an anonymous source.

Page 145 "'In South Carolina,' Frank Rich wrote . . ." This editorial by Frank Rich appeared in the *New York Times* on February 23, 2000.

Page 149 "'One of the entertaining vignettes' . . ." This unpublished quote comes from my interview with John McCain, August 2001.

Page 150 "On February 19, the polls would be open . . ." The details of Primary Day were confirmed by Peter Rinfret as well as coverage in the *Washington Post,* the *Arizona Republic,* the *New York Times,* and other newpapers.

Page 151 "As he had in New Hampshire . . ." Details in this paragraph were confirmed with an anonymous source.

Page 151 "As McCain, Murphy, Weaver, Salter, and Davis . . ." The details of this and the next three paragraphs were confirmed with John Weaver.

The Best Man

Page 155 "'They sent out a press release' . . ." This unpublished quote comes from my interview with Paul Galanti, August 2002.

Page 159 "'I was with McCain on the bus' . . ." This unpublished quote comes from my interview with Peter Rinfret, February 2002.

Page 162 "'I am no longer an active candidate' . . ." Certain details about McCain's speech at Sedona were confirmed by John Weaver and an anonymous source.

Page 162 "At some point, Bush called McCain . . ." The information concerning the telephone call from George W. Bush to John McCain was supplied to me by an anonymous source.

Page 163 "Despite more-or-less constant tension . . ." Details about the McCain-Bush meeting in Pittsburgh were confirmed by the Office of John McCain.

Man of the People

Page 167   "'I realized when we were about to organize' . . ." This unpublished quote comes from my interview with Thad Cochran, June 2002.

Page 168   "'What happened was,' John Edwards says . . ." This unpublished quote comes from my interview with John Edwards, June 2002.

Page 171   "'I was in my office' . . ." This unpublished quote comes from my interview with John McCain, August 2002.

Page 172   "'We had pre-conferenced the bill' . . ." This unpublished quote comes from my interview with Christopher Shays, August 2002.

Page 173   "'The ceremony the White House chose' . . ." This quote comes from Ari Fleischer's daily press briefing in the White House, March 27, 2002.

Page 174   "On March 20, 2003, the Senate . . ." David Firestone, "Drilling in Alaska, a Priority for Bush, Fails in the Senate," *New York Times,* March 20, 2003.

Page 174   "Calling it a real-time war' . . ." David Sanger, "As a Quick Victory Grows Less Likely, Doubts Are Quietly Voiced in Washington," *New York Times,* March 30, 2003.

Page 174   "Twelve days before . . ." Ibid.

Page 175   "In order to appeal . . ." Elizabeth Bumiller, "Bush Would Give Illegal Workers Broad New Rights," *New York Times,* January 7, 2004.

Page 176   "As the gossip began to surface . . ." Sheryl Gay Stolberg and Jodi Wilgoren, "Undeterred by McCain Denials, Some See Him as Kerry's No. 2," *New York Times,* May 15, 2004.

Page 179   "'The agreement signed by the 14 Senators' . . ." Editorial, "The Center Can Hold," *New York Times,* June 12, 2005.

Page 179   "'I would hope that no one' . . ." Eric Schmitt, "Senate Votes Again for Ban on Abusing Prisoners," *New York Times,* November 5, 2005.

Page 180 "'For Mr. Bush' . . ." Eric Schmitt, "President Backs McCain Measure on Inmate Abuse," *New York Times,* December 16, 2005.

Page 181 "'Look, hang on, things are bad' . . ." Jim Rutenberg and Adam Nagourney, "A New Partnership Binds Old Republican Rivals," *New York Times,* July 3, 2006.

Page 181 "Heading into the midterm elections . . ." John M. Broder, "McCain Mines Elite of G.O.P. for 2008 Team," *New York Times,* August 21, 2006.

Page 182 "'They tried to control McCain' . . ." This unpublished quote comes from my interview with an anonymous source, February 2008.

Page 183 "'I walked into the headquarters' . . ." Ibid.

Page 184 "'In effect, they were fired' . . ." Ibid.

Page 185 "'John McCain came back' . . ." This unpublished quote comes from my interview with Orson Swindle, March 2008.

Page 186 "'That's John McCain for you' . . ." Ibid.

Index